HARD TIMES in the
MARVELOUS CITY

Bryan McCann

HARD TIMES in the
MARVELOUS CITY

From Dictatorship to Democracy in the Favelas of Rio de Janeiro

Duke University Press · Durham and London · 2014

© 2014 Duke University Press
All rights reserved
Printed in the United States of America on acid-free paper ∞
Designed by Courtney Leigh Baker and typeset in Quadraat
by Tseng Information Systems, Inc.

Library of Congress Cataloging-in-Publication Data
McCann, Bryan, 1968–
Hard times in the marvelous city : from dictatorship to
democracy in the favelas of Rio de Janeiro / Bryan McCann.
p. cm
Includes bibliographical references and index.
ISBN 978-0-8223-5523-6 (cloth : alk. paper)
ISBN 978-0-8223-5538-0 (pbk. : alk. paper)
1. Slums—Brazil—Rio de Janeiro. 2. Poor—Political activity—
Brazil—Rio de Janeiro. 3. Rio de Janeiro (Brazil)—Social
conditions—20th century. I. Title.
HC189.R4M39 2013
305.5′6909815309046—dc23
2013025532

Contents

Illustrations

MAPS

Acknowledgments

I closed the Epilogue with Ratão Diniz and will open the acknowledgments by thanking him for his talents as a *cicerone* through Maré and other *complexos*. João Roberto Ripper and the community leaders at Imagens do Povo, CEASM, and the Observatório de Favelas also contributed unstintingly to my education. Christina Vital, Cristiane Ramos, Marcelo Monteiro, and Rita de Cássia of Favela Tem Memória shared their vast knowledge and allowed me to participate in their discussions. Theresa Williamson of Cat-Comm fulfilled the name of her organization, catalyzing my engagement with multiple communities. Eliana Athayde of the Fundação Bento Rubião shared her unswerving commitment to justice and her honest reflections. Paulo Muniz shared his memories of the events that open the book.

Officers of many favela associations offered their deep, local knowledge, most importantly those representing Chapéu Mangueira, Babilônia, Morro Azul, Borel, Formiga, Cabritos, Pedregulho, Providência, Asa Branca, Vila Autódromo, Horto, and Cantagalo. Association officers from the neighborhoods of Botafogo, Bairro Peixoto, Vila Valqueire, and Cruzada São Sebastião were equally generous.

Many scholars, organizers and students in Rio de Janeiro went out of their way to lead me to sources and insights. Paulo Knauss shared his deep grasp of Rio's history and his understanding of *brizolismo*. Mário Brum, Mauro Amoroso, Bruno Aragão Bastos, Mário Grynszpan, Dulce Pandolfi, Itamar Silva, Márcia Leite, Américo Freire, Marly Motta, Marieta Ferreira, Luciana Lago, Cristina Buarque de Hollanda, Sílvia Muylaert, Lígia Segala, and Lígia Mefano all shared generously and pardoned my naïveté. Mariana Cavalcanti and Paulo Fontes stimulated further reflections. Alba Zaluar was both encouraging and inspiring.

Tatiane Pereira Nunes Costa and Kizzy Couto helped me see the structure of favelas in transition. Cecília Azevedo, Ana Mauad, and Martha Abreu were gracious hosts and colleagues. Angela Magalhães *amiga fiel de muitos anos*, never hesitated to do anything possible to make my experience in Rio more enjoyable and productive at the same time.

The staff of libraries and archives at IUPERJ, Arquivo da Cidade, APERJ, CPDOC-FGV, Arquivo Pastoral das Favelas, SMDS, IBAM, UFRJ, the Secretaria de Habitação, and the Instituto Pereira Passos facilitated my research.

Latin Americanist colleagues from the US encouraged, re-shaped and improved my work, particularly Janice Perlman, Leandro Benmergui, Michael Donovan, Ben Penglase, Maite Conde, Alex Dent, and Amy Chazkel. Matt Karush, Karin Rosemblatt, Ted Cohen, and Mary Kay Vaughan helped broaden the perspective. Jeff Lesser and Barbara Weinstein have been constant sources of support. Mark Healey has shared his understanding of the ways cities work. Brodie Fischer has been an unfailingly energetic and magnanimous friend and colleague.

Several students at Georgetown University have provided research assistance or helpful readings: my thanks to April Yoder, Djuan Bracey, Amanda Earley, Juan Pablo Barrientos, Juan Carlos Garzón, and Andréia Motta. The Americas Seminar and the History Department at Georgetown gave me my first opportunity to share this work with colleagues and benefit from their comments. Several Georgetown colleagues read parts of the manuscript and provided constructive feedback, including Jim Shedel, David Painter, Michael Ferreira, Shiloh Krupar, Katie Benton-Cohen, Michael Kazin, David Goldfrank, Alison Games, Aviel Roshwald, Denise Brennan, Doug Reed, Joe McCartin, and Adam Lifshey. A few read the whole thing—John McNeill, Shobana Shankar, Amy Leonard, John Tutino, Erick Langer, and Adam Rothman—and their help was decisive.

Beyond Georgetown, Desmond Arias and Robert Gay shared the kinds of insights that only scholars with deep knowledge of the subject could dispense.

I thank Valerie Millholland and Gisela Fosado at Duke University Press for believing in the project and sticking with it. This project would not have been possible without research funding from the ACLS-Charles Ryskamp Fellowship, the National Endowment for the Humanities, and the Graduate School of Arts and Sciences at Georgetown University.

My greatest debt is to my family: Sean McCann, Moira Moderelli, Helena Moraski, and Jay McCann, thank you for your confidence in me. To my wonderful boys, Booker and Seamus, I hope we enjoy many more happy times in Brazil. And to Mary Hunter, my undying gratitude and love.

VIDIGAL, RIO DE JANEIRO, JANUARY 6, 1978

As the sun rose over the hillside favela of Vidigal, local residents stood anxiously in front of their humble shacks, steadfastly defending them against the municipal workers sent to evict them. The men from COMLURB, Rio de Janeiro's sanitation company, were there to cart away their belongings, removing them to a housing project in distant Antares, in the swampy western flatlands of the city. The *favelados*, favela residents, looked down the hill, toward the upper middle-class neighborhood of Leblon, with its new apartment towers rising from blocks that had been occupied by another favela only a few years before, and to the shimmering Atlantic that lapped at Leblon's shore. They knew that the city's mayor, Marcos Tamoio, wanted to make way for more oceanfront apartment towers on Vidigal's hill and was pushing for a speedy removal of the favela to facilitate a lucrative real-estate deal.

Like most favelas in the 1970s, Vidigal was a collection of *barracos*, or shacks, assembled by their residents from wood, metal scraps, and anything at hand. A few of the homes were more stable, constructed of brick and concrete, but these too had mostly been built by their own residents in ways that defied any architectural code. Vidigal had a precarious, irregular electrical network, no paved roads within the community, and no schools or public buildings, unless one counts the chapel that doubled as a community center. Although a few homes had piped water diverted from springs higher up the slope, most residents still relied on two central *bicas*, or water spigots. None of the residents had legal title to his or her home or the lot it sat on. Most had been paying monthly rent for the use of their lots to a local resident who acted as an agent of the putative land-

owner. The lease of unserviced lots violated municipal laws but had been common practice across the city since the early twentieth century. In all these ways, Vidigal was typical of favelas in 1978. The term *favela*, as we will see in the following chapter, is difficult to define, in part because favelas have changed so dramatically over the past thirty-five years. About the only things that today's Vidigal has in common with the same neighborhood in 1978 is the absence of property title and the continuing discrimination against its residents, yet everyone still recognizes it as a favela. Vidigal was, however, unusually well located, making it a lucrative target for real-estate development.

Paulo Muniz, at the time a young resident of Vidigal, recalls that the municipal government had justified removal based on the risk of landslide. "They came with that story of risk of landslide. But if Vidigal was at risk, so were half the favelas in Rio, along with many of the luxurious homes in Gávea [a middle-class residential neighborhood nearby]. When we found out they had plans for development, we knew it was really about profit."

FIG. I.1–I.3. Vidigal, January 1978. This Vidigal resident appears to go through the process of mobilization in front of the photographer, at first lamenting the order to evacuate, then raising her arm as if hoping for inspiration, and finally pointing vehemently at the ground as if to swear she will not be moved. The smiles of the girl behind her in the first two images indicate this is, to a certain extent, *jogo de cena*, playacting. But all onlookers share her vehemence in the third image. The roughhewn shack and muddy hillside show Vidigal's characteristics in 1978. Photographs by Rogério Reis, CPDoc JB.

Muniz's friend Armando de Almeida Lima, along with several other young residents of Vidigal, mobilized local residents to resist the attempt. A few months earlier, they had founded a new favela resident's association to represent the community in its struggle against removal, with Almeida Lima as its first president.[1]

Up the hill came Bento Rubião and Eliana Athayde, a pair of lawyers from the Pastoral das Favelas, an office of the Archdiocese of Rio de Janeiro. The activists in the Pastoral das Favelas, and Rubião and Athayde in particular, were inspired by the principles of liberation theology, a blend of Christian social teaching and radical theory that animated the left wing of the Catholic Church in Latin America from the 1960s through the 1980s. Like many pastoral activists inspired by liberation theology, Rubião and Athayde sought to defend poor communities against the depredations of capitalists. Vidigal was a perfect test case for their commitment. Rubião and Athayde understood Vidigal's struggle to be a microcosm of the broader struggle against the right-wing military regime that had controlled Brazil

FIG. I.4. Bento Rubião in Vidigal. January 1978. Surrounding Rubião and in the background are an assortment of reporters, favela association leaders, residents and sanitation workers, participants in Vidigal's moment of truth. Photograph by Ronaldo Theobald, CPDoc JB.

for over a decade. They joined Almeida Lima and his comrades, produced judicial staying orders to delay the proceedings, and helped summon local reporters to document their efforts.[2]

Together, the favelados of Vidigal and the liberation theology lawyers fought a successful battle against Mayor Tamoio, his allied real-estate developers, and the dictatorship that ruled Brazil from 1964 to 1985. They mobilized to present a strong popular defense against eviction and hustled to file a series of injunctions against removal, saving one shack at a time. All but a few residents managed to avoid removal. By the middle of 1978, the residents of Vidigal had won a crucial victory in court, annulling the municipality's standing order for removal. The judge conceded that if Vidigal was at risk of landslide, so was every hillside favela in the city, and therefore risk of landslide could not itself justify removal of an urban community.[3]

Vidigal's successful self-defense set off a wave of favela mobilization throughout the city. By the end of 1978, dozens of favelas had joined the struggle against removal and for infrastructural upgrading. Basing their strategy on that of Vidigal, they founded new favela residents' associations or revived stagnant ones. In many cases, the new associations joined forces with the Pastoral das Favelas, where Rubião and Athayde coordinated legal efforts while ranks of volunteer pastoral assistants conducted outreach in favelas across the city. Frequently, the new association officers were themselves pastoral assistants. In favelas across the city, a new generation of favela association leaders challenged long-standing practices of marginalization. Together, they led a movement that challenged municipal and state governments to recognize and uphold their rights.

The favela association movement became a vanguard in the national mobilization against the dictatorship, pressuring the regime to speed its transition toward redemocratization. The favela movement, however, heralded something more than a mere return to electoral democracy: it held out the promise of a new imagination of Rio de Janeiro, one in which the gulf between rich and poor could be bridged and the children of Vidigal and Leblon would attend the same schools and share the same opportunities.

These were well-founded aspirations. For several years, it seemed not only that they would be realized, but that they already had been. Before Vidigal's successful resistance, favelas were subject to peremptory removal by private landowners or the state. Between 1962 and 1978, dozens of favelas were razed and tens of thousands of favelados were forcibly relocated, usually to distant housing projects.[4] It is no accident that this age of favela eradication largely coincided with a right-wing military dictatorship that endured from 1964–85. Although favela removal was under way before the armed forces seized power, it picked up pace dramatically under military rule. Vidigal's successful resistance marked a success for favela autonomy and a blow against the dictatorship.

The wave of mobilization for urban reform unleashed by Vidigal's success helped pressure the military government to legalize the formation of new political parties in 1980, and to hold democratic elections for state governors in 1982. Socialist candidate Leonel Brizola won the gubernatorial election in the state of Rio, based largely on his cultivation of favelado support. Brizola brought favela leaders into leadership positions in his party, Partido Democrático Trabalhista (PDT, Democratic Labor Party), and into state administration, overturning decades of practice that had consigned favelados to the role of humble supplicants before political power. He dedicated his administration to a series of projects designed to bridge the gap between Rio's rich and poor, particularly the poor residing in Rio's favelas.[5]

In 1985, the first democratic mayoral elections in Rio's history brought further victories: Saturnino Braga, another socialist—and temporarily Brizola's ally—won mayoral office. His vice-mayor, Jô Resende, was himself a leader of the urban reform movement. Like Brizola, Braga and Resende sought to bring favela activists into their administration and to make government a tool for favela improvements.[6]

In the same year, the generals finally turned over power to a civilian president, one chosen in a democratic, albeit indirect, election. These mayoral, gubernatorial, and presidential elections constituted a strengthening and expansion of the franchise that in effect gave many poor Brazilians, including favela residents, the power to vote not just for the first time since the beginning of the dictatorship but the first time ever. Citizens eager for further reform looked forward to the prospect of participating in the impending drafting of a new constitution, one that they hoped would reinforce the urban reform under way. By the mid-1980s, there were many good reasons to believe that Vidigal's victory had triggered wholesale changes in local politics, laying the groundwork for the construction of a truly democratic city.

A FEW TROUBLING DETAILS

It is an inspiring story and it is a true story. Yet it is not the whole truth. In its interstices—in the crucial details this inspiring summary leaves out—lie clues to the complexities of Rio's history over the past half-century, and in particular to the knotty relationship between Rio's favelas and the rest of the city. To begin with, it helps to know that Vidigal's community leaders served breakfast to the COMLURB workers who had been sent to evict them. This "café dos garis," or breakfast for the garbagemen, was a key element in the fight against removal. The local leaders understood that the COMLURB workers were not any better off than the favelados, had every reason to sympathize with them, and would really appreciate a hot meal. So on January 6—and on successive mornings, as the conflict unfolded—Almeida Lima and his friends met the COMLURB workers with hospitality and good humor and explained why they did not want to move, while enjoying numerous *cafezinhos*, small black coffees.[7] The carioca ritual

FIG. I.5. Garbagemen move a refrigerator, Vidigal, January 1978. This image reminds us that some Vidigal residents chose to move to the housing project in Antares. The refrigerator, symbol of upward mobility, reflects the way some residents perceived a move from a favela shack to a new home in a planned community. Photograph by Ronaldo Theobald, CPDoc JB.

of chatting over cafezinho can be a great way of getting business done, but it is even better as a way of making sure nothing gets done. The *garis* soon made it clear to their superiors that they would not remove any belongings of favela residents who did not clearly wish to leave.

That brings up the next complication. Some of the residents *did* want to leave. Despite growing disillusionment with reports of life in the projects, several favela residents were happy to trade a precarious shack in Vidigal for a single-family cinderblock home in a state-subsidized project in distant Antares. Contrary to fond memories, the favelados of Vidigal were not united. The new association leaders found themselves in a war of ideas with rivals from the Fundação Leão XIII, an organization that had started as a social services project of the Catholic Church but that had become a part of local government in the 1960s. Organizers of the Fundação Leão XIII encouraged favelados to seize the opportunity to acquire a decent home in a new neighborhood, fleeing what they characterized as the squalid promiscuity of the favela. Opponents of removal argued that this was a real-estate swindle designed to push the poor farther to the margins of urban life.[8] At bottom, the Fundação Leão XIII offered a vision of the moral sanctity of the individual nuclear family in its struggle for progress. The new favela association, in contrast, offered a vision of the moral sanctity of the larger community, where all worked together to protect the common good from outside exploiters.

The ensuing contest between the Fundação Leão XII and the favela association was one of door-to-door persuasion and careful stagecraft. Paulo Muniz worked as an assistant manager in a clothing store in nearby Ipanema, a job that required him to wear a suit and tie. When Muniz returned home each evening, Almeida Lima and Carlos Raimundo Duque warned the Fundação Leão XIII workers, "Here comes our lawyer. You'll have to talk to our lawyer!"[9] According to Muniz, the subterfuge helped put Fundação Leão workers on the defensive. The Fundação Leão XIII functionaries, for their part, alleged that Vidigal's new resident's association had "catechized everyone to appeal to the judge," a choice of words that suggested that the liberation theology lawyers were the real force behind the resistance movement. The lawyer Bento Rubião, for his part, observed that he and his colleagues could only win judicial protection for those residents who had solicited their help. Rubião's observation simultaneously defended the lawyers against allegations of outside agitation and implicitly suggested to unaffiliated favela residents that they would be wise to enlist the services of those lawyers if they wished to avoid eviction.[10]

A handful of families accepted offers of relocation, while the majority stayed put. Not all those who stayed, though, shared the new association's communitarian vision. The local resident who had long collected rents for the absentee landowner continued to live on the hill and remained a thorn in the side of the communitarian activists for years.[11] There are further complications to the Vidigal story. Mayor Tamoio was an appointee of the military regime, but he had exceeded his authority in pressing for Vidigal's removal. Key administrators in the dictatorship had already begun to distance themselves from favela removal. Tamoio was not so much a representative of the dictatorship as a middleman unaware of the real limitations on his power.[12]

Leonel Brizola, who rode the wave of favela mobilization to the governor's office, was a Socialist—he served as vice-president of the Socialist International for fourteen years—but a younger generation of leftist activists in Rio considered him just an updated version of a long Brazilian tradition of *caudilhos*, political strongmen who dispensed favors to their loyal followers. When the military regime legalized party politics in 1980, the university Left rejected Brizola and his party, opting for the new Partido dos Trabalhadores (PT, Labor Party), which they believed would advocate for more thoroughgoing change.

What do these complexities demonstrate that was not evident in the inspiring summary at the beginning of this introduction? Vidigal was already enmeshed in an informal real-estate network well before 1978. Its residents were neither defenseless before the threat of removal nor united during the struggle against it. The claim of the new favela associations to communitarian unity conflicted with the continued existence of divisive internal interests in favela real estate.

The military dictatorship was riven by internal disputes and at the local level it remained sensitive to popular mobilization. The political left wing in Rio would be split between Brizola and his favela ward-heelers on the one hand and the university Left of the PT on the other. Perhaps most important, favelados were participants in a war of ideas about the future of their neighborhoods and of their city, one whose future was more open ended than most residents cared to acknowledge.

THE DARK SIDE

These complexities help to explain the rest of the story. If 1985 was the high watermark for urban reform, the rest of that decade constituted a rapid decline. As governor, Leonel Brizola attempted to revolutionize public education for favela children and to grant property title to favela residents. These reforms were beset by deep problems and were largely scrapped by the subsequent administration. Saturnino Braga's mayoral administration was even less successful: by the end of his term, the city had gone bankrupt and his social programs came to a screeching halt.

More perniciously, drug-trafficking networks targeted key favelas as bases for their operations. The traffickers seized on the communitarian vision that had stoked the favela association movement and perverted it, turning it toward their own ends. They took over favela associations, or at the very least kept association officers on short leashes, not permitting anyone to speak for the "community" in a way that might undermine their own interests.[13]

In Vidigal, the local drug-trafficking crew initially kept its distance from the association and gradually asserted greater leverage. Then, in the 1990s, the leader of the local traffickers sent a note to the existing association president, making it explicitly clear that the traffickers had taken charge of the hillside and the association functioned at its pleasure. It seemed as if a lifetime had passed since 1978.

The prominence of criminal networks in the favelas appeared to vindicate the prejudices of Brizola's detractors. Their resentment fueled a backlash, ostensibly aimed at drug traffickers but in practice targeting favela residents in general. A wave of police violence washed across Rio in the late 1980s and early 1990s. The victims were overwhelmingly favelados, thousands of whom died in suspicious incidents at police hands.[14]

As police violence made headlines, a new phenomenon took shape covertly. Militias made up predominantly of off-duty police began expelling low-level drug-traffickers from favelas on the city's west side. Characterizing themselves as community defense units, they quickly turned into turf bosses, exploiting local commerce and exacting protection money. Like the traffickers, they established networks and cultivated political leverage.[15]

Vigilante executions became a horrific feature of urban life, most notoriously in two massacres that took place in 1993. The first was the July murder of eight street children as they slept outside the Candelária Church, carried out by members of the military police. The second, a month later, was the massacre of twenty-one residents of the north side favela of Vigário Geral. Again, military police were responsible.[16]

As a result, the fortunes of Rio's favela dwellers changed in contradictory ways between the late 1970s and the early 1990s. Life improved in immediate material respects. The threat of large-scale removal had been eliminated, and in response favelados invested in their homes. Eliana Sousa Silva, president of the favela association in Nova Holanda during Brizola's first term as governor, observes, "When we won infrastructure—water, sewer, *et cetera*—the quantity of works undertaken by individual residents was enormous. . . . People had lived there for twenty or thirty years and had never seen anything happen, and suddenly in four years, water, sewage, light."[17] Wood shacks lacking in any services evolved into three-story brick and concrete structures connected to electric, water, and sewage networks. These services, although irregular, constituted an enormous improvement over previous decades.

Brizola's schools plan failed to reach its lofty goals but succeeded in expanding access to primary and secondary school for favela children. And for the first time, favelados gained entrance into higher education, including Rio's selective public universities. Favela commerce expanded exponentially, as every favela became home to minimarkets, beauty salons, gyms, auto mechanic shops, and building supply stores. The great majority of this commerce was irregular, but few favela residents perceived that as a problem. Favela health posts expanded across the city. In sum, favelas consolidated and diversified internally.

In other, striking ways, however, life deteriorated dramatically. Favelas became stigmatized as the source of pervasive urban violence, a vastly oversimplified perception but one hugely consequential for favelados. This stigma of favela residents as the carriers of violence seemed to replace an older one based on class prejudice. Rio's public and private institutions eliminated codes that in practice had barred the entrance of favela residents, but deeper class divisions did not disappear. Instead, those divisions, hardened into new forms of discrimination and exclusion, as the border between the favela and the rest of the city was increasingly enforced through heavy armament.

Rio's elite retreated into closed condominiums, private schools, and shopping malls guarded by private security; they fortified their apartment buildings and coveted armored vehicles and personal weapons. Even the beach, theoretically Rio's most democratic public space, became the site of entrenched territorial claims and lingering conflicts.[18]

The spirit that had characterized favelado mobilization in the late 1970s dissipated or was hollowed out by the bogus communitarian claims of drug traffickers and militias. The battle of ideas between individual familial security and communitarian defense that had characterized the late 1970s was not so much settled as exhausted: neither option seemed attainable for favela residents by the early 1990s.

THE GLOBAL, THE REGIONAL, AND THE LOCAL

Rio's favelados were living through a period of momentous change at global, national, and local levels. For a brief period in the late 1970s and 1980s, they seemed to be in control of that change, or at least in control of the changes in their own lives and neighborhoods. By the early 1990s, that control and the opportunity it represented were lost, for at least a generation.

The world moved to the city in the second half of the twentieth century. The green revolution of high-yield crops and mechanized agriculture simultaneously freed most of humanity from the need to raise its own food and destroyed sustenance agriculture, sending former peasants, *campesinos*, *camponeses*, and other former farmhands and their descendants in search of urban employment. Galloping urbanization took on many variations but in the Global South was generally characterized by the proliferation of self-built housing for the urban poor in any perch they could secure long enough to nail together a rough shelter.

Rio de Janeiro had a head start on this pattern of urbanization, as Rio's favelas already had fifty years of history behind them: new waves of urbanization then drove their expansion in the second half of the twentieth century. Partly as a result, Rio's pattern of urban settlement differed from the "cup and saucer" model of a formal core ringed by informal peripheries common in most cities across the Global South. In Rio, favelas were scattered throughout the city, including within its downtown core and adjacent to luxury residential neighborhoods. As a result, the urban poor could never simply be pushed to the outskirts of the city, and conflict over urban space became central to urban life. As elsewhere, however, the population of the urban poor and the percentage living in self-built housing on irregular lots expanded dramatically during the second half of the twentieth century.

Most of Latin America fell under the power of right-wing dictatorships at some point during the 1960s–80s. These dictatorships presented themselves in varying forms across the region — Brazil's was one of the longest enduring but far from the bloodiest — but in general regarded poor urban neighborhoods as potential foci of radical leftist revolt. They eradicated poor neighborhoods where possible, evicting their residents and moving them to housing projects. When this solution proved untenable, they opted to contain the urban poor, suffocating popular mobilization while distributing material benefits in the guise of patronage to loyal supporters. In all these ways, Brazil's regime was typical.

The decline of military regimes across the region opened Latin America up to the creation of new democracies and to new political opportunities for the urban poor, among others. This was technically redemocratization, as Latin American nations had experienced previous periods of democratic rule, but in most cases amounted to the attempted creation of an inclusive democracy — one in which all citizens would have equal rights under the law—for the first time. Brazil was in the vanguard, as its regime began to cede power in the late 1970s, while others across the region were tightening their grip. And Rio's favelados were in the vanguard of the vanguard, pushing for the right to remain in their homes, as well as the rights to habeas corpus, to public education, to freedom of speech and freedom of assembly—rights all routinely denied under the dictatorship and in scant supply for the urban poor in earlier periods of democratic rule.

Across the region and indeed across the Global South, the expansion of democratic rule coincided with the exacerbation of urban violence. A small percentage of the rise in violence can be attributed to the inability of the new democratic governments to exercise the kind of arbitrary containment characteristic of their military predecessors. But not much of it: in Rio, the police became far more homicidal under democracy than they had been under dictatorship, though this violence only produced further violence, rather than suppressing it. This too, was not unusual, as partially demobilized security forces of the Latin American dictatorships became interest groups in the new Latin American democracies, exacerbating violence in attempts to secure their own position.

These militarized interest groups, along with their rivals and occasional collaborators in criminal networks, operated in an expanding illegal economic sector. The two principal commodities were cocaine and guns. Rio's favelas had little of the former and few of the latter in the 1960s, when a bandit with a .45 was a notable rarity and domestically grown marijuana the only common illegal substance. The favelas were awash in both these things by the end of the 1980s, undermining the democratic experiment in progress within them.

Rio's transitions over the past fifty years have thus been typical in some ways (sharp rises in population and informal housing) and prefigurative in others (an earlier expansion of democracy than in much of the Global South, coupled with an earlier spike in urban violence). Its transitions have also been more intense than in most places. On the one hand, popular mobilization swept a socialist governor to power in the midst of a right-wing military dictatorship. On the other, as the drug and turf wars raged from the late 1980s into the twenty-first century, Rio became one of the most violent cities in the world.

MAP 1. Map of Brazil, with inset map of the metropolitan region of Rio de Janeiro. The municipality of Rio de Janeiro dominates the metropolitan region. The municipalities along the northern border of the city of Rio constitute the Baixada Fluminense, or Fluminense Lowlands. Like the municipalities north of Niterói, those that make up the Baixada Fluminense are characterized by a high density of irregular subdivisions. Cartography by Bill Nelson.

THE ARGUMENT IN BRIEF

Between the late 1970s and the mid-1980s favela activists led a movement to bridge the long-standing divide between favelas and the formal city in Rio de Janeiro. They challenged the practices that had long consigned favela residents to difficult lives—insecurity of land tenure, limited access to formal employment and public education, and the expectation of routine harassment by the forces of law and order—demanding equal rights to the city. In a rush of *Mobilization*, they built a movement that redrew the political map of the city and helped push the nation toward redemocratization.

Having played a decisive role in the election of a crusading left-wing governor, these favela activists joined forces with political allies and attempted to institute a thorough process of *Reform*. The reforms this alliance instituted—particularly in regards to land titling, education, and public security—shaped the city for the next two decades. Although these reforms brought some benefits, they fell well short of early aspirations. Their shortcomings owed partly to external and partly to internal forces. Externally, national recession and hyperinflation hampered attempts to upgrade Rio's favelas. Changing patterns of international drug trafficking turned Rio into a valuable export node, triggering violent turf battles. Internally, each of the reforms had two key strategic flaws. They assumed the continuation of popular mobilization but provided few incentives for its support, and they strengthened middlemen who connected favela residents to municipal and state benefits without instituting any conditions to enforce the middlemen's accountability. These middlemen became irresistible targets for corruption. In consequence, these reforms did not unite favela and city, but reconfigured the boundaries that separated them.

Through the mid-1980s, energetic reformers struggled to hold together a fraying coalition against mounting odds. By 1988, Rio de Janeiro reached a *Breaking Point*. Floods and landslides wracked the city. Municipal government went bankrupt trying to respond to the emergency while staving off the effects of hyperinflation. Drug wars and police violence ravaged the city. Self-styled *donos do morro*, owners of the hill—well-armed traffickers who protected their turf through a combination of violence and patronage—became the new lords of Rio's favelas. Criminal turf monopolization became the new expression of the barrier between favela and city.

Things got worse before they could get better, in the *Unraveling* of the 1990s. Drug lords formed criminal networks, intimidating and co-opting local political and civil representatives. Favela associations, recently the spearhead of mobilization, became moribund husks lightly concealing criminal turf monopolization. Emergent nongovernmental organizations (NGOs), powerless to confront this state of affairs, instead operated within it, making necessary accommodations while achieving what they could. Defense militias ostensibly organized to drive out traffickers themselves became new criminal interest groups, exercising leverage over local commerce while limiting political representation.

Favela leaders began their movement in order to guarantee the right of favela residents to remain in their homes. By the early 1990s, that right of occupation and possession—albeit not the legal title to favela land itself—was largely guaranteed. But rising urban violence and criminal turf monopolization imposed new limits on the rights of favela residents. In practice if not in law, favelados lost the right to choose their own political representatives and the right to circulate through the city free of police harassment. This attenuation of rights became routinized in the daily operations of the city, in everything from policing strategies to provision of public utilities.

Mobilization and *Reform* had offered an opportunity to erase the boundary between favela and city. After reaching the *Breaking Point* and enduring the *Unraveling*, that opportunity seemed more distant than ever, and favelas were perpetuated as zones of exception, where the rule of law and guarantees of citizenship did not apply.

At each of these stages, the fates of Rio's favelas and their residents were determined largely at the nexus that connected the favelas to the rest of the city. For this reason, most of this book is devoted to the rise and evolution of political leaders within Rio's favelas and their interaction with civil servants, elected officials, and public intellectuals. More than any other factor, these interactions determined where the bold strategies of *Mobilization* and *Reform* would succeed and where they would fail. The drug lords and militia leaders were also political actors, and I analyze their role in pushing Rio to the *Breaking Point* and in exacerbating its *Unraveling* with that understanding.

"Mobilization," "Reform," and the "Breaking Point" each get one extensive chapter exploring their inner workings. The "Unraveling"—because it has been treated in depth elsewhere and because, in my analysis, it largely played out in accordance with conditions already determined—gets a shorter chapter.[19]

These chapters are followed by an epilogue, which considers the current state of Rio de Janeiro and the fragile new beginning under way. Although the reforms of the 1980s failed, the dream of the extension of full and complete citizenship to the residents of Rio's favelas did not die. Many of its staunchest advocates, along with their acolytes, remain influential policy-makers, civil servants, and organizers. Over the last several years, they have seized a new opportunity to build a Rio de Janeiro that lives up to its democratic promise and to its nickname: the Marvelous City. The strategies they have crafted explicitly seek to revive the animating vision of the reforms of the 1980s while eliminating the design flaws that undermined them in their earlier incarnation. Like those earlier efforts, current experiments are both hugely promising and risky. Favela residents stand to gain tremendously in the current transitions — many already have — but those gains are not universally shared among all favela residents and do not always offset associated risks. This new beginning is far too indeterminate for a historian to treat it in depth. As a result, the epilogue is short and speculative. But first, we must take a brief look at the big questions.

THE BIG PICTURE

Rio de ladeiras	("Rio of steep hills
Civilização encruzilhada	civilization crucified
Cada ribanceira é uma nação	Each ravine is a nation
À sua maneira	In its own way
Com ladrão	With thieves
Lavadeiras, honra, tradição	Washerwomen, honor, tradition
Fronteiras, munição pesada	Borders, heavy munitions")

—CHICO BUARQUE, "Estação Derradeira" (song) 1987.

OCTOBER 1, 1991

My first visit to Rio coincided with a garbage strike. Employees of the municipal garbage company walked off the job, demanding better wages. Mayor Marcello Alencar refused to negotiate. Alencar was Leonel Brizola's protégé, a legacy that should have stood him in good stead with the organized working class, but in the early 1990s he began to separate himself from his socialist mentor, cutting municipal expenses and moving toward the fiscal center. Trash piled up in the street, reaching ten feet high on some corners, adding a particular ripeness to the humid carioca spring. Cariocas went about their business, confident that workers and mayor would eventually compromise and that inflation would outpace their negotiations in any case.

It was not a particularly significant strike: it was one in a hundred of similar labor conflicts during the hyperinflationary period of the 1980s and early 1990s. Government wages were indexed so that pay would rise along with inflation, but wage earners often watched the real value of their pay drop precipitously between the opening of a month and the indexing that took place at month's end. This devaluation made for constant tension between public employees and local administration. By 1991, cariocas were accustomed to temporary work stoppages and seemed unfazed. For a visitor, though, it made for a pungent introduction to the Marvelous City.

I remember one afternoon in particular. I was resting on the steps of my hotel, the Venezuela, a budget traveler's joint in the middle-class neighborhood of Flamengo. Fifteen feet from where I stood, a skinny boy of about twelve was attempting in vain to remove the radio from a Chevette with a bent kitchen knife. As the car alarm blared, patrons at the nearby bar and passersby glanced over, deemed the matter not worth their attention, and went back to their business. The child operated with the dedication and lack of skill of the ambitious novice—attacking the radio from left, right, top and bottom—to no avail. Eventually he gave up and trudged down the street carrying nothing but a few cassettes, skirting the garbage pile on the corner on his way. One of the patrons of the bar walked over to the car and ever so gently closed the passenger door, a gesture that did not diminish the ongoing noise of the car alarm.

It occurred to me that Rio's problems might go beyond the gulf between rich and poor for which Brazil was justifiably notorious. Inequality explained the boy's poverty in the midst of Flamengo and perhaps the resentment suggested by his grim hacking away at the radio. Yet it did not explain how administrative sclerosis and street crime had become so routinized into the workings of the city that residents did their best to ignore both and carry on as usual.

Even as a first-time visitor I realized that the incident did not indicate that cariocas tolerated petty theft. Rio and São Paulo had already become infamous for the operations of death squads that regularly harassed and in some cases murdered boys like the one I watched that day in Flamengo. But the incident made clear that no one on the street saw any likely benefit in intervening in any way, certainly not by alerting the authorities.

I had a great time that week, in any case—it is famously difficult not to. But perhaps the seeds of this project were planted on that Flamengo street in 1991. At some level, I wanted to find out how Rio had reached that point. As I pursued that question over the next twenty years, at first casually and then with sustained focus, I kept circling back to the complex and evolving

FIG. 1.1. Nova Holanda, 1969. The image captures the favela in the early stages of transition: in the foreground, a toddler in diapers stands in the doorway of a shack perched on *palafitas*, or stilts, in the marsh; in the background rises a newer, two-story, brick construction. Photograph by Rubens Barbosa, CPDoc JB.

relationship between Rio's favelas and the rest of the city, which seemed to underlie so many of Rio's challenges and conflicts.

WHAT IS A FAVELA?

The division between "favelas" and "the rest of the city" is partly real and partly imaginary. Real distinctions between favelas and other parts of the city have often been oversimplified in the public imagination, in ways that exaggerate a binary tension. Favelas are obviously *part* of the city, and yet for over a century *favela* and *cidade* have been counterposed to each other as mutually exclusive terms, suggesting that the favela is what the city is not, and vice versa. In 2004, I attended a seminar entitled "Favela é Cidade," the Favela Is the City. The activists who organized the seminar intended the title to call attention to all the ways in which favelas are part of the fabric of Rio de Janeiro, but the need to do so suggested that most people still see them as irrevocably different. This calls for a more careful consideration.[1]

What is a favela? In practice, the term describes a variety of neighborhoods. The first favelas got their start when the working poor and demobilized soldiers, with former slaves and their children strongly represented in both categories, settled hillsides near Rio's commercial center in the last years of the nineteenth century. Providência, Rio's iconic "first favela," was partly settled by soldiers returning from a campaign to wipe out a millenarian peasant village in the harsh backlands of Canudos, in northeastern Brazil. The term *favela* came from the name for a hardy weed that grew around Canudos. Although this origin story indicates both the social and economic profile of early favela residents and the poetic resonance of their struggle to survive, Providência was only one of several similar communities. From the start, local strongmen and property owners divided these areas into rough lots and rented them out, using political leverage to protect their irregular real-estate operations. The razing of crowded tenement housing in the first years of the twentieth century spurred the growth of early favelas, as former residents—pushed out of the formal real-estate market—resorted to the informal market.

Even by this early date, the two factors that would shape favela expansion for the next century were already established: the formal sector was not structured to provide housing for the urban poor and working class, and actors in the informal sector stood ready to extract profit from their ability to control access to terrain. The first factor has always been clear and has had obvious consequences. The second is more subtle but equally decisive, and is best summarized by the popular expression "todo pedaço tem dono," or every piece has an owner. There is no such thing as free urban soil. Instead, informal landlords have used their practical control over unoccupied land to extract rents from the urban poor in exchange for permission to build or occupy space.

Through the middle of the twentieth century, the lowest-paid workers of enterprises such as factories and hospitals were often permitted to erect shacks in the rear of the property, a solution that guaranteed their employers a local workforce while suppressing wages. Employees of public and semipublic institutions such as pension institutes and the water company often followed similar practices. Over time, as families grew and residents rented subplots to newcomers, these nuclei grew into small favelas.[2]

The consolidation of the formal real-estate market in the middle de-

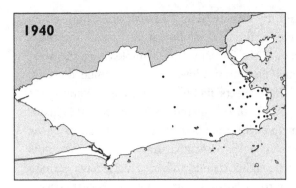

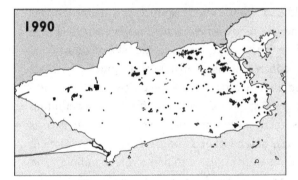

MAP 2. Favela growth over time. Favelas first emerged in the central city, near the residential neighborhoods on the south side, and adjacent to the industrial factories on the north side, densifying along with that industrial growth. Between 1960 and 1990 favela growth spread to the west side of the city, often accompanying highway construction and nearby infrastructural expansion, and grew increasingly dense throughout. Over the past two decades, that densification has continued, accompanied by the emergence of isolated and often temporary smaller favelas. Cartography by Bill Nelson, based on material from the Instituto Pereira Passos.

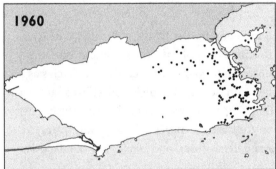

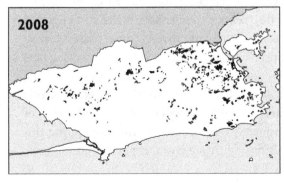

cades of the twentieth century swallowed up most available land, setting aside much of it in reserve for future development. Strict building codes and caps on rent increases in the formal market, coupled with the near-absence of mortgage loans, discouraged investment in popular housing. Sporadic attempts at housing projects did little to alleviate the shortage of worker housing, to say nothing of the unemployed poor, and this insufficiency speeded the growth of informal housing in the interstices of the formal city. Favelas such as Vidigal and Rocinha grew on former farm plots close to growing residential neighborhoods. Informal real estate became a more lucrative market than truck farming, giving property owners strong incentives to demarcate and rent lots.[3]

Up until the turn of the millennium, the Instituto Brasileiro de Geografia e Estatística (IBGE, Brazilian Institute of Geography and Statistics), keeper of Brazil's official census and geographic data, defined favelas as a type of "subnormal agglomeration," consisting of "a collection of at least fifty-one housing units, occupying or having occupied in the recent past terrain that is not the property of the residents (public or private), arrayed, in general, in disorganized and dense form, and lacking, in the majority, essential public services."[4]

Adequate in the middle of the twentieth century, this definition was already out of date by the late 1970s, when iconic favelas such as Jacarezinho and Rocinha had grown to populations in the tens of thousands, with nuclei of brick and concrete homes surrounded by more precarious dwellings, and with irregular hookups to public electricity and water networks. The massive changes that ensued made the official IBGE definition a relic. By the mid-1990s, many favelas had public services as extensive as those in other working-class neighborhoods, with a crucial distinction: in favelas, residents themselves were expected to play a role in building and maintaining public infrastructure. Favelas remained dense and disorganized, but these are hardly distinctive characteristics in Rio de Janeiro.

Although the criterion of an absence of property title is more relevant, favelas are not "squatter cities."[5] Squatting, in the sense of occupying land that legally belongs to someone else without paying rent, was never the rule in Rio's favelas. As we will see in chapter 3, the election of Leonel Brizola triggered a brief wave of land invasions on Rio's north side, and several of these land invasions subsequently turned into enduring favelas, but this was an anomaly in Rio's history. Squatting is at this point almost entirely absent. The vast majority of Rio's favela residents either bought their lot on an informal market or pay rent. The "title of possession," a document that helps protect them from eviction, possessed by some does not give them legal right to sell or pass on the property.[6] Only a tiny minority of residents has legal title to property. Absence of property title, then, has remained the single most consistent characteristic of favelas for more than a century. Yet it has done so in ways that reveal the existence of a deeply rooted informal real-estate market, a system that complicates efforts to confer property title on current residents.[7]

Absence of property title is invisible, and is therefore not enough to define a category of urban neighborhood. Favela architecture is a more obvious identifying characteristic, particularly in the labyrinthine communities that climb the hills above Rio's south side. On these steep slopes, brick complexes of several stories rise off of tiny, bending alleys, propped on wooden stilts, strung together by knotted electric wires. Open space in these communities is almost nonexistent; every square meter of usable space has been claimed and developed.

Favelas in the flatlands of Rio's west side look quite different, however, with regular street grids and defined building plots. What these differences immediately make clear is that there is no such thing as a typical favela; nothing comes close. "Cada favela é um mundo" — each favela is a world — as a popular saying has it. Or, as composer Chico Buarque put it in lyrics that open this chapter, "Each ravine is a nation."[8]

There are a number of identifiable types of favela, however, defined largely by location, size, and length of settlement. They have experienced the transitions of the past forty years in different ways. Favelas on Rio's south side experienced both material consolidation and rising violence earliest, in the mid-1980s. As the favelas located closest to expanding employment opportunities and to middle-class drug consumers, they offered material advantages to residents, as well as to criminal networks.

Favelas on the north side and near the old city center were hit hardest by deindustrialization and rising unemployment in the 1980s. Many of these had been symbiotic with adjacent factories. As São Paulo's industrial belt boomed, Rio's shrank. Factories closed down or relocated, and nearby favela populations expanded — in several cases colonizing the abandoned factory itself. Working-class neighborhoods became reservoirs of the unemployed urban poor. Because these favelas offered a smaller economic base and were farther from middle-class consumers, they were typically targeted later by expanding criminal networks. But when turf wars came, they often came with greater intensity and lasted longer than those in the south zone, where the presence of local media encouraged police to contain violence.

Favelas on Rio's west side, most of which grew along with the expansion of middle-class construction in this area in the 1970s and 1980s, were more likely to be taken over by defense militias by the end of the 1990s. Although these favelas tended not to experience years of violent turf war, their residents often faced greater limitations on their civil rights, given the militias' intolerance of dissent.

One common feature across these different types is that homes are never finished. Favela dwellings nearly always have *lajes*, flat roofs, so that residents can construct another story at some point in the future. The unfinished nature of favela architecture is a more consistent characteristic than the apparently chaotic or organic style of the iconic south side favelas.

Favelas are not slums. They began as the only available housing option for the urban poor, but over the past thirty years they have diversified economically. Many favelas contain subneighborhoods characterized by high rental prices, public utilities, schools, health posts and a full array of commerce. Despite economic mobility and social investment, however, they are still considered favelas both by residents and outsiders. There are poor neighborhoods in Rio, moreover, that are not favelas. Poverty is no longer a consistent identifying characteristic.[9]

What these variations make clear is that favelas are not defined by a clear set of physical characteristics; rather, they are defined by their history. They began as unplanned and unserviced settlements nurturing an informal real estate market and progressed through stages of consolidation and diversification without ever being fully incorporated into the surrounding formal city.

This has not been for lack of trying. Planners and politicians have attempted to solve the "problem of the favela" for nearly a century. The creation of a model favela—or, alternatively, a model neighborhood for the working poor to replace the favela—has been the animating desire behind several high-profile interventions over the past eighty years.[10] These interventions have typically been designed as emergency responses to urgent problems, designed to fix all that ails favelas in a brief flurry of reform. That sense of urgency has often hindered gradualist reforms that have proven

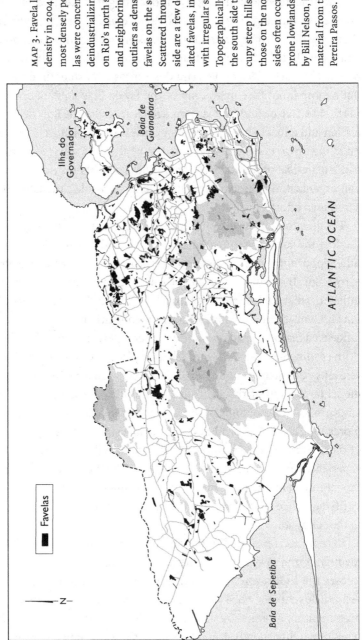

MAP 3. Favela location and density in 2004. By 2004, the most densely populated favelas were concentrated in the deindustrializing stretches on Rio's north side. Rocinha and neighboring Vidigal are outliers as densely populated favelas on the south side. Scattered throughout the west side are a few densely populated favelas, interspersed with irregular subdivisions. Topographically, favelas on the south side typically occupy steep hillsides, whereas those on the north and west sides often occupy flood-prone lowlands. Cartography by Bill Nelson, based on material from the Instituto Pereira Passos.

Favelas

Ilha do Governador

Baía de Guanabara

Baía de Sepetiba

ATLANTIC OCEAN

N

more successful on the outskirts of the city and elsewhere. When urgent reforms fail to reach their goals, they are typically abandoned, leaving favelas to await the next crisis.[11]

Until the 1960s, model interventions sought to replace favelas with planned worker housing. As the experience of housing projects such as Cidade de Deus demonstrates, these plans proved insufficient in both scale and vision. In the late 1960s, a team of visionary architects and urban planners led by Carlos Nelson Ferreira dos Santos won state funding to carry out a more innovative upgrading of the favela Brás de Pina on the city's north side. Nelson and his team worked closely with the Brás de Pina association and a local liberation theology priest to enable favela residents to build their own new homes on lots demarcated and serviced by the state, using materials provided by the state. The architects provided basic plans and organizational assistance, but residents provided the labor through communal effort.[12]

The dictatorship, still committed to favela removal, discouraged state funding for subsequent upgrading projects, and Nelson did not have another opportunity to carry out a similar project on the same scale until the early 1980s. In the meantime, he earned a PhD in anthropology, writing an influential dissertation that focused on the Brás de Pina experience. Brás de Pina became internationally celebrated among urban planners, and deeply influenced favela upgrading projects of the 1980s and 1990s.[13]

In ensuing decades a rise and fall took place in terms of renewed interventions. Chapters 3 and 4 explore Leonel Brizola's attempt to make model favelas out of the adjacent communities of Cantagalo and Pavão-Pavãozinho, overlooking Copacabana and Ipanema. Chapter 5 briefly explores the Favela-Bairro program of the late 1990s and early 2000s. Each of these efforts yielded significant gains while falling short of goals. Their experience lends a cautionary note to considerations of the most recent model intervention, the Unidade de Policiamento Pacificadora (UPP, or Pacifying Police Unit) strategy of the past several years, discussed briefly in the epilogue.

Urgent interventions bring much-needed resources to the favelas. In identifying the favela as a problem to be solved, however, they also reinforce the separation between favelas and the rest of the city. This tendency helps explain why Providência is still universally considered a favela over a century after its initial settlement. Comparing favelas to two other types of neighborhoods, irregular subdivisions and housing projects, will help clarify the endurance of the favela as a distinct part of the city, viewed as separate and different from surrounding formal zones.

COMPARING FAVELAS, IRREGULAR SUBDIVISIONS, AND HOUSING PROJECTS

Informal land tenure, or lack of property title to one's dwelling, is not limited to favelas. Irregular loteamentos, or subdivisions, and conjuntos habitacionais, or housing projects, share this characteristic. Comparing favelas to these neighborhoods helps reveal the function of favelas within the city, explaining why, even after a century of history, they are commonly perceived as something other than the city.

Irregular subdivisions are common in the western zone of Rio de Janeiro and in neighboring municipalities, common enough that their irregularity—defined primarily by their residents' absence of legal property title—has been the rule rather than the exception. The origins of many irregular subdivisions do not differ dramatically from that of many favelas. Land developers bought tracts on the expanding periphery of the city, divided these into lots, and sold the undeveloped lots to individual families, who then built their own homes. Irregular subdivisions were already emerging on the west side of the city by the 1930s, but their most rapid period of growth came between the 1950s and the 1980s, as Rio's population boomed. When settlement in these subdivisions became dense enough to support collective action, local residents banded together to lobby for infrastructure and services.

In many cases, the original developers had only the shakiest of legal claims to these tracts, and in almost all cases, these irregular developers failed to register their subdivided lots with state and municipal authorities. As a result, residents of the irregular subdivisions held documents of negligible legal value, purchased from shady developers. As one property manager summed up the process to a researcher: "An idiot surveyor drew it up for an idiot owner. The idiot owner bought off a corrupt official, in the time when the mayor was an imbecile. . . . You can write it up that way, because the story is always the same."[14]

There is no consistent juridical way to distinguish between irregular subdivisions and favelas. In the early stages of their growth, both have typically been characterized by absence of legal property title, self-built housing, and the growth of informal real-estate markets sheltered by political protection. But they have had strikingly different functions in

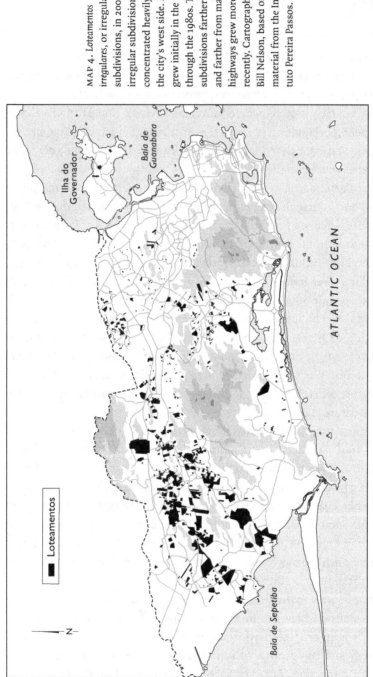

MAP 4. *Loteamentos irregulares*, or irregular subdivisions, in 2008. The irregular subdivisions are concentrated heavily on the city's west side. Most grew initially in the 1950s through the 1980s. The subdivisions farther west and farther from main highways grew more recently. Cartography by Bill Nelson, based on material from the Instituto Pereira Passos.

Ilha do Governador

Baía de Guanabara

Baía de Sepetiba

ATLANTIC OCEAN

Loteamentos

—N—

the political machinery of Rio de Janeiro. The irregular subdivisions have gradually been incorporated into the surrounding fabric of the city to the point that there is no visible or cultural indication of their difference.[15] The favelas, in contrast, continue to be recognized as nodes of difference within the surrounding city.

The preponderance of characteristics of the overall neighborhood, rather than any specific individual action, has determined the contrasting trajectories of irregular subdivisions and favelas. The great majority of residents of irregular subdivisions had enough resources to purchase lots upfront, and many of them subsequently acquired formalized ownership. Overall levels of legal title often remain low, but where the neighborhood in general is perceived as part of the legal framework of the city, that perception redounds to the benefit of all its residents. Architectural tendencies have also come into play: in contrast to favela homes, always under construction and ready for the next stage of expansion, subdivision homes typically look finished, and the appearance of completion has facilitated the process of regularization. This is more an issue of presentation and perception than of raw percentages: residents of irregular subdivisions mobilized as homeowners and gained recognition in that way. Residents of favelas, perceived as squatters even when that has not been the case, have been consigned to a different category, receiving lesser treatment and suffering greater consequences.[16]

Irregular subdivisions fit more neatly into global patterns of urbanization than do favelas. Evidence from Mexico City and Lima, for example, suggests similar processes of gradual incorporation, diversification, and regularization of neighborhoods that had their inception as poor, peripheral and irregular.[17]

Rio's housing projects have followed an opposite trajectory: they started in the formal sector and gradually became part of the informal sector. Most of the housing projects were built in the 1960s and early 1970s. Many of their initial residents were former favelados recently evicted in the favela removal campaign. They were moved to projects where water and sewage networks were, at best, still under construction; where schools were planned but not built; where roads were unpaved and public transportation did not reach. These residents were given nontransferable property titles and required to make low monthly mortgage payments. Despite legal restrictions on transfer, some original deed holders sold their keys and the documents that went with them on an informal market, using the profits to buy or rent elsewhere—often in favelas near the one from which they had been recently removed.[18]

Residents often did not keep up with their required monthly payments, partly in protest over the state's failure to deliver on its promises of infrastructure and services. Again, the preponderance of characteristics was decisive: as growing numbers of residents failed to make monthly payments, incentives for remaining residents to keep up their payments diminished. In turn, as growing numbers of residents fell delinquent, the state's incentives to complete infrastructure and deliver services diminished. Residents who were behind in their payments or who were not the legally registered occupants of their homes were in a weak political position. They could not demand that the state fulfill its obligations. They could only seek political patronage—the exchange of votes for political favors—to ameliorate conditions sporadically.[19]

As conditions in the housing projects deteriorated, newcomers built their own housing between the apartment blocks, and irregular occupants of the projects could not protest. As a result, by the late 1980s, the housing projects were themselves perceived as favelas, both by outsiders and by their own residents. Cidade de Deus, or City of God, is the best-known example, thanks to the book and film that chronicle that neighborhood's transition from rudimentary housing project to violent favela. There are numerous other examples: samba singer Bezerra da Silva included shout-outs to several projects-turned-favela in his 1985 hit "Saudação às Favelas" (Salutation to the favelas), demonstrating that the understanding of these projects as favelas was well established by that date.[20]

What do these contrasting fortunes tell us about the political function of irregular subdivisions, housing projects, and favelas? The irregular subdivisions built in the great wave of the 1950s through the 1980s have changed in ways that accompany and support the upward mobility of their residents. Although they are not an example of successful prescriptive urban planning, over the long term they demonstrate a successful capacity of the city to expand and incorporate new sectors. The favelas and housing projects have also been incorporated into the political machinery of the city, but in ways that reproduce informality and vulnerability.

The irregular subdivisions have been characterized by the gradual strengthening of rights, both the right of property and rights to public services, to political association, and to freedom of movement—the third of which Brazilians ritualistically cite as "o direito de ir e vir," the right to come and go. For residents of favelas this same process of strengthening of rights stalled, even where they achieved material upward mobility. For residents of housing projects, it not only stalled; it slid backward.

Favela dwellers have historically been "rights poor": they have been treated as second-class citizens by official bureaucracies and representatives of the law, in regard to property and also in regard to public services, political association, and the right to come and go.[21] Residents of housing projects were consigned to this same status. Agents of municipal and state government—the police, above all—have often treated both favela dwellers and residents of housing projects as illegal aliens in their own city: as long as they make no trouble, they are free to go about their business. Once entangled in the workings of the law, they are likely to find themselves caught in a knot that can only be severed with the assistance of a political patron. This has maintained favelados and residents of the housing projects in a vulnerable state, dependent on the intercession of political middlemen. In contrast to residents of irregular subdivisions, who passed through a stage of vulnerability to a stage of security, residents of favelas and housing projects have been consigned to indefinite insecurity. Over the past thirty years, this uncertainty has reinforced the real and imagined boundaries between these neighborhoods and the rest of the city.

RACE AND RIGHTS IN THE FAVELAS

The "rights poverty" of residents of favelas and housing projects connects in direct but complex ways to the history of racial discrimination in Brazil. Contrary to the impressions one might glean from high-profile popular depictions, this is not because being a favelado is synonymous with being black, as this is definitely not the case. Many of the inhabitants of Rio's favelas are black, but the percentage varies widely from one favela to the next, and every favela is home to many nonblack residents.[22] There are many black cariocas who have never entered a favela, much less lived in one. More important, the historical trajectory of favelas with a high percentage of black residents has not differed dramatically from that of favelas with a relatively low percentage of black residents, suggesting that discrimination against black residents has not in itself determined the continued exclusion of favela residents from the full protections of civil rights.

That said, black favela residents have faced particular hurdles in achieving civil rights, and persistent racism does explain part of the stigma against favela residents.[23] In chapter two, figure 2.1 showing Leonel Brizola visiting the *barraco* of an elderly black resident of Cantagalo gives a strong sense of these connections. The woman in the photograph seems to be emerging not only from her humble, wattle and daub shack, but from Brazil's past. The image reminds one how late abolition came to Brazil—not until 1888—and how deeply the legacy of slavery marked the unequal distribution of rights and opportunities to Brazil's black population in the twentieth century. Black residents were inevitably concentrated more heavily in the substandard, precarious urban spaces effectively reserved for those without full rights: Rio's favelas. Furthermore, their blackness reinforced dominant understandings of these as zones beneath the protections of law and guarantees of citizenship.

Favela residents recognized this and fought against both racism *and* discrimination based on place of residence. For many participants, the favela movement of the late 1970s and early 1980s was intertwined with a black movement that also helped push Brazil toward redemocratization.[24] Black residents of the predominantly black Santa Marta favela, for example, helped form a local group militating against apartheid in South Africa, because they recognized a resonance between their own struggle and that of the residents of the black townships of Soweto. Throughout the early 1980s, that group met at a vacant lot next to the metro station under construction in the Botafogo neighborhood, just a few blocks from Santa Marta. In 1985, acceding to this group's request, Mayor Saturnino Braga named the adjacent street the Rua Nelson Mandela, a fitting reminder of the way global trends of black mobilization against racism informed the favela movement and the struggle over urban space in Rio.[25]

Leonel Brizola's new party, the PDT, recognized the connections between the black and favela movements and eagerly brought leaders of both into key party positions. More than any other factor, this explains the PDT's regular trouncing of its foremost rival on the Left, the PT, in municipal and state elections through the 1990s. The PDT drew the support of black favela residents based on appeal to their sense of both racial and residential identity, something the PT at least in Rio, proved unable to do.

Like the story of Vidigal's resistance that opened the book, however, this summary leaves out crucial details. In this case, it leaves out the ways race in the favelas has been complicated by discrimination against migrants from northeastern Brazil. Although these migrants are known collectively as *nordestinos*, they are often stereotyped as *baianos* or *paraíbas*, names that refer to specific state origins in the Northeast but that have taken on disparaging overtones in Rio. Northeastern migrants run the phenotypical gamut from pale to dark skinned. They rarely self-identify as black, and are not generally perceived by native cariocas as black. Instead, they self-identify and are perceived as nordestino, which becomes, in effect, its own ethnicity.

Like black cariocas, northeastern migrants are strongly represented in Rio's favelas. In the early 1980s, there were some favelas that were largely black and others that were almost entirely northeastern. Cantagalo, for example, was predominantly black, whereas the neighboring favela of Pavão-Pavãozinho was overwhelmingly northeastern. Over the course of the 1980s, drug traffickers from the two neighborhoods engaged in a series of turf wars, and quasi-ethnic hostilities played a role in these hostilities.[26] As these turf wars became part of larger conflicts between rival criminal networks, however, they lost that quasi-ethnic resonance. By the early 2000s, both neighborhoods had diversified demographically and economically and were increasingly understood as parts of the same favela "complex," or cluster of several favelas. Their shared history suggests that both racism and discrimination against northeastern migrants have exacerbated challenges for favela residents and imposed obstacles to pan-favela organization. Antiblack racism has been one element, inconsistently present, of the relegation of favela dwellers to second-class status. Although it is a key part of understanding favela history, it is not in itself explanatory of continued separation between favelas and the surrounding formal city.

MOBILIZATION, REFORM, AND RIGHTS TO THE CITY

The favela mobilization of the late 1970s and early 1980s and the reforms that followed were an explicit, urgent attempt to break the cycle of rights poverty and become "rights secure." That attempt almost succeeded. It did change the relationship of favela dwellers to city and state government. Mobilization and reform forever ended the expectation that favelados would come as supplicants before state power. They brought into common use a discourse of rights to the city, of expectation of equal treatment that itself helped to change perceptions of the favela.[27]

One of the most striking features of this movement was the prominence of young women, often in their early twenties, in positions of leadership. These young women challenged not only economic stratification and political marginalization, but also expectations of the submission of young women to elder males. In an odd way, these expectations may have created opportunities for young women in the context of Brazil's redemocratization. Because women — particularly those from the favela — were not expected to become political leaders, strong women activists were seen as unthreatening community builders rather than as aspiring politicians. Many rose to the fore of their favela associations based on this understanding.

Eliana Sousa Silva was prototypical in this regard. She was born in 1962, in Paraíba, in northeastern Brazil. Her family migrated to Rio in the late 1960s, and found housing in the favela of Nova Holanda, or New Holland, so named because its canals distantly recalled Amsterdam — with the difference that in Nova Holanda, the canals were brackish malarial inlets flanked by rough wooden shacks on *palafitas*. Silva attended the nearest Catholic church, took her first communion and then her confirmation, and became a "catechist," or lay religious instructor. She soon grew disenchanted, as she was more interested in political mobilization than in religious orthodoxy. Several years later, when a younger priest — a passionate liberation theologist — was posted to the parish, she began to work closely with the church again. Her approach to communitarian mobilization and her understanding of socialist reform were profoundly shaped by the ideas of liberation theology, and she worked closely with the Pastoral das Favelas on strategy within Nova Holanda and across the city.[28]

She began working with a health post coordinated by a nearby hospital, whose researchers encouraged her to continue with her own studies. She won admission to the prestigious federal university in 1982. The main campus of the Universidade Federal do Rio de Janeiro (UFRJ) was separated from Nova Holanda only by a narrow marsh (replaced by a major highway later that decade), and many residents of the favela worked there, but Silva was one of the first to attend.[29] As she continued her studies, Silva and a cohort of fellow organizers spearheaded communitarian mobilization in Nova Holanda, ensuring that federal initiatives to replace the canals and homes on stilts with landfill and solid construction brought advantages to local residents rather than driving them out. In the early 1980s, they won control of the favela's association and used that as a platform for establishing connections to neighboring favelas in a long stretch of low-lying, flood-prone neighborhoods becoming known as the Complexo da Maré. Silva subsequently served two terms as the association's president, then left the association in the 1990s in order to work with NGOs and pursue graduate study, becoming one of Rio's foremost engaged scholars on questions of urban violence.

Eliana Sousa Silva was particularly energetic, smart, and persistent, but the basic details of her story reflect that of many young favela women who took on political leadership in the 1980s. Their emergence was one of the profound achievements of the decade, one whose significance took decades to become fully apparent.

Despite their accomplishments, in the short term, mobilization and reform did not put an end to treatment of favela dwellers as second-class citizens. Instead, the setbacks of the late 1980s reconfigured the rights poverty of favela residents. In the early 1970s, state government treated favela residents as the reserve pool of patronage politics. By the early 1990s, state government treated favela residents as the contagious source of urban violence plaguing Rio de Janeiro. In both cases, that treatment reflected and reinforced broader understandings.

During the military dictatorship from 1964–85, federal, state, and municipal legislative bodies continued to function, albeit in ways limited and distorted by the regime. Dictatorial manipulation of the elected legislature exacerbated long-standing tendencies toward patronage in local politics, and the favelas and housing projects proved fertile ground for this practice. Favela activists in the late 1970s made patronage politics one of their first and most prominent targets. They insisted on cutting out the middlemen, the political brokers who had delivered occasional material improvements such as a paved road or a sports court in return for political support. They strove to represent themselves in the halls of state and municipal power.[30]

The activists succeeded in that regard: by the mid-1980s, veterans of the favela movement largely staffed the Municipal Secretariat for Social Development and were well represented in other municipal and state agencies. Incorporation into city and state government, however, did not in itself secure the rights of favela residents; nor did it entirely eliminate the middleman. Instead, it raised the political value of internal favela representation. The new middlemen, mediating between favela residents and local government, came from within the favela. This development initially seemed like a positive one, as favela associations became more influential and electoral competition for their offices intensified. This was local representation in action. Increased value of representation, however, was not accompanied by any mechanism to support the accountability, transparency, and efficacy of that representation. Nor was it accompanied by effective measures to guarantee civil and property rights. This made favela associations lucrative targets for takeover by criminal interest groups, just as drug-trafficking crews and militias were establishing bases of power in the favelas. And it left individual favela residents with no leverage with which to challenge those criminal interest groups. By the late 1980s, both drug traffickers and militias were aggressively taking over favela associations in order to gain political leverage and secure their control of territory.[31]

THE BRIZOLA YEARS AND THEIR CONTEXT

In the minds of many cariocas, the transitions just described have become strongly identified with the two gubernatorial administrations of Leonel Brizola: 1983–87 and 1991–94, particularly with his epochal first term. Brizola was one of the most influential Brazilian politicians of the past half century. Nonetheless, it is as implausible to assign him individual blame for creeping criminal turf monopolization in Rio's favelas as it is to assign him individual credit for the expanding democratic participation in the state of Rio in the mid-1980s. Both transitions were partly shaped by local policymakers — Brizola first among them — but both stemmed from deeper causes.

Brizola made mistakes, analyzed in detail in the pages to follow. He ultimately could not control the party he founded, much less the other forces that conspired to undermine his experiment in socialist government.[32] His ambitions exceeded his war chest and his mandate. Even so, São Paulo suffered a similar spiral of violence and corruption in the same period, with no Brizola. Belo Horizonte, Salvador, and Recife — Brazil's next-largest cities — experienced similar transformations a half decade or so later, under dramatically different political leaders, suggesting that urban violence in Brazil had little to do with Brizola, specifically.[33] Rio was at the leading edge of similar transitions that unfolded in many of the major cities of Latin America and the Global South.

The simultaneous rise in urban violence and return to or expansion of democracy across the Global South, has plagued both right-wing governments (Guatemala, El Salvador) and left-wing ones (Venezuela). The link between them is not one of simple cause and effect, but is more than a coincidence. The rising demands of expanding democracy coincided with diminished state capacity and the privatization of security. The U.S. War on Drugs and other changes in international enforcement triggered rapid transformation in international drug- and arms-trafficking networks. Local governments responded to this deadly combination by seeking short-term security, giving tacit endorsement to police violence or accommodating criminal interest groups. The result of either tactic, or the combination of the two, has been to produce short periods of "peace" punctuated by cycles of violence.[34] Rio's experience was paradigmatic in that regard.

As the defining political figure of the 1980s and 1990s in Rio de Janeiro, Brizola is inevitably associated with this broader transformation. Like Jimmy Carter and the national malaise of the 1970s, like Herbert Hoover and the Great Depression, he will forever be linked to calamities that out-sized him. It is worth noting, however, that many of the current policies credited with recent improvements in Rio de Janeiro clearly and explicitly draw on Brizola's experiments.

The most controversial and oft-invoked allegation against Brizola is that he ordered Rio's state police to stay out of the favelas. Did he? It depends who you ask—and I have asked many people, from rank-and-file police officers to former secretaries of security, from favela residents to pent-house dwellers. I could not find any evidence that Brizola gave a direct or explicit order that police should stay out of Rio's favelas. On the contrary, he entrusted his chief of military police, Colonel Magno Nazareth Cerqueira, with the creation of a new security policy emphasizing community policing in favelas. Beginning in his 1982 campaign for governor, Brizola vowed to put an end to the *polícia pé na porta*, the foot-in-the-door police who barged into favela homes with neither warrant nor permission, in search of alleged suspects. His goal, he stated, was to give favela dwellers the same expectation of privacy in their own homes enjoyed by middle-class cariocas.[35]

Nevertheless, as subsequent chapters explore in detail, Nazareth Cerqueira did not have strong support in the police officer corps, and Brizola had less. His reforms rubbed most officers the wrong way, and several commanders sought to undermine Brizola and Nazareth Cerqueira at every turn.[36] Others instructed their rank and file to stay away from favelas simply to avoid violating new restraints. Brizola forbade the kind of aggressive policing that had been customary in the favela but was unable to win support for effective community policing. The result was an absence of effective policing in the favelas when they most needed it.

Criminal turf monopolization and stunted political representation imposed new limitations on favelado rights. By the early 1990s, the most
obvious expression of those limits were the lack of habeas corpus—the
freedom from arbitrary, secretive arrest—and the limitations on freedom
of political association and the right to come and go. Police treated all
favela dwellers as suspects and detained them without cause, while drug
traffickers and militias took over favela associations and controlled access to favela turf. Both city and state government tacitly accommodated
or reinforced criminal turf monopolization. City government did so by
working through corrupt associations, state government by assuming the
criminality of all favela residents, raising the value of the protection of
local strongmen. The rise and reproduction of criminal turf monopolization stymied progress toward guaranteeing the rights of favela dwellers as
equal citizens of Rio de Janeiro.

The case of property rights is paradigmatic in this regard. Absence of
property title has played a key role in the reproduction of favelas as separate zones that lack the full protection of the rule of law. This separation
has not happened, however, in ways described by influential Peruvian
economist Hernando de Soto. De Soto's celebrated book from 2000, *The
Mystery of Capital*, argues that property rights are the magic bullet of capitalist development. Their creation, distribution, and protection set off processes of exponential growth of investment, savings, and rising wealth.
In de Soto's analysis, residents of poor urban neighborhoods cannot afford to seek work aggressively or invest in their own homes, because their
tenancy is insecure.[37] In Rio de Janeiro, this was not the case. Once large-
scale favela removal was eliminated from political consideration, favela
residents eagerly invested in upgrading their own homes. During the same
years, their employment networks spread throughout the city, for reasons
of improved transportation as much as security of land occupancy.

The real costs of lack of title were not economic, but political.[38] Favela
residents, accustomed to improvised and unreliable water and electricity,
got improvised and unreliable political representation, as well. Favela
associations became the necessary mediators between individual favela
residents and state agencies. Those associations, in practice, became the
guarantors of possession of property. In the opinion of the association
president in the west side favela of Rio das Pedras in 1984, "When a favela
is small, people are afraid of removal. They know the police can evict them,

when there are only ten or twenty shacks. But from the moment a favela grows and has a residents' association with a certain structure, that is able to attend to the interest of residents, there is a lot of confidence that we will not be leaving. And really, who is going to be able to evict 20,000 people that have a kind of headquarters [in the association]."[39] This analysis was spot-on. What it left out was that, in this case, the association had ties to a faction of local military police that would grow into the prototypical favela militia, silencing dissent, extracting protection money from residents, and controlling elections through force. The militia cast itself as the defender of the favela's residents. Its ability to exploit the advantages of that role, however, depended on the weakness of favelado rights — starting with, but not limited to, the weakness of their property rights. The legal marginality of favelas made political corruption and exploitation almost inevitable.

Under these circumstances, many of the gains of the 1970s and early 1980s were reversed or undermined in the 1990s. Although material conditions continued to improve, that improvement was not accompanied by a strengthening of rights — the discourse of rights to the city notwithstanding. Instead, favelas were perpetuated as zones where the rule of law did not necessarily apply and where civil rights could not be guaranteed.

MOBILIZATION

Podem me prender	("They can arrest me
Podem me bater	they can beat me
Podem até deixar-me sem comer	they can even leave me without food
Que eu não mudo de opinião	I won't change my opinion
Daqui do morro eu não saio não	I will not leave this hill")

—ZÉ KETI, "OPINIÃO" (song) 1970.

They called it the *política da bica d'água*, the politics of the water spigot. A populist politician would visit a favela and promise delivery of a basic infrastructural improvement, such as a communal water spigot, in return for the community's votes. If the favela residents got out the vote, the politician or one of his subordinates returned to the community and ceremoniously announced delivery of the promised improvement.

Governor Antônio de Pádua Chagas Freitas was the acknowledged master of the politics of the water spout. Chagas Freitas knew how to use government resources to create and oil a political machine and how to trumpet that machine's defense of the people in the media—as the owner of two daily newspapers, he had particular advantages in this department. His deft use of these tactics made *chaguismo*—support for the Chagas Freitas machine—the dominant political force in Rio's favelas through most of the 1970s.

On November 10, 1982, five days before the gubernatorial election to choose Chagas Freitas's successor, the governor's wife, Zoe, was in the favela of Morro dos Cabritos to celebrate the inauguration of a communal laundry—a facility consisting of long rows of wash troughs and clotheslines. The event had all the trappings of the typical water spigot ceremony: Rio's first lady, wearing an elegant dress and flanked by her husband's assistants, spoke in grandiose terms of the momentous occasion, and humbly dressed *favelados* applauded gratefully.[1] It was the kind of event Chagas Freitas had orchestrated hundreds of times.

Chagas Freitas had ample opportunity to hone his strategy during two terms as governor. The first, from 1971 to 1975, was as governor of Guanabara, the tiny city-state created when Brazil's national capital was moved from Rio to Brasília in 1960. What had been the Federal District became the state of Guanabara. At the end of that term, the military dictatorship "fused" Guanabara with the surrounding state of Rio de Janeiro. Guanabara became the municipality of Rio de Janeiro, capital of the "fused" state. Not long afterward, Chagas Freitas returned as governor of the "fused" state of Rio de Janeiro, from 1979 to 1982.

In both cases, Chagas Freitas's election was tightly circumscribed, if not entirely controlled, by the military regime. The regime vetted a short list of candidates from the only two parties permitted under the dictatorship, the right-wing Aliança para a Reconstrução Nacional (Arena, Alliance for National Reconstruction) and the Movimento Democrático Brasileiro (MDB, Brazilian Democratic Movement), the legal opposition party. The regime kept the MDB on such a short leash that it did not represent any threat. (Brazilians joked that there were two political parties under the dictatorship: the party of yes and the party of yes, sir!) Chagas Freitas was the MDB candidate, but his politics of the water spigot fit well within the regime's strategy of accommodating the moderate opposition while repressing radicals.[2]

In 1980, when the regime legalized the formation of new political parties, the MDB became the PMDB, or Partido do Movimento Democrático Brasileiro, and set out to occupy the mushy center of Brazilian politics. For the next decade, its primary competition in Rio de Janeiro would come from two parties on the Left: Leonel Brizola's new PDT and the PT, a party linked in Rio primarily to the campus Left and the liberation theology wing of the Catholic Church. For all these parties, the first real test came with the gubernatorial elections of 1982, which was Brazil's first open, democratic gubernatorial election since 1960.

Chagas Freitas and his machine survived a frenetic scramble for control of the PMDB in Rio, and the governor activated his machine in an attempt to guarantee the election of his handpicked successor. His strategy depended on the politics of the water spigot to guarantee the favela vote. By 1982, however, favela leaders wanted more than water spigots. And on that November day in the Morro dos Cabritos, Arlindo Marinho—president of the favela's residents' association—altered the script: he thanked Chagas Freitas and the first lady perfunctorily and then praised Father Ítalo Coelho, leader of the Pastoral das Favelas, more effusively. Father Ítalo was the parish priest in Santa Cruz da Copacabana, just down the hill from Cabritos, and had played a key role in the emergence of a new spirit of political activism in the favela. Marinho suggested that Father Ítalo and the favela association were working toward more profound change than the new wash troughs. The first lady was upstaged at her own event while the president of the favela association and the liberation theology priest seized center stage.

The event captured a broader transition in favela politics. In the late 1970s, a new generation of favela leaders allied with liberation theology activists, kindling an ambitious favela movement across the city. The leaders of this movement explicitly rejected clientelist politics as usual, demanding a seat at the table of power. As José Luis Pires—a favela leader from Cabritos—put it during the campaign of 1982, "People are becoming conscious that they have rights."[3] By that time, the movement had become a powerful force in city politics. Five days after the inauguration of the laundry facility in the Morro dos Cabritos, Leonel Brizola won the gubernatorial election in a surprise, come-from-behind victory. Brizola owed his victory in large part to the urban poor and working class, and to favela residents in particular. Chagas Freitas's PMDB candidate finished a distant third. In Rio's favelas, chaguismo was out. Brizolismo was in.

Brizola's election would prove hugely consequential for favela residents, but it was not an unalloyed victory for the favela movement. Favelado support for Brizola was neither foreordained nor unified, and it would not necessarily endure. Understanding the temporary convergence of the favela movement with Brizola's gubernatorial campaign, and the importance of each for the evolving relationship between favelas and the rest of the city, requires closer investigation.

Mobilization in the favelas required three steps: the first was stitching together an uneasy alliance and challenging an entrenched older generation at the local level, the second was winning control over both individual

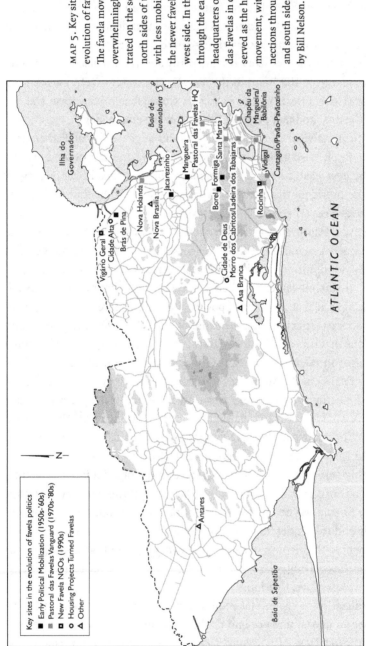

MAP 5 · Key sites in the evolution of favela politics. The favela movement was overwhelmingly concentrated on the south and north sides of the city, with less mobilization in the newer favelas of the west side. In the late 1970s through the early 1980s, the headquarters of the Pastoral das Favelas in downtown Rio served as the hub of the favela movement, with strong connections throughout the north and south sides. Cartography by Bill Nelson.

Key sites in the evolution of favela politics

- ■ Early Political Mobilization (1950s–'60s)
- ■ Pastoral das Favelas Vanguard (1970s–'80s)
- ▨ New Favela NGOs (1990s)
- ○ Housing Projects Turned Favelas
- △ Other

N

Ilha do Governador

Baía de Guanabara

Vigário Geral
Cidade Alta
Brás de Pina
Nova Holanda
Nova Brasília
Jacarezinho
Mangueira
Pastoral das Favelas HQ
Borel
Formiga
Santa Marca
Morro dos Cabritos/Ladeira dos Tabajaras
Chapéu da Mangueira/Babilônia
Vidigal
Rocinha
Cantagalo/Pavão-Pavãozinho
Cidade de Deus
Asa Branca

Antares

Baía de Sepetiba

ATLANTIC OCEAN

favela associations and the statewide favela federation, and the third was reaching rough consensus on movement goals and strategies. As the favela movement reached these three steps, it sought new alliances with parallel popular movements in the irregular subdivisions and in middle-class neighborhoods. By the early 1980s, each of these movements had achieved momentum and coherence, giving them leverage in the 1982 elections. Brizola recognized these gains earlier and more enthusiastically than any other candidate and moved to incorporate these urban popular movements into the PDT. That was the key to his victory, and the subsequent basis for his mandate as Rio's new governor.

THE MORRO DOS CABRITOS AND THE FOUNDATION OF THE PASTORAL DAS FAVELAS

The Morro dos Cabritos presents a prototypical case of the local mobilization that converged into a broad favela movement, in part because it was the neighborhood that gave birth to the Pastoral das Favelas. Along with the adjacent favela of the Ladeira dos Tabajaras, it occupies a U-shaped hillside overlooking Copacabana.[4] Like many favelas under the military regime, the Morro dos Cabritos had a *comissão de luz*, or light commission. It was composed of a small group of residents that maintained the favela's irregular electric hookup, charging all residents a monthly fee for service. The light commission was a kind of neighborhood association. It mediated disputes in the favela and had emerged from an early process of community mobilization, but it had devolved into a conservative, rent-seeking junta by the early 1970s.

Members of a younger generation of residents began to chafe under the authority of the light commission. They had watched as several neighboring favelas were razed, their residents removed to distant housing projects. They knew that Cabritos presented a likely target for removal, as well, and they longed for new leadership that might stave off that threat. As long as the military regime kept a tight lid on favela politics, these younger residents had few outlets to express their dissatisfaction. Several of them founded a samba *bloco*, or Carnaval parade band, Unidos da Villa Rica, in order to build neighborhood solidarity. This was ostensibly an apolitical organization, but it helped them earn the respect of the favela.[5]

Father Ítalo, in the meantime, was striving to strengthen the parish of Santa Cruz da Copacabana's commitment to social justice. He was part of the liberation theology vanguard that had emerged from Brazil's seminaries in the 1950s and 1960s, and like most priests of his generation, he had embraced the ideas of French Catholic Humanist Jacques Maritain, urging priests "to see, judge and act": to see injustice, judge it as immoral, and act to ameliorate it. Like many, he had gone further, embracing a radical reading of the gospel as a call for profound social change and a commitment to communitarian mobilization.[6]

In the early 1970s, Father Ítalo began climbing the hill to the Morro dos Cabritos one day a week to minister to residents. Like the young generation of Cabritos residents, he found the light commission to be an obstacle rather than a boon. He began working instead with the *sambistas* from Unidos da Villa Rica on projects such as building a sewage ditch, replacing a dirt pathway with a concrete stairway, and building a daycare center in the favela. These projects had several purposes: they met specific needs, fostered communitarian bonds, and reinforced the solidity of the favela, raising the stakes of any prospective removal attempt.

Father Ítalo and his young assistants referred to these projects as the *mutirão*, a Tupi-Guarani term for collective labor. The mutirão quickly emerged as a touchstone in Cabritos' mobilization and in that of the larger favela movement across the city.[7] Growing participation in the mutirão demonstrated that the old light commission had outlived its usefulness. In 1976, Father Ítalo encouraged the Villa Rica organizers, led by sambista José Luiz Pires and his friends, to found a new favela association. Even a year earlier, the regime would not have permitted this; by 1976, though, it had begun to ease restrictions on popular organizations. This turned out to be the odd alliance necessary to jumpstart a movement. Father Ítalo was a reedy, reserved priest, and the sambistas of Villa Rica were extroverted musicians, accustomed to playing for late-night jams. Their interests converged in their shared commitment to resisting removal and strengthening community in the favela. Together, they worked out a template for a new association that would "awaken the conscience of residents such that they might reflect . . . and motivate themselves for greater participation."[8]

Father Ítalo understood that the experiment in Cabritos could only be nurtured and magnified if it were echoed and allied with similar experiments in other favelas. He approached Dom Eugênio Sales, archbishop of Rio de Janeiro, with the proposal for a Pastoral das Favelas. Although Sales was not a liberation theologist, he did believe strongly in what he described as the "fixação do homem à terra," or the rooting of man to the earth. In Sales's eyes, the government sinned in its policies of favela removal. He granted Father Ítalo authority to create a pastoral office, led by the priest in collaboration with lay assistants, to advocate against removal and in favor of material investment in the favelas. The Pastoral das Favelas quickly made the foundation of new favela associations the key to its strategy, using the statute drawn up for the Cabritos association as a template.[9]

THE MORRO DOS CABRITOS AND THE PRODUCTION OF THE CITY

As Vidigal's case wound its way through the courts, similar conflicts over removal broke out all over the city, including in Cabritos. In 1978, a real-estate conglomerate that claimed title to much of the hillside struck a development deal with Chicaer, a cooperative representing air force personnel. The deal called for the construction of five apartment buildings with parking and recreational areas that would require eradication of much of the favela. Chicaer would offer low-interest mortgages to air force personnel to purchase the apartments.[10]

The cooperative's subsidized mortgages were a crucial element of construction, as private mortgage banking in Brazil was practically nonexistent. The Banco Nacional de Habitação (BNH, The National Housing Bank), a federal mortgage bank, offered mortgages to middle-class buyers, and in theory these middle-class mortgages would provide a capital base for development of popular housing. In practice, however, the BNH could not back enough mortgages to satisfy demand and failed in its promise to build popular housing. The BNH mortgages, contracted at floating rates, also left borrowers vulnerable to rising interest rates. In the late 1970s, those rates had begun to climb steadily, part of a worldwide trend triggered by the petroleum crisis of 1976–77. Many BNH mortgage-holders fell delinquent, and the Housing Bank began its own slide toward bankruptcy. This climate increased the attractions of mortgages from semiprivate cooperatives.

Chicaer and other white-collar pension institutes were connected to federal or state government but could operate as private banking concerns, eliminating the need to reserve funding for popular housing. Because they were limited to members of certain labor "classes" — the air force, in this case, or bank workers or civil servants, in others — they were functionally off limits to the most of the working class, particularly to favela residents.[11]

These factors combined to give Chicaer leverage and momentum, advantages that the favela residents generally lacked, in developing the hillside on the Morro dos Cabritos. As in Vidigal, several families in Cabritos chose resettlement, accepting payment in return for vacating their shacks. In this case, however, most of the families in question simply relocated higher up the hill, above the rest of the favela and out of range of the Chicaer construction. Most residents, emboldened by the new association, resisted removal.

In contrast to Vidigal, the Pastoral das Favelas was able to mediate a negotiated solution between the association and Chicaer. Eliana Athayde and Bento Rubião, the same lawyers defending Vidigal, notified the developers that they planned to request a Judicial Engineering Survey. This bureaucratic hurdle, if approved, would delay construction by at least two years. Like the foundation of the new association itself, this tactic took advantage of the early stirrings of redemocratization. Whereas in 1970, there would have been no chance of winning approval for a court-ordered engineering survey, by 1978 it was a distinct possibility.

This brought the developers to the bargaining table. In February 1979, Chicaer agreed to pay about US$12,000 to remove about a few dozen families, offering them land further along the same hillside, and to contribute US$23,000 in low-interest financing for construction of cooperative housing for these uprooted residents. The Pastoral das Favelas recruited a team of young architects inspired by the Brás de Pina experiment in favela upgrading and oversaw the drafting of plans for an innovative housing cooperative constructed through mobilization of the Cabritos community mutirão.[12]

The cooperative was never built. Before construction began, uprooted residents promptly settled the new areas "donated" by the developers, building their own shacks there. This small nucleus quickly sent off spurs further along the hillside. Building the planned development, as a result, would have required a new process of negotiation and resettlement.[13] The favela residents were not the only ones who failed to fulfill the terms of the agreement. The Chicaer apartment blocks flagrantly violated local zoning restrictions, and though the terms of the agreement limited occupancy to members of the air force, Chicaer sold off many of the apartments to citizens with only tangential connections to the armed services, many of whom subsequently sold to third parties. Within a few years, the apartment blocks had lost any connection to the air force.

The Chicaer/Cabritos accommodation was a perfect example of what might be described as the production of the city in the 1970s: this involved the simultaneous and linked expansion of formal and informal development in ways that defied attempts at restrictive planning. Both middle-class apartment buildings and favelas were marked by consistent irregularities, with the crucial distinction that in the middle class those irregularities were masked by the orderly façade of apartment blocks. Middle-class apartment buyers were often able to access sheltered mortgages through restrictive cooperatives, even when the terms of those cooperatives technically excluded them. When middle-class apartment dwellers fell behind on floating-rate mortgages in massive numbers, they could rely on state bureaucracy to avoid mass foreclosure. In the favela, in contrast, irregularity was written in the architecture, and its residents were exposed to potential removal.

The genius of the Pastoral das Favelas and of the new associations that allied with it was to understand this game and to intervene in ways that guaranteed possession of their homes to favela dwellers. With the victory against removal proceedings in Vidigal and the Morro dos Cabritos, the Pastoral das Favelas had two striking success stories, and favela leaders from across the city rushed to forge alliances with the growing organization.

The Pastoral's work received nothing less than a papal blessing with the visit of John Paul II to Vidigal in July 1980. Archibishop Sales and Father Ítalo, working in conjunction with the Vidigal association, coordinated the visit. The Pope toured the favela, entering the humble homes of local residents and praying in Vidigal's chapel. Upon leaving, he removed his papal ring and bestowed it on Father Ítalo, a powerful symbolic donation to the cause. The gesture provided further invigoration and justification for participants in the pastoral wave: with the pope himself on their side, who could oppose them?[14]

USEFUL CONTROVERSY IN THE FAVELA FEDERATION

The Pastoral's strategy of founding new associations gave it a rapidly growing presence throughout the city, but no individual association had significant political leverage in citywide politics. In the aftermath of the Chicaer agreement, the Pastoral das Favelas supported a move to seize control of the Federação das Associações das Favelas do Estado de Rio de Janeiro (FAFERJ, Federation of Favela Associations of the State of Rio de Janeiro). Although it was an umbrella organization that represented all favela residents in the state of Rio, in practice its membership was limited to favelas within the municipality of Rio. The federation of associations was the descendant of a once-vigorous favela federation created in the early 1960s, during the fifteen-year Guanabara period, when the city of Rio was coterminous with the state of Guanabara. Under the military regime — including the first several years of the existence of the new, "fused" Rio de Janeiro — the favela federation had been powerless and ineffectual. The stirrings of redemocratization created the opportunity to revive the favela federation as a key player in city politics.

The Fundação Leão XIII, the state charitable services organization that sought to facilitate removal of Vidigal, maintained effective control over the favela federation. In 1978, the sitting president was a *chaguista*, leery of confrontational politics. His five-year term had ended late in 1978, but he had not organized elections and no one had pressed him to do so.

In March 1979, the Pastoral leaders called on the federation to hold elections in accordance with its own bylaws, a request the federation president could hardly deny, given the momentum of redemocratization. But the young leaders associated with the Pastoral did not believe they had yet achieved enough authority to guide the favela federation on their own. Instead, they sought another alliance, this time with most ideologically committed faction of the old guard. They turned to Irineu Guimarães of Jacarezinho, the largest favela on Rio's north side, as candidate for the federation presidency. Guimarães had his own reasons to accept the invitation. He was a longtime communist and had been a strong community leader in the early 1960s. He had kept a low profile through most of the dictatorship, participating quietly in the radical underground organization MR-8.

In the late 1960s, the MR-8 had engaged in guerrilla actions such as kidnappings and bank robberies and had suffered harsh repression in consequence. Guimarães survived the crackdown unscathed, an immunity he attributed to the disdain of both the regime and middle-class radicals for favela residents: "They didn't pay much attention to us. I was never treated with hostility. They never believe we had the capacity to make them uncomfortable."[15] By the late 1970s, the organization had long since abandoned guerilla actions in exchange for broad, popular-front organizing.[16] The favela federation was a logical target for this strategy, and installing Guimarães as its president would be a valuable prize for the MR-8.[17]

Nilton Gomes Pereira, an ally of the Pastoral cohort, ran for vice-president on Guimarães's ticket. Pereira was from Itararé, another north side favela. Although the early Pastoral was stronger on Rio's south side, its leaders recognized that most favela residents lived on the north side, and sought to solidify its presence there through Pereira's nomination.[18]

In April 1979, Guimarães and his slate won the elections, but the sitting president and the Fundação Leão XIII refused to recognize the results, and insisted on maintaining power. Guimarães and the Pastoral refused to back down. The favela federation split into two factions, with each claiming to represent the real federation.[19]

The Fundação Leão XIII faction emphasized its ability to get along by going along: "Their case is one of pressure. And we work much more through dialogue. They force the government, and we beseech. Their rhetoric is much heavier."[20] The Pastoral faction, in contrast, put the split in terms of consciousness and rights. Only "conscious favelados," they stressed, were capable of contributing to a real democracy: "Our function is more to organize residents to understand their true problems. Only favelados organizing themselves can resolve their own problems."[21]

The controversy was useful to both Guimarães and the Pastoral, and the split proved more advantageous than winning control of the federation outright. Local newspapers gave extensive coverage to the controversy, rewarding Guimarães's strategy of broadening the popular front. For the Pastoral, the split gave weight to the argument that entrenched powers would never cede authority willingly. The Fundação Leão XIII unintentionally reinforced this message by firing three hundred social service assistants, residents of favelas throughout the city, who had joined the breakaway federation.[22] The dismissals cemented the image of the Fundação Leão XIII as fundamentally antidemocratic. During the ensuing months, the Pastoral rushed to seize the advantage, founding clusters of new associations across the city.[23]

The split endured for eighteen months — not coincidentally, the period of greatest growth for both the Pastoral and for the foundation of new favela associations.[24] Governor Chagas Freitas finally mediated a compromise early in 1981. Guimarães would officially take office as president of a united federation, but the Fundação Leão XIII would retain strong representation among the federation's officers. The compromise served Guimarães's purposes, making him a key interlocutor in the upcoming elections. It also fulfilled the MR-8's mandate to seek cross-class alliances in the service of ousting the generals: as one MR-8 communiqué put it, "At the same time that we denounce the ambiguities of bourgeois opposition, we should be ready to establish with these sectors . . . all the agreements necessary and useful to the growth of the revolutionary struggle against the dictatorship."[25]

The Pastoral leaders found themselves outflanked. Despite loathing any solution that included the Fundação Leão XIII, they could not risk a public break with Guimarães after pushing his candidacy. They accepted the compromise reluctantly. This proved a crucial step not only in the evolution of the favela movement, but in the path toward the elections of 1982. A reunited favela federation presented an attractive ally for candidates. Although the Pastoral das Favelas played a key role in reinvigorating that federation, it did not achieve extensive influence over its direction.[26]

LAND TITLE AND THE COMMUNITARIAN VISION OF THE PASTORAL DAS FAVELAS

In other regards, the Pastoral's influence proved decisive, nowhere more so than in regard to the central issue of land tenure in the favelas. Following the successful defense of Vidigal, Bento Rubião and Eliana Athayde found their services in demand in favelas across the city. Within months, they plunged into a dizzying number of legal battles against removal, often undertaken to forestall proceedings as yet uninitiated. Archbishop Sales raised no objection to their work but provided no direct funding. Rubião and Athayde not only needed to sustain their own efforts; they needed to hire more lawyers and assistants. In 1979, they persuaded Sales to sign off on a successful application for funding from the Ford Foundation.[27]

The terms of the Ford Foundation grant explicitly forbade involvement in electoral politics, a stipulation in clear conflict with the Pastoral's heavy involvement in the founding of new favela associations. Both the Ford Foundation and the Pastoral das Favelas, however, were willing to look the other way. The Pastoral activists drew a distinction between community politics and party politics. They viewed the favela associations as tools for community mobilization, above the fray of party politics, and therefore presumably exempt from the Ford Foundation's restriction against electoral activity. This notion, barely sustainable in 1979, would become increasingly untenable as the 1980s wore on.

A similar ambiguity informed the Pastoral's approach to land tenure. The Pastoral vigorously defended the general right of favela residents to ownership of the land their shacks rested on, based on their long and productive occupation. In practice, however, the Pastoral discouraged favela residents from filing claims for individual property ownership. This apparent contradiction hinged on the implications of Brazilian land law, specifically the concept of *usucapião*, a doctrine known in the United States as adverse possession. Brazilian land law differs from Anglo-Saxon law in several important regards, but the concepts of adverse possession are similar in the two systems. This doctrine holds that occupants of land eventually acquire property rights, provided their possession is public, continuous, and exclusive—that is, as long as their possession is not shared with anyone else, including the nominal holder of title to the land. This possession must also be adverse, that is, undertaken without the permission or agreement of the nominal title-holder, and characterized by an effective claim to ownership against the interests of that titleholder. The essence of adverse possession is that if a squatter holds land under these conditions for a defined statutory period, he or she becomes legal owner of the land.

In Brazil, statutes regarding adverse possession have changed over time, and this evolution informed the debate over land tenure in Rio's favelas. Brazil's Civil Code of 1916 allowed for property rights based on adverse possession of urban property over a span of thirty years. The Constitution of 1934 provided for expropriation of land based on adverse possession during only ten years, specifically in order to fulfill the "social function" of land—language that became part of every subsequent popular struggle over Brazilian land. The adverse possession clause of the Constitution of 1934, however, was understood to refer only to rural land, implicitly leaving favela residents without any claim to property rights. The Constitution of 1946 did not alter these terms. The Constitution of 1967, the constitution of the dictatorship, weakened the protections of adverse possession and bolstered the rights of absentee landowners. But as Brazil moved toward redemocratization, adverse possession was once again up for debate. Advocates of urban reform, including Pastoral activists, pressed for strengthening its protections, applying it to urban land, and decreasing the length of continuous possession required. Five years of adverse possession, they reasoned, should serve as an adequate basis for expropriation in both urban and rural areas.[28]

The unsettled nature of the doctrine of adverse possession shaped the Pastoral's approach to land tenure. In emergency cases, when the favela in question was under threat of planned removal, the Pastoral's lawyers used the same mechanisms that had worked in Vidigal: requesting staying orders and technical reports that might delay proceedings while the resident's association and other allies sought to mobilize the community, raising the effective cost of removal. In communities not under immediate threat, they encouraged favela residents to gather any documents that indicated their long-term residence in order to prove *posse*, or possession, of the land in question. Then they conducted inquiries into title history, preparing to generate legal doubt about the property claims of titleholders. Conflicting titles were common, arising from a history of vague royal land grants, multiple claims on property based on disputed inheritance, state expropriations, and outright double-dealing that had characterized previous generations of Rio's land market. The Pastoral lawyers learned to expose these conflicting titles, arguing that in the absence of clear legal ownership, the land should be granted to those currently residing upon it.[29]

The Pastoral lawyers became strong public advocates of strengthening the right of adverse possession. They persuaded the Archdiocese itself to adopt this position, helping to place it on the national political agenda over the course of the 1980s.[30] Despite this public advocacy of adverse possession, however, the Pastoral lawyers rarely filed a case seeking expropriation based on adverse possession and to my knowledge never carried such a case through to conclusion. They invoked adverse possession as one factor protecting residents of a given favela against removal, but held back from using it as the justification for delivering property title to current residents.

Their caution had both practical and ideological foundations. In practical terms, filing a claim based on adverse possession required clear definition of an individual lot, including precise coordinates of the separation of that individual lot from adjacent public property, a road, for example. Clear delineation of individual lots was impossible in many favelas, where shacks abutted or even overlapped one another, and where the property status of alleyways and muddy hillside paths was as vague as that of the shacks themselves. Ideologically, the Pastoral lawyers were hesitant to file individual claims because they strongly believed that favela property should be communal. The existing constitution made no allowance for collective adverse possession. As a result, the legal office of the Pastoral stressed the importance of the doctrine of adverse possession but did not use it as a tool for delivering property title to favela residents, an apparent contradiction arising from the Pastoral's deepest principles.[31]

This approach was not merely an issue of juridical strategy; rather, it shaped the evolving favela movement. In the late 1970s, Pastoral lawyers and the young cohort of leaders allied with the Pastoral understood *posse* and *título*, possession and property title, to be mutually reinforcing. By the early 1980s, that sense of mutual reinforcement began to disappear from Pastoral discourse. Pastoral leaders began to worry that individualized property title would bring taxation and thus increase the costs of possession. They also feared that property title would facilitate sale of favela homes on the open market, causing values to rise as some sold off and others invested and accumulated. They began to speak of the danger of *remoção branca*, veiled removal (literally, white removal): the risk that rising values would inevitably lead the poorest residents to sell and move elsewhere. Although the neighborhood might "improve," its poorest residents would be pushed out nonetheless, likely to worse circumstances. For these reasons, use of adverse possession as a means of delivering individual property title never gained traction in Rio's favelas. In both the field and the courtroom, Pastoral activists sought to put into practice a particular definition of community that strengthened favela associations and resisted individualization of property rights. Like the struggle over the favela federation, this was a development that would help determine the fate of favela residents over the remainder of the 1980s.

SANTA MARTA AND THE COMMUNITARIAN VISION IN PRACTICE

Santa Marta, a prominent favela plunging down a steep hillside toward the middle-class neighborhood of Botafogo, was a particularly strong example of this adoption of a communitarian vision by young leadership.[32] Santa Marta had a long history of Catholic activism before the rise of the Pastoral das Favelas. Many of its residents worked at a Catholic private school near the base of the hill. Father Belisário Velloso Rebello, a Jesuit who had graduated from the Colégio Santo Inácio, became an early advocate for the community. Father Velloso served as dean of Rio's Pontifícia Universidade Católica (PUC) in the 1950s and again in the 1970s, giving Santa Marta powerful connections in Rio's academic world, as well as its ecclesiastical networks. Father Agostinho Castejón, a Spanish Jesuit and like Velloso an administrator at PUC, embraced Santa Marta even more deeply, moving to the hillside. Fathers Velloso and Castejón preceded the liberation theology generation, but embodied a Jesuit dedication to a combination of pastoral work and academic rigor.[33]

The two priests proved crucial in organizing early community improvement projects in the 1950s and 1960s, and in bringing in the necessary material to sustain them. In the 1960s, drawing on this assistance, Santa

Marta's residents constructed a network of overhead water pipes, which was a technical necessity, given the sheer rock face of much of the hillside. The military crackdown on favela organizing at the close of the 1960s held these pastoral communitarian efforts in check but did not eliminate them. Santa Marta, consequently, was ahead of the curve of pastoral mobilization in the end of the 1970s.

Late in 1976, eight of the hill's young residents began circulating a mimeographed newsletter called *Eco* (Echo), intended to connect Santa Marta to the unfolding process of redemocratization. Raised in Santa Marta's tradition of pastoral community action, participants in the Eco group also brought two other strong influences to their early work. Several of them were participants in Santa Marta's famed Folia dos Reis parade band, which descended the hill in lavish costume and full-throated song during the annual Feast of the Kings. In several favelas, the Feast of the Kings was considered more important than Carnaval, and Santa Marta's Folia dos Reis was a linchpin of community identity. Several members of the Eco group also participated in the Movimento Negro Unificado (MNU, Black Unified Movement), an umbrella federation for black organizations, directed by black university students and professors committed to radical social transformation led by a black vanguard.

In another context, these diverse connections might have proven contradictory. Indeed, a few years later they would lead in incompatible directions. The marxist directorate of the MNU had little patience for either pastoral work or for festive parade groups, and the sentiment was mutual. But in the late 1970s, these diverse organizations were briefly pulling in the same direction, toward redemocratization and its undefined promise of broad social change. The Eco group drew its strength from this convergence of interest.

Itamar Silva, a reflective, iron-willed resident in his early twenties, became the group's most prominent leader, typifying its characteristics. His parents had migrated to the city from the rural hinterland and settled in Santa Marta in the early 1950s, where they participated in the Folia dos Reis and the community's religious network. Silva worked part time as an office helper through high school, then put himself through college while working full time at the state telephone company. As a college student he participated in the MNU but ultimately found the organization too focused on theory. He turned his energies toward Santa Marta itself, where his activism could yield immediate results.[34]

Silva made connections to the Pastoral das Favelas shortly after its foundation, not surprising, given the similarities and geographic proximity of Santa Marta and the Morro dos Cabritos. He soon became one of the most prominent young favela leaders linked to the growing organization. In Silva's words, "The Pastoral was the great umbrella of the left, at least in the urban area. Later, when redemocratization and new political parties came, we found out who was who, who was in party A, B or C, who was communist, who wasn't. The Pastoral gave shelter to everyone. It was a group of militants, volunteers who camouflaged themselves as Catholic activists, and that coexistence was very productive. Later, each one went finding his own niche."[35]

Within Santa Marta, the Grupo Eco began taking on mutirão projects, organizing cleanup brigades on the hillside, helping residents construct or reinforce their homes, and pushing for more substantial infrastructural improvements. As in the Morro dos Cabritos, this soon brought group members into conflict with the existing association, one that had not held an election since the early 1970s. The Eco group pushed for new elections in 1979, temporarily allying with an older community resident in his successful campaign for association president. In a process that reflected the simultaneous conflict within the citywide favela federation, they soon broke with this ally over conflicting visions for community improvements: he wanted to retain the association as a mediator between residents and government while they pushed for robust democratic participation. They forced new association elections two years later, this time nominating their own slate of candidates. Late in 1981, the twenty-five-year-old Silva took office as the president of Santa Marta's association, and other members of the Eco group filled roles of vice-president and treasurer. They immediately pressed city and state officials for more direct communication and investment. The Eco group was on the cusp of bringing about a profound transformation within Santa Marta and in its relationship to the city below, putting it in the vanguard of the gathering favela movement.[36]

MOBILIZATION IN THE IRREGULAR SUBDIVISIONS: ALLIANCES AND DISTINCTIONS

A parallel process unfolded in the irregular subdivisions, most prominently in Nova Iguaçu, a municipality directly north of the city of Rio de Janeiro. Like most of the municipalities surrounding Rio, Nova Iguaçu had a small formal nucleus with long historical roots, surrounded by seemingly endless irregular subdivisions of recent vintage. As one researcher put it, "You can travel for several hours through these areas with the sensation that you have remained in the same place, monotonous and disagreeable, lacking notable references of any kind of order."[37] In contrast to the powerful inhabitation of dramatic space in favelas such as Vidigal or Santa Marta, climbing up steep hillsides above dense urban neighborhoods, the subdivisions had a frustrating placelessness. They seemed interchangeable.

Nova Iguaçu's population quintupled from approximately 150,000 in 1950 to over 700,000 by 1970, a period in which the old agricultural hinterland became the new urban periphery. Most residents were relatively recent migrants from farther out in the countryside, and although their new neighborhoods were increasingly densely populated, they lacked most features of modern urban infrastructure and services. Throughout the 1960s and 1970s, short-term improvements depended entirely on trading votes for political favors, resulting in highly localized patterns of investment. On a long street in one subdivision, for example, residents at one end cultivated ties to the Arena Party and got streetlights as a result. On the other end of the street, residents allied with Chagas Freitas and the MDB and got both streetlights and a paved roadway. In between, residents failed to ally with either party decisively, and got neither streetlights nor a paved road.[38] The short-term lessons of such patterns were clear: trade votes for services, or remain in the dark, sinking in mud.

As in Rio's favelas, liberation theology priests helped mobilize residents to push for deeper transformation. In 1976, Dom Adriano Hypólito, bishop of Nova Iguaçu, was kidnapped and tortured by a paramilitary hard-liner seeking to intimidate him. Hypólito survived and emerged unbowed; if anything, the kidnapping emboldened him, along with his followers in a growing movement. In the peripheral subdivision, the Pastoral da Terra (Land Pastoral), and the Pastoral Operária (Worker's Pastoral)—along with Cáritas, a church-organized charitable organization—filled the role played by the Pastoral das Favelas in the central favelas. Hypólito nurtured all three of these organizations, connecting them to individual neighborhoods and parish priests throughout his diocese.[39]

As in the favelas, the liberation theology leaders encouraged the formation of new neighborhood associations and broad federations uniting these associations. Nova Iguaçu's federation, the Movimento dos Amigos do Bairro (MAB, Friends of the Neighborhood Movement), organized rallies of tens of thousands of participants at the municipality's city hall, pressing for delivery of city services. The subdivision federation on the west side of Rio de Janeiro, the Grupo de Terra e Habitação (GTH, Land and Housing Group) was similarly active.[40]

Journalistic coverage of these rallies helped connect favela leaders with their counterparts in the irregular subdivisions. By the end of 1979, favela and subdivision leaders issued joint calls for greater investment in infrastructure in poor and peripheral neighborhoods and were regular presences at each other's rallies. That alliance helped raise the profile of the urban popular movements but could only go so far: ultimately, public power treated the subdivisions and the favelas differently, and their leaders reacted accordingly.

In 1979, the federal government issued a new law regulating the division of urban land and facilitating regularization of irregular subdivisions. The law, primarily a response to the exponential expansion of subdivisions on the periphery of São Paulo, proved equally relevant in the metropolitan region of Rio. It conferred on municipalities the ability to grant legal title to residents in irregular subdivisions even if their lots and infrastructure did not conform to municipal codes, a devolution of government power from the federal to the municipal level typical of the passage to redemocratization. The law of 1979 did not explicitly exclude favelas, but it may as well have: its language specified regularization of well-defined lots and excluded lands in flood-prone areas and on steep hillsides, leaving most favelas out of consideration.[41]

The subdivision movements in Nova Iguaçu and on the west side of Rio responded by stepping up their demands for property regularization. In Rio's favelas, demands for property title began to diminish as possession of land became more secure, that is, as the threat of removal was lifted. In the subdivisions, in contrast, the urban land law of 1979 encouraged residents to focus on property regularization, making that the key to related infrastructural improvements. This did not result in an immediate division between favela and subdivision movements, but it did set them on a path toward gradual divergence.

THE MIDDLE-CLASS MOVEMENT

An emerging middle-class association movement presented a different set of challenges and opportunities. In contrast to the subdivision movement, which emerged simultaneously with the favela movement, the middle-class association movement started later, directly inspired by the favela movement.[42] Although its goals were different, it shared an interest in blocking the kind of apartment towers that threatened both Vidigal and the Morro dos Cabritos. Middle-class associations were primarily concerned with the restriction of runaway development and had much to gain from alliance with a popular movement stressing the rights of poor residents to stay where they were.

The most prominent middle-class leaders also shared an ambition for reimagining the city, bridging the gulf between rich and poor. Jó Resende was president of the resident's association in Cosme Velho, an upper middle-class residential neighborhood in the midst of rapid transformation, as stately single-family homes were torn down to make way for apartment blocks—the dreaded *espigões*, or big shafts, that became the object of resentment for the middle-class associations. Cosme Velho was also adjacent to the favela of Guararapes, and Resende recognized that the neighborhood's future was inextricably tied to that of his neighbors. The Guararapes association, for its part, was one of the earliest participants in the Pastoral wave, and its leaders were eager to establish cross-class ties.

Inspired by the favela federation, Resende and like-minded middle-class association leaders founded the Federação de Associações de Moradores do Estado do Rio de Janeiro (FAMERJ, Federation of Resident's Associations of the State of Rio de Janeiro) in 1978. FAMERJ was by no means limited to the middle class; associations from peripheral, working-class neighborhoods participated in the federation from its inception and in the mid-1980s came to its fore. In its early days, however, representatives from middle-class and upper middle-class neighborhoods such as Cosme Velho and Saens Peña dominated the organization. Resende served as the federation's president from 1980 to 1984, and looked to consolidate a strong alliance with the favela movement. In Resende's understanding, the favela federation's model—specifically, the breakaway federation led by Irineu Guimarães and the Pastoral cohort in 1979–80—was crucial not only in inspiring the middle-class federation but in giving it citywide reach. "Community leaders from the favelas created the bridge that enabled FAMERJ to exist ... and the next step was when the action we developed made possible connections between the south side community, that of the west side, and the favela federation itself. We created a broad movement that had joint meetings, where the president of the favela federation, Irineu Guimarães, participated as well."[43]

As in the favela federation, this broad movement contained divergent ideological tendencies. The key middle-class participants can be grouped into three categories: the revolutionaries, the operators, and the new Left. The revolutionaries though few in number were influential. They were veterans of the guerrilla struggle against the military regime who, like Irineu Guimarães, had turned their energies toward popular-front organizing. Typical of this process were Jair Ferreira de Sá and Ângela Borba, participants in the Ação Popular Marxista-Leninista (APML, Marxist-Leninist Popular Action), one of the revolutionary factions on the Brazilian Left. Ferreira de Sá had participated in the guerrilla struggle of the late 1960s and then gone into exile. Upon returning in the early 1970s, he met and married Borba, a university student who had joined one of the APML's remaining fragments. Together, they helped guide the remnant through the early stages of redemocratization, pursuing new strategies. They helped lead the middle-class association movement and encouraged APML veterans throughout Rio to use their local associations as a platform to press for broader reform. In their understanding, the immediate goals of associations were less important than mobilization itself, which could lay the groundwork for more radical change. As Ferreira de Sá put it in a communication in 1979, "The true importance to us of these struggles for improvements within existing society will not be the improvements themselves, but the growing union of residents." For this reason, it was fundamental to ensure that residents "were not deluded with petty conquests and appeased." Residents should therefore be urged "to defend not only the particular interests of a neighborhood, but the interests of the masses in other neighborhoods in other regions in their assault on bourgeois society."[44] Ferreira de Sá and comrades were hoping the middle-class associations would be a tool for revolutionary consciousness-raising.

The revolutionaries eagerly sought an alliance with favela activists: they had disavowed violent guerrilla actions but remained committed to revolutionary transformation, and joining the struggle of Rio's most disenfranchised citizens could only hasten that transformation. Toward that end, Ferreira de Sá urged fellow militants "to understand the favela federation as a space to be occupied . . . to fight for the popularization and democratization of the favela federation . . . and to fight for a combative federation, that leads struggles, that puts itself at the service of the workers' and popular movement."[45]

Ferreira's description of the favela federation as "a space to be occupied" reveals the influence of Antonio Gramsci on the Brazilian revolutionaries of the post-1960s. In the wake of the bitter defeat of guerrilla efforts by the early 1970s, many members of the APML and other factions adopted Gramsci's ideas of revolution through capillary action—"occupying spaces" in civil society and local government and turning them toward radical ends. Similarly, Ferreira de Sá also insisted on the importance of electing cultural officers in favela and middle-class associations because, they believed, the real ideological transformation would come not from saving a playground or building a staircase, but through the cultural programs.[46] The revolutionaries among the middle-class movement helped establish and deepen an alliance with the favela movement.

The operators, the second main group of leaders, were middle-class association leaders who grasped the possibilities of the movement as a springboard to greater political influence. Typical of this group was Pedro Porfirio, president of the Lauro Müller Association, representing an enclave of middle-class apartment buildings on the south side of Rio. The Lauro Müller Association mobilized when construction of a nearby shopping mall threatened to gobble up the neighborhood's common space. Porfirio negotiated with the mall developers to improve Lauro Müller's facilities without slowing construction of the mall. This was hardly revolutionary; it amounted to a preservation of middle-class privilege. But the Jornal do Brasil cast the Lauro Müller Association as a spearhead of redemocratization, ushering Porfirio onto the city's political stage.[47]

Porfirio positioned himself as a political deal-maker within the middle-class movement. When the new political parties began to reach out to the urban popular movements in the early 1980s, Porfirio began to play a similar role in Brizola's PDT. By the mid-1980s Porfirio was one of the key links between the PDT and local associations in both favelas and formal neighborhoods. He would play this role, with variations, for the next thirty years.[48]

The third group of middle-class leaders comprised the young idealists of the new Left. Like the revolutionaries, they pursued the Gramscian strategy of "occupying spaces" in civil society. In contrast to the revolutionaries, who viewed this as a necessary step on the path toward radical transformation, the members of the new Left tended to see mobilization itself as the point, imagining a new democracy that depended on constant, energetic popular participation. Jó Resende, along with young leaders such as Chico Alencar of Tijuca and Sérgio Andrea of Botafogo, typified the new

Left leaders. More than either the revolutionaries or the operators, they believed that middle-class residents and favela residents shared interests, and they sought to cement the alliance with the favela movement based on that understanding.

For the favela movement, an alliance with middle-class associations brought immediate tangible benefits, such as opening public spaces within middle-class neighborhoods to use by favela residents. Nothing had explicitly prohibited favela residents from enjoying the public plazas of neighborhoods such as Ipanema, Copacabana, Botafogo and Tijuca before 1979, but decades of implicit social codes had effectively preserved these as middle-class zones. Shared popular mobilization helped break down those social codes, opening up public space to more democratic use. Associations in all these neighborhoods began farmer's markets, youth soccer teams, and adult literacy programs in deliberate attempts to break down barriers between favela and middle-class residents. These changes were real and dramatic though also deliberately limited: the hopes of radical participants that these might pave the way for a fundamental redistribution of resources were destined to remain unrealized.

THE MILITARY REGIME AND CHAGAS FREITAS RESPOND TO THE FAVELA MOVEMENT

The presence of organizers from radical marxist factions such as the MR-8 and the APML in both favela and middle-class associations hardly passed unnoticed by the military regime. The regime's secret police infiltrated association meetings, cultivated informers, and kept extensive files on figures such as Jair Ferreira de Sá and Irineu Guimarães. A communication in 1979 from the federal political police to Rio's state police, for example, warned of "a plan by radical political groups to take control of all the favela and working-class neighborhood associations in the state of Rio." "These groups," it continued, "have succeeded in penetrating almost all the favelas of Rio de Janeiro, especially through the Pastoral das Favelas where they are infiltrated. Students and intellectuals offer to work in the Pastoral, in the communities, and were accepted with no resistance. Almost all are now assistants of the Pastoral."[49] The regime was keenly aware of the threat posed by the Pastoral and the broader favela movement.

But by the mid-1970s, arrest, torture and extrajudicial assassination of nonviolent opposition figures were the most repudiated features of the military regime. The notorious deaths in custody of several nonviolent regime opponents had undermined any remaining credibility the regime held among political moderates. Increased focus on human rights from both domestic and international observers had forced the regime to commit to slow redemocratization. In this climate, the upper echelon of the military regime was unwilling to risk public backlash by arresting popular leaders, and chose to monitor radicalism in the urban movements rather than attempting to crush it.[50]

Hard-line factions took matters into their own hands, as in the kidnapping of Bishop Hypólito, carrying out a wave of kidnappings and bombings of left-wing targets in the late 1970s and early 1980s. These actions tended to target middle-class institutions suspected of aiding and abetting radicals. In August 1980, for example, a letter bomb exploded in the offices of the Rio de Janeiro chapter of the Ordem de Advogados do Brasil (the Brazilian Bar Association) in apparent retribution for that organization's condemnation of the regime. On May 1, 1981, two bombs went off outside a popular music festival at Riocentro, a convention center on Rio's west side. The only casualties were the bombers themselves, members of a hard-line faction within the Brazilian Army. The Riocentro bombing made clear that influential actors within the dictatorship would not cede power easily.[51]

The right-wing splinter groups viewed the association movements with alarm. In 1981, a faction identifying itself only as the Group for Democracy sent ominous leaflets to middle-class homeowners, warning them that FAMERJ was a "communist organization, representing danger for Brazilian society." The group called particular attention to Pedro Porfírio and Irineu Guimarães, accusing them of "using the favela associations as a standard for their anti-Christ ideas, for their dreams of a life without God, without family, without faith and without love." Anonymous informants sent letters to the political police naming alleged radicals in the associations and pressing for their arrest. Association leaders, keenly aware of these threats, operated under the correct assumption that they were being watched closely.[52]

At the same time, both the military regime and Governor Chagas Freitas sought to avert a radical turn through moderate reforms. Upon the "fusion" of the states of Guanabara and Rio de Janeiro in 1975, the regime created a planning agency intended to facilitate urban improvement projects throughout the metropolitan region of Rio de Janeiro. Its visionary projects for improved transportation, sanitation, and zoning soon ran into the obstacles presented by entrenched bureaucratic holders of power in each of the participating municipalities, most prominently in the municipality of Rio itself. Jaime Lerner, the planning agency's first director, quit in frustration and subsequently ran for mayor of his native city of Curitiba, in southern Brazil, where he instituted the reforms he was unable to put into effect in Rio. Curitiba became an internationally renowned model of urban planning. Rio did not.[53]

Upon taking office as governor of Rio in 1979, Chagas Freitas used the planning agency as a conduit to deliver urban improvement projects to political allies. It was a gambit that left planners demoralized and local populations unappeased.[54] Chagas Freitas invested more sincerely in urban reform with his appointment of Israel Klabin as mayor of Rio de Janeiro in 1979 (under the military regime, the state governor chose the mayor of capital cities from a list approved by the dictatorship). Klabin opened dialogue with representatives of the favela, subdivision, and middle-class association movements and hired a crew of able planners and technicians. He created a new Municipal Secretariat of Social Development, staffed by field agents from Rio's favelas, and dedicated a special fund to favela urbanization.[55]

In spite of these developments, Klabin found himself presiding over Rio during a spate of strikes by municipal and state workers demanding salary hikes to keep up with rising inflation, presaging recurring events in the decade to come. The strikes threatened the base of the chaguista machine, and Klabin proved unable to settle them. Chagas Freitas forced out Klabin and brought in a more trusted veteran of his political machine as mayor. (By driving out Lerner and Klabin in quick succession, Rio lost two of its most competent technocrats in a moment of delicate transition.)

Most of the innovative young planners and favela field agents left with Klabin. Chagas Freitas succeeded in settling the strikes, but at the cost of leaving the association movements in the vocal opposition. Favela, subdivision, and middle-class leaders became increasingly convinced that they needed a new kind of politician, one eager to embrace the association movements—a politician such as Leonel Brizola.

NEW PARTIES, NEW AFFILIATIONS

Brizola was hardly a newcomer to the Brazilian political scene: he had played a central role in the political crisis that led to the coup of 1964. Brizola hailed from Rio Grande do Sul, in far-southern Brazil, and had held office as governor of that state in the first years of the 1960s, winning notoriety for his eagerness to seize the holdings of international corporations and redistribute resources to the poor. Along with his brother-in-law, President João Goulart, Brizola was one of the most prominent leaders of the Partido Trabalhista Brasileiro (PTB, Brazilian Workers' Party), the labor party founded in the 1940s by populist dictator Getúlio Vargas. In 1962 Brizola jumped from Rio Grande do Sul to the more prominent stage of Rio de Janeiro, where he won election as a member of Congress. In 1963 and 1964, as political tension mounted, Brizola called for popular militancy in defense of Goulart's labor-oriented reforms. When the military seized power in 1964, Brizola instantly became one of the regime's most wanted adversaries. He quickly fled into exile, spending the next fifteen years consolidating a political network of fellow exiles and international allies.

In 1979, the regime declared amnesty for alleged political crimes, permitting the exiles to plan their return. No homecoming was more eagerly awaited than that of Leonel Brizola. He spent the two years preceding his return in Portugal, a nation still basking in the glow of its own recent emergence from long dictatorship. The Portuguese interlude exposed Brizola to the enthusiasm of young citizens for a new social democracy that emphasized popular participation and incorporated social movements. This experience proved crucial: before the coup of 1964, Brizola had pinned his hopes for radical resistance primarily on organized labor. Upon his return in 1979, he would look to new social movements, and particular to the favela associations, as his base of support.

The regime also announced the impending legalization of new political parties in 1979; and in the last months before return, Brizola and fellow exiles entered a frenzied process of the construction of new party alliances. Although far from Brazil, they were keenly aware of the industrial labor movement that had galvanized the periphery of São Paulo, the association movements in Rio de Janeiro, and similar manifestations of popular mobilization and were in at least indirect contact with the leaders of these movements. The alliances and schisms established through these communications played a large role in defining Brazil's political left wing for the next twenty years.

In June 1979, Brizola hosted a summit in Lisbon where participants debated strategies for a broad left-wing alliance. A clear split emerged between those who favored building a new party around São Paulo's strong industrial labor movement and its charismatic leader, Lula, and those who favored reinventing Getúlio Vargas's old PTB, drawing on its nationally respected political brand. Brizola was understood to be the heir to the PTB mantle, and he was unwilling to risk that precedence through deference to the São Paulo faction. He laid plans for rebuilding the PTB from a base in Rio de Janeiro, securing the commitment of a core of exiles who referred to him as *Nosso Homem* (NH, Our Man). This deference indicated Brizola's prestige among the exiles but also underlined the contrast between his approach and that of the São Paulo faction, which treated individual political charisma with suspicion and idealized collective leadership and consensus. Brizola and his acolytes issued an open letter to sympathizers in Brazil, declaring "Analyzing the Brazilian conjuncture, we conclude that it is necessary to assume the responsibility that this historical moment demands and to invite the forces committed to the interests of the oppressed, the marginalized, to all Brazilian workers, that we might combine our efforts in the task of creating a National, Popular and Democratic Party." Although dozens of allies signed the letter, it was immediately understood and circulated as "Brizola's Letter from Lisbon," and it clearly signaled his intent to reach out to the new social movements.[56]

In the last days of 1979, Brizola returned to a hero's welcome, as well as to unexpected challenges. The regime was deeply wary of Brizola and denied him permission to refound the PTB, conferring that right instead on Ivete Vargas, Getúlio's grandniece. This gave Ivete Vargas the inside track on appealing to old PTB loyalists and left Brizola and his allies to invent a new party from scratch. This challenge proved to be an advantage: from the start the PDT would be *brizolista* rather than *getulista* and would allow Brizola to craft a broader conception of the Brazilian working class, one defined more by place of residence—in the favelas and irregular subdivisions—than by employment.

The PDT would have stiff competition for this electorate. In Rio, the PMDB could count on the Chagas Freitas machine, one that, however discredited, still gave the party an army of ward heelers throughout the state. These included figures such as Jorge Leite, who had made a political career out of negotiating with favela leaders. Irineu Guimarães's MR-8, in a move surprising to many of its own members, allied with the PMDB, pursuing its commitment to seek "bourgeois" alliances as long as they hastened the fall of the dictatorship. This decision had crucial consequences for the favela movement. Irineu Guimarães tried to persuade Brizola himself to scotch plans for his own party and join the PMDB, while Brizola pleaded with

Guimarães to break with the MR-8 and join the PDT, but neither made any headway. As a result, the PMDB could count at least temporarily on the support of an older generation of favela leaders such as Guimarães.[57]

The São Paulo faction, meanwhile, founded its own party, the PT. Although not nearly as strong in Rio as it was in São Paulo, the PT offered compelling competition for the votes of Rio's poor and working classes. The liberation theology wing of the Catholic Church played a key role in the initial articulation of the PT, establishing connections between industrial workers and university intellectuals. Liberation theology activists also strongly influenced much of the early PT's rhetoric on local initiative and participation. The Pastoral das Favelas, not surprisingly, was heavily pro-PT, and became the most influential disseminator of the PT's appeal in Rio.[58]

Pastoral leaders in Rio's favelas, however, were never able to transfer the grassroots support for the Pastoral and its initiatives into support for the PT, a disjuncture that suggests that Rio's favelados drew a careful distinction between the communitarian efforts of the Pastoral and party politics. The PT in Rio could thus count on the support of several high-profile favela leaders, such as Itamar Silva of Santa Marta and Benedita da Silva of Chapéu Mangueira. The majority of favela residents, however, remained unconvinced by the party's appeal.

THE ELECTIONS OF 1982

Brizola was not only the PDT's candidate for governor in 1982; his candidacy was the primary reason for the party's existence. Although the regime was finally opening itself up to democratic elections, it still imposed rules designed to impede the new left-wing parties. Voters were required to maintain a strict party line in their votes for governor, national Congress, and state Congress. They were not permitted to vote for a PMDB ward heeler for state Congress while voting for Brizola for governor. Brizola and his staff scrambled to fill the rest of the party's electoral slate. Rather than nominating veteran politicians, they turned to figures known for their activities outside politics. Agnaldo Timóteo, a black popular singer of melodramatic ballads, was a PDT candidate for national Congress, as were Abdias do Nascimento, Brazil's most prominent black activist, and Mário Juruna, chief of the Xavante Indian tribe. This selection was anything but random; it demonstrated Brizola's strategy to maintain the popular touch while reaching out to black and indigenous movements. Persuading voters to elect candidates who had not previously held any elected office nevertheless required them to take a risk; voting for the PDT slate meant voting for Brizola and an unlikely assortment of untested candidates. Not surprisingly, Brizola's initial polling figures were low. As late as March 1982, polls indicated only 4 percent of the electorate supported Brizola for governor.[59]

Each of Brizola's opponents had clear weaknesses, as well. Those weaknesses played crucial roles in the elections of 1982 and continued to structure local politics for the next two decades. The way they shaped the elections of 1982, moreover, reveals the political shoals that both Brizola and favela leaders would navigate in subsequent years.

The Partido Democrático Social (PDS, Social Democratic Party), notwithstanding its name, was the right-wing inheritor of Arena's mantle. It nominated Wellington Moreira Franco, scion of a powerful political clan. Moreira Franco's connections throughout the state guaranteed him a large turnout in the rural hinterlands, but he struggled within the city. Moreira Franco's difficulties revealed that if the PDS hoped to secure any support in the favelas, it would need to do so by shoring up individual alliances with leaders in a few key favelas, while seeking to undermine Brizola's base elsewhere.

The PMDB nominated Miro Teixeira, Chagas Freitas's handpicked successor. As the campaign reached its final months, Teixeira tried to distance himself from Chagas Freitas in a desperate bid to broaden his electoral base, a move that alienated the Chagas Freitas machine while failing to draw votes from other candidates. Teixeira learned that for all the disadvantages of the machine, forsaking it in midcampaign was sure to please no one. Teixeira's difficulties revealed that chaguismo was weakened but not yet dead.

The PT nominated Lysâneas Maciel, another former exile and cosignatory of Brizola's Lisbon Letter. Maciel initially joined the PDT, but recoiled at Brizola's cultivation of operators such as Pedro Porfírio and jumped to the PT. Maciel's ambivalence typified the PT's love-hate relationship with Brizola through the 1980s, sentiments shared by leaders in the Pastoral das Favelas.[60]

The unlikely frontrunner early in the campaign was Sandra Cavalcanti of the PTB. Cavalcanti had first made her name as the spokesperson for favela removal in the early 1960s. This role made her notorious among many favela residents, particularly the young generation of favela leaders. Cavalcanti's moralistic discourse of a need to rescue favela dwellers from unhygienic conditions, however, would remain a strong element of city politics for years to come.[61]

Cavalcanti's early lead worked to Brizola's advantage, as he ably used her as a foil for his own projected policies: she favored a vigorous crackdown on crime, whereas he favored addressing poverty and marginalization, which he described as the social causes of crime. She favored favela removal, whereas he strongly advocated granting property title to favela dwellers. Brizola's recognition of the favelas as part of the city helped to place them at the center of the electoral debate.[62] In full-page ads taken out in Rio's daily newspapers, the PDT spoke directly to the concerns of favelados, promising both concrete and intangible improvements in a Brizola administration: "The favela can no longer be treated with discrimination as a marginalized parcel of society. Favelados will be assured their human rights in their entirety. Families will be guaranteed property of the land where they dwell. Conditions to bestow them with water, sewage, public transport and urbanization will be created. . . . Educational centers will be created in the favelas . . . that will function as daycare centers and schools, during the day, as centers for remedial education at night, and houses of culture and recreation on weekends."[63] The message combined promises of material upgrading and access to public education with recognition of the need to strengthen civil rights of favela residents. No other candidate came close to grasping the significance of this combination for Rio's favela population.

Brizola and the PDT described their vision as *socialismo moreno*, or brown socialism, a brilliant political coinage attributed to Brizola's candidate for vice-governor, the anthropologist Darcy Ribeiro. The phrase suggested an adaptation of the redistributionist practices of socialism to particular Brazilian characteristics of racial and cultural hybridity. Yet the discourse of socialismo moreno also bore strong traces of dependency theory, the idea that Brazil's problems stemmed from its long history of exploitation by first-world powers. In Ribeiro's description, "Brazilian socialism will spring from our history, with our flesh and our color, brown. A Brazilian socialism begins by acknowledging proudly the brown people that we are, but above all our poverty. Acknowledging that poverty proudly, while knowing that it gives profits to many people. Many people want the country to continue like this. We are against that."[64] Socialismo moreno managed

FIG. 2.1. Brizola and an elderly resident of Cantagalo, 1984. Brizola was by no means the first politician to go after the favela vote, but he was the first to embrace favela residents as equals. Black favela residents found that *brizolismo* resonated with their sense of both racial and residential identity. This mud wattle-and-daub shack was typical of early favela construction. Such homes largely disappeared over the course of the 1980s, replaced by brick construction. Photograph by Ronaldo Theobald, CPDoc JB.

to stress racial pride, emphasize hybridity and flexibility, blame foreign exploiters, and promise redistribution of wealth—all at the same time.

Although Ribeiro described socialismo moreno as a political practice that could include all Brazilians, it was clearly designed to appeal primarily to black and brown Brazilians. The nomination of Nascimento and Timóteo represented socialismo moreno in action, not merely because both candidates were black but because Nascimento's militant, rigorously reasoned denunciations of racism and racial inequality balanced the raw emotion of Timóteo's melodramatic love songs. These characteristics were the sense and sensibility of socialismo moreno. It came as no surprise that Brazilians of color and favela residents overwhelmingly backed Brizola.[65]

The PT in Rio, in contrast, had the sense without the sensibility, the logical argument without the emotional appeal to citizens who were downtrodden but proud. As one political scientist has put it, the PDT deliberately presented itself as "a little dirtier, more tattered and ugly" than the PT, with great success.[66]

Appealing directly to the association movements on an emotional basis was an essential part of this strategy. The key moment came in a mid-1982 debate organized by the middle-class federation. The debate was held in the unpretentious north side neighborhood of Olaria and was strongly attended by association officers from the middle-class, subdivision, and favela movements. Brizola, a brilliant rhetorician, gave his listeners the sense that they were key players in a vast, hopeful remaking of the state. They began to believe that by joining Brizola and building socialismo moreno they would achieve the influence to which they had been aspiring all along. Following the Olaria debate, association leaders began to join the PDT in droves.[67]

Brizola was also extraordinarily effective in individual meetings with association officers. He could turn PT or PMDB sympathizers into enthusiastic supporters of the PDT within an hour. In contrast to some of his opponents, he was obviously comfortable among the urban poor. He had an unforced habit of placing a hand on the shoulder of his interlocutor and looking him or her in the eye, his own bushy eyebrows flexing like quizzical caterpillars with obvious interest in the conversation. He peppered that conversation with the folksy expressions of his *gaúcho* (from Rio Grande do Sul) youth, not hesitating to include remarks such as "Listen up, because one jackass lowers his ear when another snorts," meaning that interlocutors should quiet down when he started to speak. This style proved a winning combination and over the last six weeks of the campaign, Brizola's poll numbers suddenly soared. In the words of one PMDB candidate for Congress, "Brizola was an avalanche, a flash flood. He took everyone by surprise."[68]

On election day, November 15, the PDT began celebrating early: the enthusiastic popular display in the streets seemed to indicate their electoral triumph. Exit polls appeared to confirm this impression—IBOPE, Brazil's most reliable polling organization, gave Brizola 31 percent of the vote and the runner-up Moreira Franco 27 percent—a margin that would give Brizola a clear victory in the single-round election, where plurality determined the victor.[69] The next day, the results were muddier. Reports of balloting irregularities began to emerge from across the state. Proconsult, the private agency hired to tabulate the votes by computer, alleged that its computers had crashed and that its original electoral data had been lost. The powerful

FIG. 2.2. Brizola visits the Alemão favela, 1983. Brizola loved the crowd—the humbler and more bedraggled the better—and the crowd loved him. Here, he inaugurates a new sewage network. Opponents characterized it as a new expression of patronage. Adherents happily flushed these fears down their new drains. Photograph by Frederico Rozário, CPDoc JB.

Globo communications empire, owned by Roberto Marinho—a steadfast opponent of Brizola—began to emphasize that Moreira Franco might still emerge the victor, once the final tally was in. Brizolistas became certain that Marinho and regime hard-liners had rigged the balloting. Brizola's own team mobilized to make sure that all parties gained access to raw balloting totals from each ward. The final tallies confirmed the exit polls: Brizola took 31.4 percent of the vote, and Moreira Franco 28 percent. But the confusion merely confirmed Brizola's convictions that powerful forces were out to get him. His supporters maintained that he had been forced to win the election twice, "na lei e na marra" (once by law, once by struggle). The ballot controversy reinforced the sentiment of brizolistas as embattled crusaders.[70]

Brizola's victory demonstrated the appeal of socialismo moreno in the midst of redemocratization. Moreira Franco's strong showing made clear that rural oligarchs still held great power in the state. Miro Teixeira garnered 20 percent of the vote, showing that chaguismo was in rapid decline, but that the remnants of the Chagas Freitas machine still constituted a valuable reserve of power. Any party that could tap that reserve would reap the benefits in future elections. Sandra Cavalcanti dropped to 10 percent of the vote, demonstrating that though her brand of moralism was not likely to win democratic elections, it was also not going to disappear. Maciel garnered a mere 3 percent, a total artificially suppressed by the candidate's own ambivalence. In the last weeks of the campaign, he virtually dropped out and quietly encouraged supporters to vote for Brizola. His poor showing demonstrated the fragility of the PT in Rio and raised the possibility of a PT-PDT alliance.[71]

BRIZOLA'S ELECTION BROUGHT RIO'S favela movement to the governor's palace, effectively bringing the movement's grassroots stage to an end. Overnight, favela leaders went from being the impassioned opposition to being participants in government. This transformation brought both great rewards and new risks. As some favela leaders cemented their alliance with the PDT, others retained their loyalties to competing parties or eschewed party politics altogether, making consolidation of pan-favela solidarity unlikely. The threat of removal, moreover, had been the most prominent cause of favela mobilization from 1977 through the 1982 election. Brizola's election took favela removal off the table for at least the next four years, leaving in doubt the basis for continued popular participation in the favela movement.

The grassroots stage of the favela movement left an enduring mark on local politics and on the city itself. It ended the brief age of favela removal. It awakened a sense of communitarian struggle. It popularized and made meaningful a new rhetoric of favelado rights. And it made clear that whatever was to become of Rio de Janeiro in the future, the residents of the city's favelas would play a crucial role.

REFORM

Sou produto do morro	("I am a product of the hill.
Por isso do morro não fujo e nem corro	And because of that I will not flee or run from the hill
No morro eu aprendi a ser gente	On the hill I learned to be somebody
Nunca fui valente e sim conceituado	I was never a tough guy but I am esteemed
Em qualquer favela que eu chegar	In any favela I go to
Eu sou muito bem chegado	I am very well received
E no Cantagalo, na linha de frente	And in Cantagalo, on the front line
Naquele ambiente sou considerado	In that environment I am highly considered")

—BEZERRA DA SILVA, "Produto do Morro" (song), 1983.

In the months between Brizola's election in November 1982 and his inauguration in March 1983, three things happened that indicated how profoundly his administration would change the relationship between favela residents and state government. The first was Brizola's appointment of key favela leaders to positions in state and city government. The second was his announcement of ambitious reforms in housing, education and public security, and his appointment of controversial ministers in these three key sectors. The third was the mass invasion of public lands along rail and metro lines on Rio's north side and the overnight establishment of squatter settlements. These transitions showed that Brizola was prepared to dedicate enormous resources and energy to improving the lives of Rio's favela residents. They also showed that "the problem of the favela" was a moving target, one perhaps moving faster than the incoming governor realized.

Welcoming favela leaders into local government was an innovation of historic dimensions; never before had favela residents been given such direct political power. This incorporation indicated that Brizola's government would not be bound by traditional restrictions of social prestige in choosing its civil servants. It also ushered the favela movement into a stage of institutionalization and made partisan loyalties a key component of that process. The appointment of controversial reformers in housing, education, and public security indicated Brizola's eagerness to overhaul entrenched bureaucracies and challenge convention. Two of these reformers—Carlos Magno Nazareth Cerqueira, in Public Security, and Carlos Alberto Oliveira, in Housing—were black and from working-class backgrounds themselves, characteristics that alone defied the predilections of Rio's elite. The third was Darcy Ribeiro, who would serve simultaneously as Brizola's vice-governor and secretary for special projects, in charge of a new experiment in public education. Ribeiro was the white father of *socialismo moreno* and a prominent left-wing academic. The three new ministers shared Brizola's sense that the moment presented a unique opportunity for dramatic innovation in government. Their appointments underscored Brizola's insistence that the key to resolving Rio's pernicious inequalities lay in social reform.

The land invasions were also an innovation in a city where favelas had tended to grow through irregular real-estate markets. According to Rio's newspapers, the squatters' mantra was "invade, que Brizola legalize" (invade, and Brizola will legalize it). As disputes over the ballot count in the 1982 election dragged on, poor and working-class citizens voted with their feet.[1] This development showed that Brizola's reforms—even before they were put in place—created unanticipated incentives, threatening to overwhelm the government's capacity. Policies that did not respond to the changing nature of favelas would quickly become outmoded. The land invasions also revealed that Rio's urban poor and working-class residents were not content to wait for the governor to fulfill his campaign promises; even before the whistle blew on his new administration, they started the game with the equivalent of a full-court press.

FAVELA ASSOCIATIONS AND THE PDT

Under the military regime, state governors controlled appointments to municipal government in state capitals, such as Rio de Janeiro. This gave Brizola decisive leverage over both state and municipal administration.

He began by appointing a pliant PDT operative—Jamil Haddad—as Rio's mayor in 1983, then replaced him a year later with a more dynamic young protégé—Marcello Alencar. He instituted the Single Treasury System for state and local government, giving him immediate control over both state and municipal spending: regardless of who sat in the mayor's chair, Brizola would be holding the purse strings. Using this power, Brizola proceeded to bring favela leaders into city and state government. José Martins de Oliveira was president of the residents' association in Bairro Barcellos, the commercial core of Rocinha—a favela so large that it had three different associations in the 1980s, each representing a different subregion.[2] Martins de Oliveira, originally from the northeastern state of Ceará, had emerged as an influential leader in Rocinha in the late 1970s. Brizola named him a community manager of social services. Two years later, Martins de Oliveira rose to the position of regional administrator for Rocinha, an influential post in determining disbursement of public funds and one that paid him ten times the minimum wage—a middle-class salary.[3]

Martins de Oliveira's experience was not unusual. Brizola made clear that he planned to invest heavily in favela social services using local workers, meaning residents of the favelas in question. The Municipal Secretariat for Social Development became the office responsible for hiring favela residents, and it turned to favela association officers first. This approach followed partly on Israel Klabin's use of the Secretariat during his brief terms as mayor, but also transformed Klabin's model. Klabin had created the Secretariat as a technocratic development office, and Brizola reimagined it as a branch of government that centralized all municipal overtures toward favelas and served as a vehicle for favela employment. The Secretariat became known as the *prefeitura dos pobres*, or city government for the poor. As Itamar Silva puts it, "It was a space of circulation for the poor, for favelados. . . . There were lots of people working in Social Development, in the municipal government, as field agents, as foremen on works projects. There was a swelling of that space of public power as public projects in favelas expanded."[4] The Secretariat, intended to offer one-stop shopping for all favela interactions with municipal government, created a parallel administration, separate from that which governed the rest of the city.

Certain favelas developed particularly strong ties to the PDT, and these were rewarded with consistent opportunities in state and municipal government. The Morro da Formiga, in the north side district of Tijuca, was one of these. Hélio de Oliveira, president of Formiga's association, soon began working in the Social Development Secretariat. In 1980, Oliveira had become the first resident of Formiga to earn a university degree, and he found employment in the Secretariat's legal department, eventually rising to the post of legal director. Oliveira's rise demonstrates that Brizola's strategy was not merely *empreguismo*, or "employmentism" — the practice of distributing public jobs strictly in order to cultivate political loyalty; rather, it was an opportunity for favela residents to advance professionally based on merit. A lawyer from the favela would not have stood a chance of finding employment under previous administrations. Under Brizola, Oliveira rose quickly. These two facets of public employment, political patronage and opportunity, became inextricably intertwined.[5]

The majority of Brizola's favela appointments were more humble. Walter Pereira, a Formiga leader who had left elementary school in third grade, parlayed his support for the PDT into low-level state employment. Early in Brizola's administration, Cedae — the State Water and Sewer Company — began to build a sewer network in Formiga. "Cedae starting hiring five *companheiros* in each community where it was installing water, sewer, those things. I entered as a *servente* [an entry-level manual laborer]." Pereira continued to cultivate his political connections and eventually persuaded a PDT state congressman to promote and transfer him to Cedae's telecommunications sector. Pereira also eventually returned to school and earned a law degree.[6]

The PDT's incorporation of individual association leaders posed challenges for the Pastoral das Favelas. In an attempt to avoid PDT co-optation, the Pastoral cohort of favela leaders advocated obligatory state funding for community work projects directed by individual favela associations. They described their demand as a "paid *mutirão*," trying to combine the enthusiasm for voluntary collective labor that had marked the grassroots stage with the new possibilities of state employment.[7] Dilza Terra, Brizola's municipal director of social development, surprisingly agreed, promising to deliver funding directly to favela associations for a Project Mutirão in five hundred favelas.

Terra, however, vastly exceeded her authority in making these rash commitments, and Brizola promptly fired her. He replaced her with Pedro Porfírio, by this point a loyal PDT operative. Porfírio delayed matters long enough to weed out his allies from his adversaries and then eliminated the project entirely. The Pastoral urged FAFERJ, the favela federation, to protest, to no avail. Too many favela leaders were already working for Brizola. The Pastoral cohort quit the favela federation, leaving both the Pastoral and the federation weaker. The termination of Project Mutirão and its consequences gave a clear indication that as long as Brizola was in office, the surest way to secure favela investment would be through alliance with his party.[8]

Brizola's opponents, both among the conservative middle class and on the doctrinaire Left, criticized this as an updated version of the politics of the water spigot. Instead of delivering the spigot himself, Brizola brought favela leaders into his administration and let them deliver the spigot. The result was the same: the use of public funds to create a partisan machine that delivered ameliorative reforms rather than profound transformation. For brizolistas, in contrast, accepting state employment constituted the active occupation of spaces of political power by the urban poor. The brizolistas had the better argument: favela leaders such as Martins de Oliveira, Hélio de Oliveira, and Walter Pereira were not Brizola's pawns. They used municipal and state employment to bring resources to their communities, as well as to further their own careers. The presence of favela residents in city and state government was itself a significant step in the direction of strengthening citizenship. And when alliance with Brizola proved more a hindrance than a benefit, they broke away. Equally important, both Brizola and his favela allies wanted more than short-term material upgrading; they hoped to redistribute power, literally and figuratively, throughout the city. Brizola wanted that distribution to happen through the PDT, in ways that he could control, but he went much farther than Chagas Freitas in granting favela leaders leverage.[9]

This contentious debate about clientelism, however, obscured a deeper transition: the Municipal Secretariat of Social Development made favela associations the conduits for public investment. This use of the associations gave them leverage but also consolidated their new role as distributors of resources rather than instigators of mobilization, a consolidation that inevitably changed their relationship both to government and to local residents. Their ability to represent the demands of their community diminished as they became conduits of funding and employment. Brizola's reforms in housing, education, and public Security would reinforce this transformation.

Brizola promised nothing less than the wholesale revision of property and land tenure in Rio de Janeiro. He pledged to deliver property title to a million families throughout the state, including 400,000 families living in favelas in the city of Rio de Janeiro. He put the full weight of state administration into the effort, pushing through state legislation facilitating expropriation and titling of irregular lots.[10] His innovative program, "Cada Família Um Lote," or One Plot Per Family, sought to channel the energy of the favela and subdivision movements into the redistribution of rights to the city.

Brizola named a housing secretary willing and able to take on entrenched interests. Carlos Alberto de Oliveira—known to admirers by the acronym of his initials, Caó—was a black union leader, the son of a seamstress and a carpenter from Bahia. He had cut his teeth in the Bahian Student Union before the military coup in 1964, when he was still in his early twenties. By the late 1970s, he was a leader of the Journalists' Union and an articulator of the broad union movement that pressured the military government to cede power. He had no prior experience in housing, but he was closely connected to the new social movements and to Brizola's base among black cariocas and favela residents.

Working closely with Brizola, Oliveira designed a titling process that would enable favela residents to file for property regularization through their residents' associations. Employees of the Housing Secretariat, working in conjunction with the favela associations, would create complete registries of favela lots and then facilitate the work of delivering a certificate of possession, known as a *promessa de compra e venda*, or promise of purchase and sale. The program required holders of these certificates to make small monthly payments, capped at one-tenth of the monthly minimum wage, for four years. At the completion of this period, the state would deliver full, legal title to the property. Favela associations would serve as the intermediary between individual favela families and the Housing Secretariat at every stage of the process. This facet of the program did not initially appear to be a drawback, given the understanding that these elected associations appeared to represent the political will of their communities.

This turned out to be a crucial miscalculation. By the end of Brizola's administration, the program had delivered only sixteen thousand certificates of promise of purchase and sale. None of these had yet been converted into

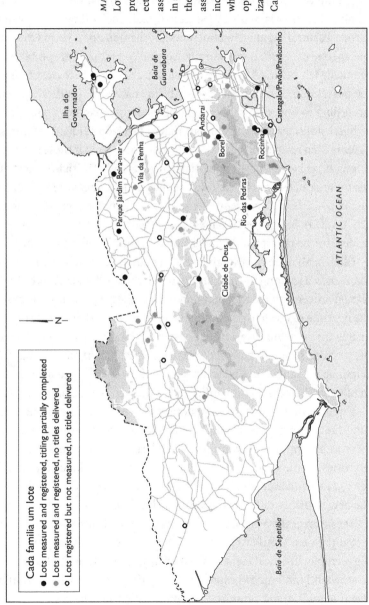

MAP 6. Cada Família Um Lote (One Plot Per Family) project sites. Neither projects in sites with strong associations nor those in sites characterized by the recent foundation of associations succeeded, indicating the degree to which favela associations opted out of title regularization in the mid-1980s. Cartography by Bill Nelson.

Cada família um lote
● Lots measured and registered, titling partially completed
● Lots measured and registered, no titles delivered
○ Lots registered but not measured, no titles delivered

Ilha do Governador

Baía de Guanabara

Andaraí
Borel
Rocinha
Cantagalo/Pavão/Pavãozinho

Parque Jardim Beira-mar
Vila da Penha

Rio das Pedras

Cidade de Deus

ATLANTIC OCEAN

Baía de Sepetiba

N

full legal title, and few would ever make that transition. In the meantime, Rio's favela population expanded at a far greater rate than it had in previous decades.[11]

Brizola and Oliveira expected association officers to collaborate eagerly in facilitating regularization of title. Property title, after all, had been close to the top of association demands in the late 1970s. But the context had already changed markedly by the time Brizola took office. In the words of former Pastoral organizers remembering the transition years later, "Once the specter of removal was eliminated, the question of property title was gradually left behind."[12] Property title was no longer necessary to guarantee possession, for that had already been ensured by political transition. According to one local scholar writing as early as January 1984, property regularization was no longer a prominent favelado demand "and in some cases is even rejected if it implies financial costs, even if these are compatible with the income of the potential beneficiaries."[13] With Brizola in office, the promise of title was to be coldly judged in light of cost-benefit analysis, and in those terms its advantages were uncertain. Title would bring property taxes, rising property values, and potential gentrification. And local leaders feared that it would undermine community mobilization.

Chapéu Mangueira, a small favela just down the beach from Morro dos Cabritos, was among the first favelas to reject One Plot Per Family. Its association officers argued that they preferred to file for property title based on the doctrine of adverse possession, a legal recourse that would, in theory, enable them to win title without passing through the intermediary stage of the Promise of Purchase and Sale, with its attendant monthly payments. But Chapéu Mangueira's residents did not file these individual claims, and in practice their association officers discouraged them from doing so.[14]

Favela leaders linked to the Pastoral das Favelas were not alone in shunning the program. As Oliveira's team stepped up its efforts in the field, FAFERJ abruptly dropped property regularization from its list of top-ten priorities. At the same moment, it ratcheted up its demands for "subsidies for FAFERJ and individual associations," a shift in priorities that reflected the new priorities of the associations as local distributors of resources.[15]

The Jacarezinho association, still under Irineu Guimarães's control, rejected the One Plot Per Family program, insisting that material upgrading—employing local residents—should precede titling. In Borel, Brizola triumphantly announced expropriation of the favela's territory from putative titleholders and promised individual title to favela residents, declaring "From today on, Borel is no longer a favela. It is a neighborhood." On the same day, however, Borel's association president criticized Brizola's "urgency" regarding property title, arguing that infrastructure should take precedence. Unbeknownst to Brizola, the game had already changed: the same association leaders who had helped propel him into office were now opting out of his titling program. Without collaboration from the associations, Oliveira's team had no ability to construct its registries, and gradually withdrew from these neighborhoods. In the understated analysis of a Housing Secretariat field agent who subsequently authored a keen analysis of the program, "Everything was supposed to be done with the agreement of the residents' association. . . . But the residents' associations did not always collaborate."[16] They did not collaborate because it was neither in their financial nor their political interest to do so. Financially, distribution of property title would have eliminated their ability to parcel out new lots in the favela. Politically, it would have weakened their role as the intermediary between local residents and state power.

ONE PLOT PER FAMILY IN PRACTICE

Oliveira's field agents were particularly stymied by the problem of favela rental properties, which they soon discovered to be far more common than previously imagined. The program called for individualization of property title, but strongly discouraged granting multiple properties to a single individual. Although project agents flirted with the possibility of overriding the interests of favela landlords and granting title directly to tenants, they found this impossible in practice: few tenants were willing to sign on to a process that would inevitably lead to local conflict, which at best would be mediated by an association with no interest in extending title and at worst end in violence. In some cases, association officers were directly involved in selling and renting lots. Not surprisingly, these officers were not enthusiastic participants in the program.[17]

Rio das Pedras, for example, was a rapidly growing west-side favela largely populated by northeastern migrants. In the early 1980s, Rio das Pedras was a small grouping of self-built wooden shacks just off a highway. In Brizola's first months in office, the Rio das Pedras association plotted adjacent areas for expansion and began selling them to newcomers who made low monthly payments. The president of the Rio das Pedras association was a tough migrant from the northeastern hinterland, known for carrying a machete through Rio das Pedras. He was not interested in the niceties of socialismo moreno. He correctly viewed One Plot Per Family as a threat to irregular real-estate ventures and sought to delay its implementation. The program's agents, meanwhile, avoided regularization that might further consolidate the power of this group by legalizing their authority as landlords and developers. The result was a stagnation of the process of regularization, even as the favela itself expanded rapidly.[18]

Because of its high profile in the wake of the papal visit, Vidigal represented an inviting target for full regularization, and in the early months of the titling program the favela was declared "subject to expropriation for social ends." This decree still required payment to the putative titleholder, however. Since the resistance of 1978, a new real-estate consortium had acquired nominal property rights to Vidigal. The consortium refused Oliveira's terms, Oliveira refused to negotiate, and Vidigal—"the Pope's favela"—dropped out of the program.[19] Although real-estate values were far lower in Morro de Andaraí, on Rio's north side, plans for expropriation there ran into similar problems. Program agents mapped the favela, conducted a census, and prepared the rolls for titling, but the funds for expropriation were never delivered, and titling of individual lots could not proceed.

In the face of these obstacles, One Plot Per Family ultimately titled fewer than 2 percent of the one million plots announced as the program's goal.[20] Continued favela expansion far outstripped the meager results of attempted regularization. Brizola and Oliveira were able to halt the rapid invasions of public lands that had characterized the period between Brizola's election victory and his inauguration, but only by recognizing most of these invasions as accomplished facts. In existing favelas, the titling program itself prompted expansion and "verticalization," as residents rushed to build before any new limitations could be imposed. The first two years of Brizola's administration, meant to be the great push toward favela regularization, were, instead, a period of intense favela growth.[21]

In the irregular subdivisions of the city's west side, in contrast, title regularization proceeded slowly but steadily. One Plot Per Family, though initially intended to include the subdivisions, ultimately concentrated almost entirely on favelas. Instead, Rio's municipal government, following Brizola's directives, created a Núcleo de Regularização de Loteamentos, or Nucleus for Subdivision Regularization, specifically to facilitate titling in the irregular subdivisions. In contrast to One Plot Per Family, which worked with the local association, the nucleus worked directly with individual residents. Also, in contrast to the favelas, where property regularization dropped down the list of association demands once possession was guaranteed, regular title remained the priority in the subdivisions, and individual residents availed themselves of the nucleus. Although its early progress was unassuming, by 1986 the nucleus was established as a reliable facilitator of regularization, a distinction it would strengthen in subsequent years. Brizola's property reforms, intended to regularize both favelas and subdivisions, ended up reinforcing distinctions between them.[22]

ELECTRICITY, WATER, AND SEWAGE IN THE FAVELAS

Infrastructural upgrading projects that were initially intended to complement the titling program had higher success rates. The Program of Electrification in the Social Interest was intended to provide regular electrical service to Rio's favelas, eliminating the old "light commissions" that had stifled favela political representation through the 1970s. The Programa de Favelas da CEDAE (Proface, the Favela Program of the State Water and Sewage Authority) was intended to extend regular water and sewage networks to favelas. Planners and field agents for both programs encountered obstacles similar to those faced by One Plot Per Family, but succeeded in surmounting them because they found association officers to have greater interests in serving as the intermediaries for infrastructural upgrading than they did in facilitating delivery of individual property titles.

Light, the municipal electric authority, initiated the electrification program on a small scale in 1979. Brizola massively expanded the program, extending it to four hundred favelas during his administration. Light turned to planners and field agents from the Instituto Brasileiro de Administração Municipal (IBAM, The Brazilian Institute of Municipal Administration), an urban-planning think tank, to carry out the project. The instituto's most influential planner was the visionary architect and anthropologist Carlos Nelson Ferreira dos Santos, the key figure in the upgrading of Brás de Pina in the late 1960s. Nelson's young assistants took over the Social Electrification project, designing a flexible program intended to respond to changing conditions. In effect, they created a subsidiary of Light to deliver electricity to favelas in the midst of rapid expansion. Although the program did not fully regularize service—an impossible task, given the dynamics of favela expansion—it did vastly improve service while lowering costs.[23]

The electrification program did not eliminate the remaining light commissions, but it forced them to evolve quickly or wither away. In a small favela adjacent to the north side residential neighborhood of Vila da Penha, for example, a local powerbroker—literally and figuratively—had run the light commission since the late 1960s. As in many favelas, the light commission served as the de facto association, negotiating on behalf of the favela with local politicians and limiting any possibility for opposition. In 1981, in the midst of the boom in the foundation of favela associations, a group of young residents held elections for a new association, challenging the old powerbroker's authority. He refused to recognize the new association or to relinquish his chokehold on the favela's electrical network.

Over the next three years, he blocked efforts by Light technicians to put in a new transfer station and bring existing connections up to code, improvements that would have circumvented his chokehold on the favela's electrical connection. Brizola's inauguration invigorated the youthful opposition, who began describing themselves as the Movimento Sangue Novo, or New Blood Movement, and waging a public campaign against the old powerbroker. Field agents from IBAM found themselves in the midst of a heated dispute for power within the community. The New Blood Movement sued the powerbroker for allegedly removing the valuable copper wire from the existing system and replacing it with cheap, unreliable aluminum wire. The powerbroker, in turn, sued Light for breaking a putative agreement to work through the light commission. Agents from the instituto had no idea whom to work with in order to carry out their project.[24]

In contrast to experiences in the titling program, where confusion and dispute yielded paralysis, popular enthusiasm for improved electrical service eventually carried the day. The New Blood Movement led rallies demanding regular public electrification, winning coverage from local newspapers and television stations. The powerbroker found himself in the untenable position of claiming to represent the favela despite widespread popular demonstrations against his power. He ultimately accepted a negotiated settlement, stepping down in return for a hefty payment from Light; the fee was ostensibly paid to the "community" in return for use of the old light commission's copper wire, which the old powerbroker duly returned. The money, however, was delivered to the old powerbroker individually, with no subsequent accounting for its whereabouts. Not to put too fine a point on it: Light and the planners from IBAM paid the old powerbroker to get out of the way so they could regularize the favela's electricity. This kind of unsavory but effective compromise had proven impossible in the property-titling project, where the Housing Secretariat was both unable and unwilling to pay off countless claimants and irregular landlords. Had they tried to do so, they would have triggered a landslide of claimants, each demanding his or her cut. In the electrification program, in contrast, paying off one light commission—in practice, one or two powerbrokers—was enough to facilitate upgrading in an entire favela. Light and the young planners from IBAM accepted these compromises as part of the cost of doing business.[25]

In favelas where new associations had already risen to power, these associations were for the most part eager to participate in the electrification program and found their own ways of turning the program to their advantage. The association in the north side favela of Bela Vista, for example, promptly purchased a refrigerator and a stereo and starting hosting weekend *forró* (northeastern Brazilian accordion music) dances as fundraisers.[26]

Proface's goals—extending sewer and water networks to 113 favelas—proved more challenging. Stringing electrical wires was relatively simple in comparison to digging, installing, and maintaining sewage and water lines without overburdening area networks. And in contrast to the electrical network, which could be extended easily as favelas grew, sewage networks were quickly overwhelmed by continued growth. Nonetheless, Proface's achievements were dramatic, if not complete. Fetid open sewers had been the worst stigma of favela residence. By installing a network of pipes, underground where possible, Proface demonstrated that there was nothing inherently insalubrious about favelas, once they were provided with the same kinds of public services middle-class neighborhoods took for granted. Public sewage networks also provided the clearest material indication that local and state government no longer consigned favelas to the contradictory category of indefinitely temporary aberrations; rather, these entities considered favelas permanent parts of the city.

There was a price for this consolidation, but it was neither the price of veiled removal feared by the pastoral nor that of the creation of perpetual clientelist "electoral corrals" feared by the PDT's opponents. Neither of these phenomena came to pass: property values rose markedly in some favelas, yet rarely so fast as to push out many previous residents. Instead, favelas themselves developed more marked economic contrasts between relatively advantaged and disadvantaged subareas. And although the PDT continued to build on the success of the outreach to informal neighborhoods that had helped secure victory in 1982, the open nature of political competition in the new democracy required that it do so through ever-renewed commitments, rather than through presumed loyalty. Even favelas such as the Morro da Formiga, strongly linked to the PDT in the mid-1980s, cultivated diverse political alliances in subsequent years.[27]

Instead, the cost was one that seemed initially more of a benefit: the fortification of the mediating role of favela associations. State government and its agencies relied on the associations to facilitate upgrading projects, and local populations began to use them as a means of gaining employment on those projects. Instrumentalization took the place of grassroots mobilization. This process was partly inevitable. Social movements cannot sustain grassroots mobilization indefinitely; they either wither or get institutionalized. The incorporation of the favela associations into the state was not the problem. The problem was that incorporation happened in ways that reinforced, rather than eroded, the distinction between the favelas and the rest of the city.

A NEW VISION FOR PUBLIC EDUCATION

As governor of Rio Grande do Sul from 1959 to 1962, Brizola had funded the construction and inauguration of dozens of new schools throughout the state. These brizolinhas, as they became known, extended public education to poor neighborhoods and villages in Rio Grande do Sul for the first time. Two decades later, Brizola hoped to do the same thing on a larger scale, planning construction of hundreds of brizolões (the plural of brizolão): massive public schools and community centers intended to transform the availability and the experience of education.

There was little doubt that massive change was required; Rio's public schools were a calamity. Its public education system had been designed in the early twentieth century for middle-class students and had only been gradually extended to students from the industrial working class. Gradual expansion had enabled schools to serve an increasingly diverse population while maintaining quality, and up through the 1960s elementary schools had offered an orderly and well-rounded education where children of lawyers and factory workers often shared classrooms. At the secondary level, these populations tended to diverge, with middle-class students proceeding through liberal arts high schools and children of the working class balancing employment with education in semipublic vocational programs.[28]

Apparent harmony and inclusion were built on an illusion, however. The rapidly expanding city population was substantially larger than the slowly expanding capacity of public schools. Favela residents remained largely excluded. Previous governors had responded to these problems by expanding class size and shortening school days so that schools could operate in two shifts, resulting in declining quality.

Chagas Freitas attempted to respond to rising demand by hiring thousands of new teachers, themselves often graduates of overcrowded normal schools. But the onset of rapid inflation in the late 1970s exacerbated difficulties: the real value of teacher salaries declined, leading to increasing dissent and high rates of double employment. Teachers often worked at one school in the morning and another in the afternoon, a solution that led to exhaustion and chronic teacher absenteeism. By the early 1980s, middle-class students had begun to desert the public school system, opting for private schools. Although this opened up some spaces in public schools for the urban poor, it left these schools with fewer well-connected advocates. By the time Brizola took office, many schools had moved to three daily shifts of fewer than four hours of classroom instruction per shift. Not surprisingly, rates of failure, grade repetition, and dropout climbed steadily.[29]

Brizola worried that the existing teacher corps and the state secretariat of education were resistant to change. To circumvent their entrenched power, he created a parallel education ministry for Darcy Ribeiro, the secretary of Special Projects, giving him power to open schools, hire and train teachers, and institute an education track completely distinct from the regular system.

Ribeiro seemed to be the right man for the job: he was a distinguished anthropologist—his research specialty was study of the Xavante Indians in the Brazilian Amazon—and a dedicated educator with extensive experience in administration as well as classroom teaching. He was a follower of Anísio Teixeira, a pioneering educator who had pushed for an expanded, modern public school system. Ribeiro was also a former communist and remained an impassioned socialist, with a fervent commitment to radical reform. He intended to realize Teixeira's vision on a grand scale, making Rio's public schools the factories for the creation of a new generation, unburdened by the prejudices and weaknesses of the past, prepared to construct the glorious future. He cut a striking profile in carioca politics—he had a thick mane of hair that swayed as he gesticulated, invoking the great future of socialist education for all—and inspired an impassioned following in local universities.[30]

Over the course of 1983, Ribeiro directed a survey of the state's teacher corps, collecting ideas for reform. In November of that year, teacher delegations from across the state met with Ribeiro and his advisers in Mendes, a small town in the hills northwest of the city. The Mendes Encounter was meant to be ground zero of Ribeiro's education revolution, and after several days of intense debates, the encounter produced a rough blueprint for radical reform. One cohort of young teachers emerged from the encounter energized and committed to these reforms, but other delegates left Mendes with the suspicion that the encounter's process had been manipulated to produce the results Ribeiro had intended all along. The divisions among the Mendes delegates would soon produce a deeper schism across the state, between those drafted into Ribeiro's parallel program and those linked to the traditional system and resentful of the favoritism Ribeiro showered on his own flock.[31]

Following the Mendes Encounter, Ribeiro announced plans for the creation of five hundred Centros Integrados de Educação Pública (CIEPs, Integrated Centers of Public Education), a new model school, across the state. Over three hundred of these would be located in the metropolitan region of the city of Rio, overwhelmingly in or adjacent to favelas. The plans for the CIEPs presented several marked contrasts from typical public schools. To begin, they would be housed in new buildings, with all but the first two built according to a striking prototype designed by the Brazilian modernist architect Oscar Niemeyer. The design was meant to offer maximum efficiency and flexibility of use. Students would attend at minimum from 7:30 AM to 5:00 PM, and in addition to academic subjects they would eat three balanced meals, take a daily shower, play sports, and pursue cultural activities directed by a special "cultural animator" at each school—ideally an artist or performer from the neighborhood itself, connecting students to local cultural traditions. At least one CIEP in each region would offer medical care to students and local residents. Students who lived a great distance from their closest CIEP or who came from troubled homes would be lodged at the school, where they would be supervised by live-in "social parents."[32]

FIG. 3.1. The CIEP Tancredo Neves shortly after its inauguration, 1985. Niemeyer's design reflected the urge to order, elevate, and inspire favela youth. Brizola, more than anything, loved the capacity of these enormous schools. Photograph by Rubens Barbosa, CPDoc JB.

After 5 PM and on weekends, the CIEP would be used for community meetings, cultural activities, and night classes for teenagers and adults. In addition to remedial education, these night classes would emphasize a "critical conscience of the world and society," following the methods of the revolutionary educator Paulo Freire. The goal was not merely to educate, but to make the CIEPs the engines of deeper social reform.

Sites were strategically chosen on the border of major favelas, close enough to a major road to be prominently visible to passersby, intended to serve both the children of the favela and those of surrounding neighborhoods. In Ribeiro's words, "Instead of camouflaging the harsh reality in which the majority of students hailing from poorer social segments live, the CIEP commits itself to that reality, in order to transform it — by feeding hungry students, giving uniforms and supplies to poor students, and treating students in medical need." The CIEPs were meant to be more than schools; they were intended to be "the public compensation for emotional, nutritional, intellectual, cultural and social needs."[33]

In order to underline the revolutionary goals of the CIEPs, Brizola and Ribeiro named each after an inspiring historical figure. Reading the list of

CIEPs today provides a snapshot of the third-world revolutionary ideal-ism of the early 1980s, as seen from Brazil. The list demonstrates that the right-wing military regime had already retreated from the field of cultural commemoration, leaving Brizola to set his own agenda in Rio, one far to the left of the comparatively moderate opposition discourse within Brazil's National Congress. The CIEPs' honored heroes fell into several clear cate-gories: figures such as Patrice Lumumba of the Congo and Agostinho Neto of Angola represented recent African marxist revolutions. Figures such as Olga Benário Prestes and Gregório Bezerra represented the long tradition of Brazilian Communist radicalism; both Benário Prestes and Bezerra had rebelled against dictatorial regimes and suffered imprisonment and abuse in retribution. Figures such as Vicente Mariano—one of the founders of the favela association federation—and Antoine Magarinos Torres—a cru-sading Communist lawyer who had helped save Borel from removal in the 1950s—represented favela leadership and mobilization. An assortment of other heroes of the Latin American Left—such as rebel slave Zumbi dos Palmares, Nicaraguan revolutionary Augusto Sandino, guerrilla Che Gue-vara, and martyred Chilean president Salvador Allende—represented aspi-rations of pan-Latin American solidarity. Each of these categories included black rebel leaders, such as Lumumba, Zumbi, and Vicente Mariano. The CIEPs, in other words, were named after pantheon of heroes of socialismo moreno. Brizola and Ribeiro clearly intended history lessons to begin be-fore students walked in the schoolhouse door.

Centro Integrado teachers, for their part, would work longer hours and face higher expectations of community involvement, and as a result would earn higher salaries than most teachers in traditional schools, despite the fact that most CIEP teachers were in their twenties. Ribeiro and his depu-ties showed an explicit preference for newly minted teachers, who had not yet been corrupted by the ingrained habits of failing schools. Teachers at CIEPs, consequently, would not be subject to the state secretary of educa-tion, but would be administered directly by Ribeiro and the Secretariat for Special Projects. In the same way that the Municipal Secretariat for Social Development became the face of municipal government for the favelas, the Secretariat of Special Projects became the face of public education for the same population. Again, Brizola's administration created a parallel, sepa-rate track, designed to eliminate long-standing obstacles to effective de-livery of services to favelas, but one that would reinforce the distinctions between favelas and the rest of the city.

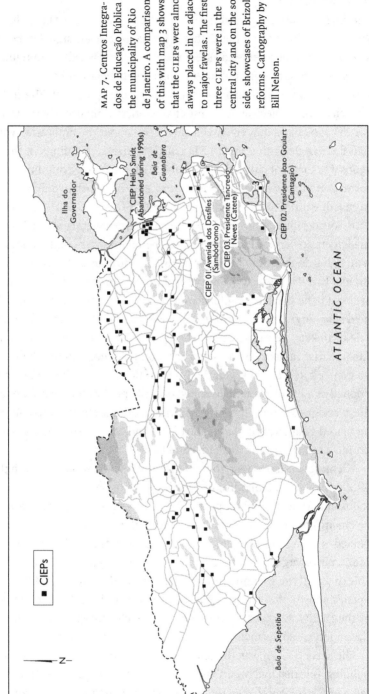

MAP 7. Centros Integrados de Educação Pública in the municipality of Rio de Janeiro. A comparison of this with map 3 shows that the CIEPs were almost always placed in or adjacent to major favelas. The first three CIEPs were in the central city and on the south side, showcases of Brizola's reforms. Cartography by Bill Nelson.

CIEP Helio Smidt (Abandoned during 1990s)

Ilha do Governador

Baía de Guanabara

CIEP 01 Avenida dos Desfiles (Sambódromo)

CIEP 03 Presidente Tancredo Neves (Catete)

CIEP 02 Presidente Joao Goulart (Cantagalo)

ATLANTIC OCEAN

Baía de Sepetiba

CIEPs

N

The first problems to be addressed were designing the CIEPs, choosing sites, and getting them built. This prioritization itself signaled both the strengths and weaknesses of Ribeiro's vision: he was willing to reimagine education from the ground up but mistakenly believed that a change in venue itself would solve many of Rio's educational problems. The architect chosen for the project shared these characteristics; indeed, Niemeyer made Ribeiro look like a moderate. His only regret about the innovative work he had done in designing most of Brasília's signature buildings in the early 1960s was that that city had not became the stage for the communist transformation of society he idealized. The CIEPs, he hoped, would go further in that direction, nurturing the new Brazilian.[34]

Before designing the standard CIEP prototype, Niemeyer faced an intermediary task—designing the first CIEP, better known as the Sambódromo, which did double-duty as the stadium for Rio's annual carnival parade. Brizola had determined to move the annual February celebration off the streets of the Estácio neighborhood, where the official parade had been held since 1931, and into a long, narrow stadium, facilitating production, sale of tickets, and post-Carnaval cleanup. Carnaval was the linchpin of Rio's tourist industry, and even a socialist governor had to take steps to guarantee a successful spectacle. Even so, Brizola knew he would be lampooned as a hypocrite if he presided over the public construction of a stadium designed primarily for the enjoyment of tourists. With that in mind, he placed Niemeyer in charge of design and stipulated that the Sambódromo also serve as the Rio's first and largest CIEP.

Niemeyer designed long rows of stands with classrooms beneath them. As a school, the Sambódromo was designed to serve as many as twelve thousand students, drawn primarily from nearby favelas of central Rio de Janeiro, particularly the adjacent São Carlos favela. The school was intended to anchor the reconfiguration of this area, facilitating the social and economic emergence of the urban poor. Racing against time, Brizola was able to unveil the stadium for the Carnaval parade of 1984, and the school opened shortly afterward, with a small pilot enrollment. Much of the rest of the facility was used for training CIEP teachers, separating them from the overcrowded normal schools attended by most teachers.[35]

The second CIEP was the only unit to take advantage of a preexisting building, one that had been abandoned for nearly a decade. The Hotel Panorama was a swooping concrete and glass structure jutting out from a hill

FIG. 3.2. Brizola visits Cantagalo, 1985. Brizola chose Cantagalo as one of his model communities, and took every opportunity to exhort its youngest residents to seize the opportunities his reforms represented. Photograph by Custódio Coimbra, CPDoc JB.

overlooking Ipanema. It was built in the mid-1960s, designed to serve well-heeled international tourists. The Panorama's nightclub, with a glorious ocean view, had been briefly popular, but the hotel itself did not succeed. By the early 1970s the favela of Cantagalo had crept up another flank of the hill, just behind the hotel, eventually prompting the hotel owners to abandon the building. Brizola seized the building and passed control to Ribeiro for the creation of another massive CIEP, serving the children of Cantagalo and the adjacent favela of Pavão-Pavãozinho. Brizola named this one after his brother-in-law João Goulart, ousted in the coup of 1964 and since deceased. Ribeiro oversaw a transformation of the building into a school designed to serve four thousand students. Brizola and Ribeiro envisioned it as the linchpin of another neighborhood development plan, this one designed to make Cantagalo and Pavão models of favela upgrading.

The third CIEP was the first of the schools built according to Niemeyer's basic prototype, the same used for all subsequent schools. This one was named for Tancredo Neves, the former ally of Getúlio Vargas, longtime opponent of the military regime and, in 1985, the victorious candidate in Brazil's first democratic presidential elections since 1960. Neves died in April of that year, shortly before the scheduled inauguration. Neves was in general too moderate for Brizola's taste, but the governor responded to the wave of popular mourning by naming the CIEP in his honor. Its design incorporated many of the signature traits of Niemeyer's work in Brasília, including swooping curves of poured concrete, massive blocks raised on slender pillars, and clean geometric lines. It consisted of two constructions: one to house the classrooms, the other to a house a sheltered assembly hall and sports court, open on two sides. Between these two buildings stretched a concrete plaza. It opened in early May 1985, two weeks after Neves's death, for a pilot population of twelve students, carefully selected from the neighboring favela of Santo Amaro. They found themselves under careful observation, not only by the school's teachers and staff—several of whom also resided in Santo Amaro—but by journalists and politicians. Brizola's opponents were eager for the school to fail, and his supporters needed it to succeed.[36]

Typical of his work, Niemeyer's striking design had both advantages and disadvantages, particularly in comparison with traditional schools. Classrooms were separated by concrete dividers rather than by complete walls, and most window spaces were unglazed. This facilitated cross-ventilation but also made for noisy classrooms. The striking design could not accommodate particularities of site; it required leveling a two-acre swathe of land, a requirement not always practical in Rio's favelas and enormously expensive elsewhere. Several communities protested when their soccer fields were seized to make way for a CIEP.[37]

Construction of the CIEPs also proved to be expensive. Niemeyer's design was meant to be relatively inexpensive to build in quantity, but the early phases of the project required the construction of a massive factory on Rio's north side, where the specific concrete molds required by the CIEPs were formed and replicated. Ribeiro noted proudly that this technology was "frequently utilized in the Soviet Union as a factor of rationalization of social works," thereby distinguishing himself as one of the last Western holdouts to emulate Soviet planning. In his estimation, the high number of workers employed at this factory was itself one of the program's great virtues, "attenuating the grave social problem of unemployment." Political opponents, in contrast, characterized it as profligate, politically motivated spending that made no direct contribution to education. They had a point: Brizola's son João Otávio controlled the bidding process for the schools factory and directed contracts to PDT loyalists.[38]

Teachers and administrators in Rio's traditional schools argued that Brizola and Ribeiro had poured all their resources into the CIEPs, leaving traditional schools to decline further. They contended that Ribeiro's plan boiled down to architecture, scheduling and hot meals, and had no pedagogical method. Ribeiro and his allies had no response to this argument; amidst all of the other immediate problems faced by CIEPs, the pedagogy was largely left to take care of itself. This rift reached a crisis point in March 1986, when the teacher's union went on strike. Twenty thousand teachers—nearly a third of the total state force—attended a mass meeting on April 10 of that year, marked by bitter denunciations of Brizola's educational strategy and his unwillingness to offer meaningful concessions. Election-year exigencies eventually forced Brizola to concede most of the demands of the striking teachers, pulling back from the state's previous strategy of preferential treatment for the CIEPs.[39]

Most discouraging, the CIEPs remained underenrolled. The super-CIEPs in the Sambódromo and the former Hotel Panorama never reached even one-quarter of target enrollments. Most other CIEPs served between three and five hundred students, half their target population. Underenrollment had two causes: Ribeiro found it difficult to hire and train new teachers quickly enough to staff the schools fully. More tellingly, after an early rush to enroll that overwhelmed initial capacity, enthusiasm died down. Middle-class parents did not respond to Ribeiro's call, and many poor families stayed away as well, as the CIEPs were soon stigmatized as schools for poor and troubled children, the last thing that many struggling families wanted.[40]

Hiring practices within the model schools also generated controversies. In keeping with the directives of Brizola's administration, Ribeiro worked closely with favela associations in recruiting staff, particularly as cafeteria-workers, security guards, "house parents," and "cultural animators." This invited charges of apadrinhamento, or nepotism—charges that tried Brizola's patience but that he proved unable to refute. Although he argued that his administration was "not like it was in the time of Chagas Freitas . . . [;] no one enters through politics," his opponents vehemently disagreed. To the dispassionate observer, the goal of bolstering local employment was difficult to distinguish from traditional clientelism, particularly when party loyalists were in charge of selecting employees.[41]

Despite these problems, the CIEPs made significant achievements:

there were 137 CIEPS functioning by the end of Brizola's term in office, and most of these made massive improvements over previously available local schools. Many of Ribeiro's young teachers felt a strong sense of educational mission and devoted extraordinary energy to the project. In the words of one young art teacher who worked first at the Sambódromo and later at the João Goulart CIEP, "It was an inspiring experiment, and we put everything we had into it. I still consider it the most important creative work of my life." Although enrollments fell short of early goals, many CIEPS eventually reached capacity. Despite the challenges faced by the CIEPS, Brizola's supporters tended to view them as both the noblest and most practical of the governor's experiments.[42]

A NEW VISION FOR THE POLICE

If the innovations in housing and education were intended to resolve the deep causes of inequality, an equally bold public security policy was designed to treat its most destructive immediate symptom: the persistent abuse of the poor by state police. If the CIEPS were the most obvious concrete manifestation of Brizola's reforms, the overhaul of public security would be the most controversial. Brizola began by creating the new posts of secretary of military police and secretary of civil police. Previously, one secretary had presided over both branches, and during the dictatorship they were understood to be complementary arms of the national security state. The military police conducted uniformed patrols and arrested suspects in the act of committing a crime, and the civil police investigated crimes and collaborated with prosecutors. Although security was constitutionally a state responsibility, the military regime had appointed state secretaries of security directly. In creating the new positions and appointing handpicked nominees, Brizola demonstrated his intent to wrest control over the police from the regime — particularly the military police, which had greater everyday contact with civilians.

He appointed Carlos Magno Nazareth Cerqueira as his secretary of military police. For all its faults, the military police was one of the few Brazilian institutions where black citizens of humble background could rise to command white subordinates. Nazareth Cerqueira's rise to the rank of colonel, however, demonstrated particular ability and tenacity. He was both an embodiment of the ideal of socialismo moreno and an officer with a deep understanding of traditional police abuses. With Brizola's support, he mapped out a plan to transform police presence in the streets, changing a truculent, arbitrary force into one that respected and protected broad democratic citizenship.

It would be difficult to exaggerate the disjuncture between previous commanders—who were directly subordinate to the dictatorship and steeped in a vision of police work as a form of combat—and Nazareth Cerqueira—who emphasized prevention, community policing, and tolerance of many nonviolent crimes. Oswaldo Ignácio Domingues, secretary of security in the state of Rio de Janeiro from 1975 to 1977, held views typical of most police in the pre-Nazareth Cerqueira corps. He believed that the best strategy for repressing crime was to set up a barrier of police battalions between the poor periphery and the central city, "to restrict the criminality that came from the Baixada . . . in order to avoid an invasion of Rio de Janeiro." In Domingues's view, "Before he is taken prisoner, the citizen is a criminal; from the moment he is captured, he becomes the responsibility of the state." In Domingues's vision, in other words, suspects were equivalent to criminals, and police abuse before or outside of custody was implicitly permitted.

Domingues was by no means a rogue officer—indeed, he was considered a model. In his own way, he modernized a police corps that had for decades been stocked with political flunkies and supernumeraries from other state agencies. He made no secret, however, of his belief that the primary responsibility of the police was to protect the property-owning classes from the poor.[43]

Nazareth Cerqueira, in contrast, argued that the primary function of the police was to uphold human rights. He was soft-spoken and studious, but a firm disciplinarian within the force. He believed that Rio's police could be modernized in accordance with the rational reforms pioneered by the world's most effective police forces, he made it his mission to accomplish this, and he did not hesitate to offend and alienate long-serving officers where he believed it was necessary to do so. His most controversial order was to recognize suspects, particularly favelado suspects, as citizens. In the words of one of his junior officers, "His order was the following: the guy that is on the hill, whether he is a favelado or a bandit, is a citizen. People distorted that, and went around saying that the police would have to treat bandits as citizens. In truth, what Colonel Cerqueira wanted was to focus police operations on citizen security."[44] As in Domingues's case, the word choice here reveals volumes about perspective. Whereas Domingues described the urban poor in general as proto-criminals, Nazareth Cerqueira and the junior officers who adopted his methods emphasized a distinction between *favelados* and *bandidos*.

Nazareth Cerqueira studied the latest international ideas in community policing, particularly from New York, and showed a clear understanding of which elements from these models would work in Rio and which would not. He recognized, for example, that repeat offenders in the United States were of high likelihood to be prosecuted whereas those in Brazil were almost certain to avoid prosecution, a reality that revealed greater flaws in Brazil's judicial system than in its policing. As a result, emphasis on prevention, rather than on catching suspects in the act, was even more important in Rio de Janeiro.[45]

This change proved to be more than most senior officers could bear. Nazareth Cerqueira instituted obligatory officer retraining, starting with fellow senior colonels. He persuaded a few, but most dug in their heels. As one of his junior officers later observed, "The colonels did not want to do it and they did not know how to do it, and why? Because until then . . . the order was 'kick in the door.' Suddenly, a new administration comes in and you have to call people citizens and treat them accordingly."[46]

Pé na porta, or foot in the door, referred to the police's authority—not legal but previously unquestioned in practice—to enter the homes of favela residents at any time in pursuit of alleged suspects. The inviolability of the favela home and its moral equivalence to the middle-class home were key tenets for both Brizola and Nazareth Cerqueira. Brizola, for his part, compared traditional police treatment of favela residents in Rio to that of residents of townships in South Africa and Jewish ghettos in Nazi Germany, arguing "The ghetto, historically serves as scapegoat and deposit of rejects. . . . For the police, it is an opportunity to demonstrate their service to the middle class and the rich and an excuse for everything. . . . Imagine armed contingents . . . arresting suspects in Ipanema or Urca . . . using the same methods they do in Rocinha, Dona Marta and Mangueira, searching everyone's house?"[47]

Brizola backed Nazareth Cerqueira completely. In the junior officer's analysis, that was all the police chief could count in his favor: "The scenario was 100 percent unfavorable, and the only thing he had on his side was the governor."[48]

Within the first month of his administration, the governor attempted to bolster Nazareth Cerqueira's position with the creation of a new council: the Council on Justice, Public Security, and Human Rights. The council's goal was to turn human rights from vague political rhetoric into an institutional concern. It had the power to investigate any human rights abuses, particularly those allegedly committed by public servants. Any citizen could bring complaints before the council, and the council had the authority to require investigated parties to turn over documents and submit to questioning. In addition to these individual cases, the council had the responsibility of forming commissions to investigate specific human rights concerns thoroughly and systematically, including commissions on racism, juvenile rights, and women's rights and a special commission to investigate allegations of torture committed in state penal institutions.[49]

As governor, Brizola was ex-officio president of the Justice Council. In practice, Vivaldo Barbosa, Brizola's secretary of justice, along with Nazareth Cerqueira, set the tone for the Council. Barbosa—one of the ideologues of socialismo moreno, along with Darcy Ribeiro—shared Brizola's vision of creating an administration that would address historical inequalities. As he described it, "Building democracy and investing individuals with their minimal rights is so relevant that we can say that it is the task which history has reserved for our time and the responsibility it has given to the generations that now exercise public service."[50]

As secretary of justice and secretary of military police, respectively, Barbosa and Nazareth Cerqueira occupied two of the permanent chairs on the Justice Council. The secretary of civil police and representatives of key civil society organizations also held permanent chairs. By far the most influential of these was the representative of the Rio branch of the Brazilian Bar Organization, a position occupied during Brizola's administration by the jurist Nilo Batista. Like Barbosa and Nazareth Cerqueira, Batista became an influential Brizola advisor and a powerful advocate for redress of historical inequalities. In 1986, Brizola named Batista the secretary of the civil police, thereby expanding his responsibilities within state government while maintaining his forceful presence within the Justice Council.

Representatives of the middle-class and favela association federations also received permanent seats. Their inclusion bolstered claims to broad popular representation and welcomed potentially disruptive organizations into the administration, subordinating them to its procedural logic. It gave these organizations—in theory, at least—permanent access to state power, reinforcing their institutionalization.

The Justice Council was split between two roles: it was both an advocate for human rights and a tool for political appeasement. In the first role, it helped bring to light long-standing practices of racial discrimination in public employment and systematic abuse in the penal system. Typical of this contribution was the council's role in passing state legislation outlawing Rio's traditional elevator codes. Most middle-class residential apartment buildings and downtown office buildings had codes requiring workers to use the service elevator and reserving the "social elevator" for wealthy residents or white-collar employees. Application of these codes was notoriously racist; doormen understood that they were expected to orient all dark-skinned visitors to the service elevator.

The elevator had long served as the capsule where Rio's tricky algorithms of race and class were calculated and enforced. Every black resident of Rio could recount moments when instructions to use the service elevator amounted to a reminder not to push beyond one's social boundaries. The Justice Council turned the elevator codes into an exemplary target. By the close of 1985, the council had succeeded in pushing the state legislature to prohibit them. This did not put an end to discrimination in Rio's elevators, but it gave citizens—black working-class citizens, in particular—a legal tool for challenging that discrimination.[51]

In its second role, the Justice Council was intended to bring civil society organizations and social movements into the machinery of the state. This transformation was particularly pronounced for the favela federation and the individual associations it comprised. The associations' engagement with the Justice Council—and with Nazareth Cerqueira's model of police work as the protection of human rights, more generally—followed a political logic that sought to maximize their own role while minimizing the role of the police.

NAZARETH CERQUEIRA'S POLICE AND THE FAVELAS

Nazareth Cerqueira attempted to put an end to long-standing police abuse of the urban poor by minimizing hostile interactions and encouraging community outreach. He believed that the most important role for the police in preventing crime lay in facilitating community cooperation: "Only a police force tied to the community, working with the community, can reduce the anxiety that perturbs the population and reduces quality of life in the great urban centers."[52] In practice, this meant reducing the presence of armed police in Rio's favelas and holding frequent meetings with community representatives. Nazareth Cerqueira himself met often with favela association and federation leaders, and he required his precinct chiefs to meet weekly with favela association officers in their area.[53]

Favela association officers used these meetings as an opportunity to chastise the military police and to argue for decreased police presence. In December 1984, Nazareth Cerqueira, Archbishop Sales, and association leaders linked to the Pastoral das Favelas held a summit meeting on the "Military Police and the Communities" at the archdiocese's hilltop retreat above Rio. (The summit's title was an early example of use of the term "community" as a euphemism for favela, a usage that would become predominant among NGOs of the 1990s.) Aguinaldo Bezerra of Chapéu Mangueira—a charismatic favela leader better known as "O Bola," the ball, likely for his barrel-chested physique—opened the discussion with a frank assessment of historic and ongoing police abuse, providing a quick overview of the traditional role of Rio's police in protecting the wealthy by harassing the poor. Strikingly, Nazareth Cerqueira made no attempt to rebut these charges and instead readily agreed, offering that he was working "to make the military police more humane." Such meetings, themselves an innovation in the first two years of the Brizola administration, were the small exemplary dramas of socialismo moreno, intended to demonstrate how much had already changed under Brizola's administration.[54]

The editors of Favelão (Big favela), a monthly newsletter circulated throughout Rio by the Pastoral das Favelas, seized on the trend to press for greater favela autonomy from police operations. In May 1984, the editors, themselves young favela leaders, urged favela residents and their association presidents to meet personally with Nazareth Cerqueira and Brizola and to demand an end to police violence. They argued, "The police are against the people," and insisted that, speaking from the favela, "a autoridade aqui somos nós" (we are the authority here). The pernicious implication was that favela associations, and not the police, held authority for guaranteeing the peace in Rio's favelas.[55]

Such protestations slid easily from objections to police violence into a defense of local residents who found themselves on the wrong side of the law, in particular low-level drug traffickers. The summit meeting with the Nazareth Cerqueira and the archbishop concluded with a list of "concrete proposals," including tolerance for low-level drug trafficking.[56] As Brizola's administration progressed, such proposals became more candidly favorable toward local traffickers. In an August 1986 meeting with Nazareth Cerqueira, the association president in the north side favela of Parque Jardim Beira Mar noted that crime was rising in the area despite the presence of a community police outpost. "The police are constantly tormenting the families that live here," he insisted, arguing the police post should be removed. "The residents prefer to be protected by the *dono da boca-de-fumo* [the chief of the drug bazaar] here, who is very respected." Nilton Gomes Pereira agreed, observing that the traffickers were more considerate than the police: "Many times, the men from the gangs let us know that there will be a shootout that afternoon. On those days, no one leaves home." Pereira was the association president from Itararé who had served as vice-president of the favela federation in 1979, strongly supported by the Pastoral das Favelas. His acceptance of the growing presence of gangs in the favela was indicative of the position taken by many leaders who had risen to influence in the late 1970s. They did not perceive low-level drug traffickers as a threat. Suggesting that the traffickers were more humane than the police became a way of defending the autonomy of the favela.[57]

Nazareth Cerqueira found himself in the role of the rejected suitor while the standoffish association officers entertained other parties. Brizola's opponents took this as evidence that the governor and his police chief were deliberately pulling their punches in an attempt to win back their key favela allies. Former secretary of security Domingues took it for granted that Brizola had ordered police to stay out of favelas: "When he prohibited the police from going up the hills or entering favelas, Brizola undermined security. It is clear that limited the efficacy of the police. Not that I agree with unnecessary violence, but sometimes violence is necessary. . . . When he prevented the police from going up the hill, that really favored the proliferation of those criminal groups." Domingues considered it axiomatic that favela associations had connections to "pernicious elements." Nazareth Cerqueira, in contrast, appeared to dismiss this possibility entirely.[58]

Nazareth Cerqueira and his supporters insisted there was never any order to stay out of favelas. One junior officer explained, "Lots of people say that was a period when police could not go up the hill [go into the favela] and Colonel Cerqueira always said, 'What they are waiting for is for me to give an order, but I always say, my order is to police everything. I never said not to police the hill, not police this or that.' I was never told not to police, and neither Colonel Cerqueira nor the governor at the time gave such an order."[59]

Nazareth Cerqueira did overtly attempt to increase nonviolent police presence in favelas and housing projects. He created new community police outposts that emphasized establishing constructive community relationships rather than apprehending criminals. The experience of Cidade de Deus, a massive housing project in the western zone, was paradigmatic. By the time Brizola took office, Cidade de Deus was already beset by infrastructural decay, spotty provision of services, and growth of favelas surrounding the original buildings. Rival drug dealers had battled for primacy in the area in the years just before Brizola's election, leaving a legacy of hostile factions within the neighborhood.[60]

The declining fortunes of the national economy complicated the local situation. In Brizola's first months in office, inflation soared across Brazil, partly in response to the military regime's inability to meet rising interest rates on its international loans. Residents of housing projects were among the most negatively affected by inflation; they tended to work in sectors vulnerable to sudden contraction during economic slowdown, but their floating-rate mortgages were subject to monthly hikes. Recession and its discontents surfaced first and most dramatically in these contexts, and sporadic street crime began to rise. Brizola and Nazareth Cerqueira responded by placing a Centro Integrado de Policiamento Comunitário, or Integrated Center of Community Policing, in the housing project. Rather than serving as a bunker from which police emerged to catch criminals, the community police post was open to the public. The precinct commander created job-registry booths to try to connect residents to local employment, an initiative integrated with the local efforts of the Housing Secretariat and other social service organizations. In an interview with the *Jornal do Brasil*, the commander maintained, "For the first time we are doing something in relation to the causes, and not merely the effects, of criminal violence: the employment crisis."[61]

At the same time, both Brizola and Nazareth Cerqueira advocated tolerance of crimes they viewed as nonviolent, in particular unlicensed street vending and illegal gambling—including Rio's renowned number racket: the *jogo do bicho*, or animal game. Early in his administration, Brizola made clear that he would not repress these crimes, and Nazareth Cerqueira carried out and endorsed this directive. The precinct commander in Cidade de Deus embraced these priorities, but many ranking officers strongly resented them. Nazareth Cerqueira hired a consultant to help persuade officers of the wisdom of emphasizing prevention while tolerating petty infractions. The consultant later recalled, "A large part of the military police in that time believed that community policing meant a lax approach to criminality; that being a community policeman meant getting preoccupied with little details and leaving the confrontation of criminality on a secondary level."[62] It proved impossible to persuade these officers to adopt Nazareth Cerqueira's methods.

Many members of the military police had practical as well as ideological reasons for opposing Nazareth Cerqueira: they were heavily involved in protection and extortion rackets. They resented official policies of tolerance because those policies undermined their ability to extract payoffs, and looked for covert opportunities — far from Nazareth Cerqueira's prying eyes — to step up intimidation of suspects.

Nazareth Cerqueira himself later recognized the implications of this opposition, and his own analysis is devastatingly persuasive: "Without doubt, we failed. We were not able to implant the democratic model we defended. We did not figure out how to arrest traffickers in the favelas without invading homes, without putting innocent lives in danger. We did not figure out how to make police investigate in order to arrest; we did not figure out how to make police understand that their principal task was to arrest and not to kill."[63]

ELECTIONS IN ROCINHA

The reforms in housing, education, and public security were part of the dramatic transformation of favela life, but often in unintended ways. One thread that runs through these reforms is the increasing institutionalization of the favela associations as the mediator between favela residents and local government. Favela associations connected local residents to city and state employment, directed public investment within the favela, and met with police precinct commanders. This changed the game of association elections, which became more contentious as rival factions competed for greater political leverage. How did these transformations unfold in individual favelas? Closer investigation of three of Rio's most prominent favelas — Rocinha, Cantagalo, and Pavão-Pavãozinho — gives a strong indication.

Rocinha's elections of 1984 were the paradigmatic case of the association as a battleground for competing interest groups. As in many favelas, Rocinha's association had initially mobilized in the 1960s, had become largely defunct under military repression through much of the 1970s, and was revived in the late 1970s. By 1981, two new associations emerged in subareas of Rocinha: José Martins's Bairro Barcellos, and Laboriaux, an area of more recent settlement. This left the original association, the União Pro-Melhoramentos dos Moradores da Rocinha (UPMMR, or Pro-Improvements Union of Rocinha Residents) to represent the majority of the favela's residents—an estimated population of thirty thousand in the early 1980s.

Even before Brizola's inauguration, two factions vied for control of this association, each claiming legitimacy. José Inácio de Assis—known to all as Zé do Queijo, or Cheese Joe, headed the first faction. Zé do Queijo was a resilient migrant from the northeastern state of Paraíba who carried a gun and brooked no disrespect. His nickname came from one of his many remunerative activities: selling cheese trucked in from the interior at the favela's open-air market. He had become better known, however, as Rocinha's foremost *grileiro*, or irregular property developer, particularly in a subarea known as Cachopa. Zé do Queijo had divided Cachopa into lots and sold them off to new residents, most of them fellow northeasterners. Although Zé do Queijo was a rough-hewn man of few words, he had an eloquent political advocate in Eleonora Castaño, a graduate student in sociology from the nearby Pontifícia Universidade Católica. Castaño had developed close ties to Zé do Queijo through social work in Rocinha, and became his unofficial press secretary. Zé do Queijo could also count on the loyalty of most of Rocinha's considerable *nordestino* population.[64]

The second faction was linked to liberation theology activists who scorned Zé do Queijo's strongman politics and Castaño's conservative understanding of charitable social work, and advocated the kind of grass-roots communitarian mobilization that was transforming neighboring Vidigal. They included an older generation of activists who had survived military repression, but by 1983 a younger cohort had come to the fore. Maria Helena Pereira—twenty-three years old, born and raised in Rocinha, and an energetic teacher at one of Rocinha's nursery schools—emerged as this faction's leader. Pereira was one of the most prominent examples of the wave of young women rising to the fore of favela associations in the early 1980s.[65]

Brizola's administrative strategy could not accommodate rival factions claiming legitimate representation of the same association and by mid-1984, Vivaldo Barbosa stepped in to mediate the fray. Barbosa persuaded both factions to accept new elections to be held in October of that year. Intense campaigning and increasing hostility marked the weeks prior to the election. Maria Helena Pereira's faction described Zé do Queijo as the "Lampião da Rocinha," in reference to a notorious bandit of the northeastern hinterlands and accused him of exploiting the residents of Cachopa.

Zé do Queijo's faction, in turn, alleged that Maria Helena Pereira was the girlfriend of Dênir Leandro da Silva, better known as Dênis da Rocinha, a local drug trafficker. Eleonora Castaño further alleged that Dênis had attempted to assassinate Zé do Queijo because of the candidate's strong condemnation of drug trafficking. As Zé do Queijo and Pereira competed for political primacy, Dênis built his own loyal base, distributing favors to local residents and hosting lavish parties. Such practices were typical of the titans of Rio's numbers racket, but were previously unknown among drug traffickers; Dênis was pioneering a new style of the trafficker as godfather. The election was crucial to his operations: a victory by Zé do Queijo would restrict his room to operate on the hill, whereas victory by Pereira would bring to power a faction that protested police intrusion in Rocinha.[66]

Barbosa's staff ran the election, registering all of the favela's residents and collecting and counting ballots, a participation with both practical and symbolic importance. Rocinha's election coincided with the peak of the national grassroots campaign for direct, democratic elections for the president of Brazil. Brizola was a leading contender for president should such elections be held. (His popularity was perhaps the most important factor leading the military regime, in its final throes, to deny direct elections, allowing only the indirect presidential elections that brought pyrrhic victory to Tancredo Neves.) By supporting free and transparent elections in Rocinha, Brizola's administration made the point that if Rocinha was ready for democracy, so was the rest of Brazil.

Over five thousand voters participated, and Pereira emerged with a narrow victory. Her supporters viewed this as the key to Rocinha's transition, sounding the death knell for old practices of strongmen and clientelism, paving the way for community solidarity.[67] Rocinha changed rapidly, but transformation did not fulfill these hopes. The big winner was Dênis, at least temporarily. He consolidated control over the hill over the next two years, arming himself and his loyal soldiers with increasingly powerful weapons. To those who had seen the democratic opening of the late 1970s and early 1980s as the dawn of a hopeful new era for the favela, this unforeseen transformation seemed to happen overnight. In the words of one anthropologist who had worked closely with Rocinha's community leaders, "Suddenly we turned around and many young men were armed." By the mid-1980s, Dênis was the city's most notorious drug trafficker, presiding over its most lucrative drug market.[68]

Zé do Queijo lost the elections and then his most lucrative business, as Pereira used her new relationships with city and state officials to put an end to her rival's practice of parceling off lots in Cachopa. Within three months, Zé do Queijo had lost much more. In the early morning hours of January 23, 1985, he was gunned down outside his dry-goods store in Rocinha. No one was ever charged in the murder, but everyone on the hill attributed it to Dênis and his crew. When asked her reaction to the murder, Pereira offered a cold assessment reminiscent of a New Jersey mafioso: "Zé already died for me last October, when he lost the elections."[69]

The election made Maria Helena Pereira the brightest star among young favela activists, though that brilliance was also short lived. The real nature of her relationship with Dênis will remain forever unknown, and by 1987 she was married to another Rocinha resident, but suspicions of her connection to local traficantes lingered.[70] She removed herself from the network of Pastoral favela leaders, pursuing short-term alliances with both right and leftwing politicians.

Pereira's position as president of one of the city's most prominent favela associations made her a much sought-after powerbroker in upcoming mayoral and gubernatorial elections. Yet the loss of the original allies that had supported her election, both in and out of Rocinha, left her increasingly exposed to the same kind of retribution that had eliminated Zé do Queijo. Late in 1987 Pereira, also, was assassinated. Again, the crime—like the vast majority of murders in Rio's favelas—was never prosecuted, but, again, everyone on the hill attributed it either to Dênis and his crew or to rival traffickers. By that time, webs of alliance in Rocinha had become so complex that only insiders understood them, and those insiders had ample reasons not to divulge secrets.

Rocinha's case was prefigurative: the favela association became closely tied to city and state government earlier than in most favelas, and Dênis was among the first of the new model donos do morro, or leading traffickers. The transitions Rocinha went through between 1983 and 1985 would become common throughout the city in subsequent years.

The favelas of Cantagalo and Pavão-Pavãozinho, sharing two hills that rise between the upper middle-class neighborhoods of Copacabana and Ipanema, were the showcase for Brizola's reforms. Like many south zone favelas, Cantagalo (Cock's Crow) and Pavão (Peacock) grew in conjunction with the middle-class areas directly below them over the course of the twentieth century, housing the service workers their neighbors depended on. The two favelas developed contrasting demographic patterns: Cantagalo was populated mostly by black cariocas and Pavão predominantly by northeastern migrants. This demographic split became more pronounced in the 1970s, as northeastern migration increased and migrants sought homes near their friends and relatives, or, in many cases, added rooms to existing dwellings.

The demographic split played into a political split that echoed that between Maria Helena Pereira and Zé do Queijo in Rocinha. By the late 1970s, a strong faction of leaders linked to Pastoral das Favelas had emerged in Cantagalo. In Pavão, in contrast, the association officers functioned as irregular real-estate brokers and developers, organizing the subdivision and settlement of a new area that became known as Pavãozinho, situated on a previously unsettled outcropping overlooking Copacabana.[71]

Both favelas were small in comparison with Rocinha; between them, they had about eight thousand inhabitants in the early 1980s. But their location and visibility gave them similar prominence. Early in his administration, Brizola prepared to invest whatever resources proved necessary to raise standards of living in Cantagalo and Pavão-Pavãozinho in order to prove that it was possible to urbanize favelas and extend the full benefits of citizenship to their residents.

Plans were barely under way when catastrophe made them more urgent. Heavy rains in late December 1984 resulted in a mudslide on Christmas Eve. The heavy water tank high on Pavão's slope toppled down the hill, crushing the homes in its path. Eighteen residents died in the slide, many more were left homeless, and the favela lay in ruins. Cantagalo also sustained considerable damage. Where previous executives might have seized this opportunity to carry out a quick removal, Brizola immediately announced plans for reconstruction and upgrading: Pavão's tragedy had accentuated the need for greater state involvement in Rio's favelas. The damage had been greatly exacerbated by the collapse of an enormous pile of trash deposited by Pavão's residents, demonstrating with painful clarity that the lack of public services consigned favela residents to permanent vulnerability.[72]

The takeover of the defunct Hotel Panorama and its transformation into the João Goulart CIEP was the first piece in this upgrading, and in consequence this school received greater funding than all other CIEPs with the exception of the massive Sambódromo. Whereas in most CIEPs the "cultural animator" was a local resident, in Cantagalo, Ribeiro hired Lennie Dale, a well-known showman and fixture of carioca nightlife. The brizolão in Cantagalo was intended to be the celebrity CIEP.[73]

The most striking feature of the school was its elevator, the former entranceway to the Hotel Panorama. It was a twelve-story elevator with only two stops, the first at ground level—on one of the most exclusive residential streets in Rio—the second at the top—at the entrance to the school. During the Hotel Panorama's brief period of operation, favela residents had been forbidden to use the elevator. Under Brizola, it became a status symbol of literal favela ascendance.

Brizola, perhaps more than Cantagalo's residents, relished the symbolism. Visiting the school under construction in February 1984, he was stopped at the base of the elevator by a resident of Ipanema, who assailed him for pouring money into the favela rather than into public security. Brizola shot back, "You have everything you need. Our priority is the people up there." Addressing another Ipanema heckler, he continued, "You look like the kind of person who supported the dictatorship. I'd like to see you living in a shack like those up there, earning a living. Then you'd see. You should give thanks for the Governor you have. If you said those things to one of those thugs during these last twenty years, you would be disappeared. And if it was in Argentina, they would stuff you in a container and throw you over the Malvinas."[74] While such comments appear hostile and surprisingly inflammatory for an electoral politician, Brizola had a way of delivering them with a smile on his face and a tone of good-natured ribbing. He was never happier than when playing the crowd in this fashion.

Investment in several concurrent initiatives bolstered the school project. Brizola charged the Geotechnic Superintendancy, the municipal government's geological engineering department, with installing concrete retaining walls to prevent future landslides. He took advantage of the damage caused by the slide to plan a new road connecting the bottom of the hills with the CIEP above Cantagalo. He planned construction of a plano inclinado, a combination hillside trolley/elevator, connecting the lower flanks

FIG. 3.3. Brizola parries middle-class hecklers in Ipanema, just outside the elevator that leads to Cantagalo, 1984. A comparison of this image with figure 3.2 gives a sense of the contrasting demographics in Ipanema and neighboring Cantagalo. Yet the photo reminds us that middle-class cariocas were also casual and gregarious and loved a good *bate-boca*, or argument. Photograph by Ronaldo Theobald, CPDoc JB.

of Pavão with its uppermost reaches—Rio's first significant public transportation project designed for favela residents. He committed state and municipal utilities to providing water, sewage, electrical, and trash services to Pavão and Cantagalo. To cap off this new development, he planned a new apartment building on top of the hill, not far from the CIEP, built to house residents displaced by the landslide and the new infrastructural projects.[75]

This confluence of projects increased the desirability of Cantagalo and Pavão as residential locations, triggering a building boom on the hill. The new retaining walls enabled expansion to previously unsettled areas. The greater expansion, however, was vertical and internal, as residents added a story to their homes or subdivided rooms, often for rental purposes. Between 1983 and 1986 rates for apartment rental in Pavão-Pavãozinho doubled. They rose in two rapid spurts, reflecting the changing political context. They spiked initially when the infrastructural projects were announced, then leveled off when agents from One Plot Per Family carried out fieldwork on the hill. The titling program delivered the promise of purchase and sale to many residents but, as in most favelas, eventually shrank

FIG. 3.4. Residents of Pavão-Pavãozinho rebuild after a landslide, 1980s. The *mutirão*, voluntary community labor, was already giving way to individual paid work, but remained fundamental in the recovery from this emergency. (One wonders what this child made of the Detroit Lions shirt, a reminder of the contingency of favela dwellers in the global economy.) Photograph by Marcelo Carnaval, CPDoc JB.

FIG. 3.5. The *plano inclinado*, or inclined traction elevator, of Pavão-Pavãozinho, 1987. The elevator, one of Brizola's high-profile favela projects, functioned for a year or two before breaking down. Subsequent administrations denied funds for maintenance. The multistory buildings, well-built stairways, and evidence of ongoing construction on either side of the elevator show how much life in Pavão-Pavãozinho—and other favelas touched by the public investments of the Brizola years—changed in the mid-1980s. Photograph by José Roberto Serra, CPDoc JB.

before the challenge of confronting the informal rental market. Once it was clear that property titling would make no further headway and would not threaten irregular landlords, rents climbed again. This showed that rental property values were remarkably sensitive both to the rising quality of life entailed by infrastructural investment and to the threat of disruption posed by One Plot Per Family. Prospective renters in Pavão-Pavãozinho clearly understood that if the state reined in the irregular rental market, they would be out on the street. Once the titling agents retreated, renters bid up values once more.[76]

The Pavão association maintained a registry of these rentals, and its officers exercised a strong influence over the market, demonstrating a strong preference for rental to fellow northeastern migrants. The association also played a decisive role in distributing state resources and connecting local residents to employment on the infrastructural projects. When suspicions arose that Luiz Carlos Dionísio, the Pavão association president in 1984, had embezzled project funds, Dionísio threatened to quit and return all the funds to Brizola in order to restore his honor. Brizola rejected Dionísio's offer of renunciation, perhaps because he could not get anything done on the hill without a strong ally in the association. As in other favelas, this accommodation reinforced both the association's authority over the hill and the separation of the favela from the surrounding city. As one local resident put it, "Up here there is no problem, because no one disobeys the association. The problem is the military police down there."[77] Again, the choice of words reveals volumes: the police, even under Nazareth Cerqueira's command, were described as violent outsiders. The role of the association was to enforce order on the hill and keep those violent outsiders away.

The Cantagalo association exercised a similarly strong role, often in competition with counterparts in Pavão. Cantagalo's officers complained that Pavão received the lion's share of relief following the mudslide, whereas Pavão's charged that Cantagalo's officers had stolen funds from infrastructural projects. The only thing the two associations could agree on was that the new road, initially planned to wind through the Pavão favela, instead run between the two favelas, where residents of each community would have equal access — and where it could function as a border between them. Brizola complied.

The mutual accusations between association officers were the political manifestations of a turf war between drug traffickers in the rival favelas.

Crews from each favela carried out armed invasions of enemy terrain, hoping to seize valuable points of sale. Throughout 1984–85, shootouts and incursions were common. Residents of each favela avoided passing through the other, a practice that often required them to walk around the base of the hill rather than make a quick shortcut across its flank. In each favela, the local dono do morro followed a strategy similar to that of Dênis da Rocinha, distributing largesse to cultivate loyalty. Bezerra da Silva, the Cantagalo sambista whose words serve as the epigraph to this chapter, became renowned throughout the city for his chronicles of these rivalries. Silva's *sambandido*, bandit samba, was the soundtrack for the transformation of carioca drug trafficking in the 1980s, extolling the new donos do morro and condemning *cagüetes*, or informers.[78]

In Cantagalo and Pavão, the local traffickers claimed to be protecting residents from the savagery of their neighbors. When police arrested "Tonho" — Antônio José Ferreira, the dono do morro of Pavão in July 1985 — over a thousand residents of Pavão-Pavãozinho, more than one-fourth of the favela's population, marched to the police station where Ferreira was being held in order to protest his arrest. Residents blocked the new road under construction, bringing all work on the hill to a halt. Luiz Carlos Dionísio complained, "The Governor has left us vulnerable to the crew from Cantagalo, who now threatens to rape, rob and even kill our children, women and workers. . . . Who will guarantee the safety of our children and women? . . . Without Tonho, Pavão and Pavãozinho will be transformed into a hell. The community can do without the security of the police, but not without his." Dionísio frantically dialed his contacts in Brizola's administration, attempting to get Tonho released.[79]

The protest did not immediately get Tonho out of jail. Nevertheless, it demonstrated to the police and to the governor the price to be paid for repression of local drug trafficking. Given the importance of "community relations" — meaning, above all, smooth relations with favela associations — in Brizola's administrative strategy, it is not a surprise that both he and Nazareth Cerqueira were generally unwilling to pay that price. The Pavão incident was the first time that favela residents took to the streets in massive numbers to protest repression of drug traffic. It would not be the last; by the end of the 1980s, this would be a recurrent spectacle of carioca politics, a rote drama played out in accordance with commonly understood codes.

WHAT IS THE BALANCE of Brizola's major reforms? None came close to reaching stated goals. The titling program did not title, the public security program did not secure. The education program did educate, and it did expand access to public education for the urban poor. But as Brizola's administration entered its final year, it was already clear that the CIEPs would not live up to the lofty goals set by the governor and his secretary of education.

No reforms could have reached those lofty goals. Socialismo moreno was not a pragmatic vision, much less a coherent plan. It was a bold dream—one the times seemed to demand, as Brazil emerged from two decades of military dictatorship as if from a cocoon and embraced the possibility of metamorphosis. Brizola had the rhetoric and the aspirations to match the moment. His plans were daring and inspiring and attempted to erase the effects of decades, centuries, of inequality. His reforms had the virtue of challenging deeply held assumptions about the place of the urban poor, particularly the black urban poor. He was far from the first politician to negotiate with favela residents. That tradition had grown throughout the twentieth century and was raised to an art by Chagas Freitas. He was, however, the first major politician to insist on moving favelados from the margins to the center of political life, the first to acknowledge that the continued relegation of one-third of Rio's population to the status of eternal supplicants was morally unacceptable and politically disastrous, and the first to attempt a wholesale refashioning of government to address this calamity.

In that regard, if his reforms failed to meet targets—even where they did so by a wide margin, as in One Plot Per Family—they were not necessarily total failures; rather, they were the initial steps toward improvements that would blossom only a generation later. In the meantime, in an unforeseen turn, the reforms of the socialist governor led to rapid capitalist expansion. One Plot Per Family did not deliver title, but in every favela where the titling program unfolded simultaneously with urban upgrading projects such as Social Electrification and Proface, economic activity increased exponentially. In favelas where commercial activity had been moribund, a combination of upgrading and regularization programs triggered the growth of a wide range of services and small businesses, including carpentry shops and lumberyards, daycare centers, beauty salons, and automobile mechanic shops. Property values—on the informal market, of course—went up, as did domestic investment. The fact that the government programs failed to meet objectives was irrelevant to this economic growth. What counted

were the provisions of basic services and the clear indication that possession and domestic investment would be respected.[80]

These effects were particularly pronounced in Pavão-Pavãozinho and
Cantagalo, the favelas that received the most per capita investment during
the Brizola years. Within two years of the beginning of Brizola's projects on
the hill, the number of commercial establishments more than doubled, and
consumption rates and standards of living rose. Some of these commercial
establishments were temporary and directly linked to the public works; as
one resident put it, "in that period everyone who had a refrigerator sold
drinks to the workers." All the same, many endured, and the general pattern of economic growth persisted.[81]

At the same time, one cannot overlook the fact that Pavão-Pavãozinho
descended in mass to demand that police release a notorious drug trafficker from jail. Public investment did not threaten the emerging donos
do morro. Quite the opposite: as experiences in Rocinha and Pavão-
Pavãozinho demonstrate, state connections to the local favela association
gave the new model drug traffickers room to operate and provided them
with political coverage. The consequences would only become evident in
subsequent years. As a result, whatever the disappointments of Brizola's
first three years in office, this period would end up looking harmonious
in comparison with what came next. That was when the wheels came off.

THE BREAKING POINT

Tem que ser ligeiriado	("You have to be light on your feet
Pra poder sobreviver	to be able to survive
Bom malandro é cadeado	A good malandro is a padlock
Nada sabe e nada vê	He doesn't know or see anything
E também se não for considerado	And if you are not respected
Você logo vai saber	You'll soon find out
Vai pagar uma taxa do pedágio	You'll have to pay a toll
Pra subir e pra descer, é a lei do morro	To go up and come down, that's the law of the hill")

— BEZERRA DA SILVA, "Lei do morro" (song) 1983.

Brizola's third year in office coincided with momentous transitions on the national stage, so much so that two journalists have termed 1985 "the year in which Brazil began again." The military regime finally relinquished executive power, but they turned it over to José Sarney, who assumed the presidency when elected candidate Tancredo Neves died before he could be inaugurated. Sarney had been the compromise vice-presidential candidate on Neves's ticket, imposed over the fierce objections of Neves's supporters on the Left. Sarney was a right-wing powerbroker from the Amazonian North and had prospered through loyal service to the dictatorship. His unlikely ascension to the presidency outraged and frustrated the millions of citizens who had mobilized for redemocratization. This new beginning was not the one Brazil had envisioned.

Sarney's inauguration complicated Brizola's life as a governor. The federal government controlled the disbursement of tax receipts to state and local government. Sarney had partisan and personal reasons to block Brizola, and he now wielded the power to cut off funds to Rio de Janeiro. Brizola faced new municipal complications, as well; the return to democracy ended the governor's privilege of choosing the mayor of the state capital. The city of Rio would elect a mayor in 1985, and Brizola's own term as governor would end the following year. The municipal election of 1985 would determine the fate of favela-upgrading projects. The state election of 1986 would determine the fate of public security. The future of Rio de Janeiro—and of the relationship between the favelas and the rest of the city, in particular—hinged on the outcome of these elections. If Brizola succeeded in getting loyal allies elected to these key positions, he still had a chance to amend his reforms and guarantee continuity. Election of anyone else would leave Brizola's appointees to struggle internally with new rivals, guaranteeing administrative sclerosis.

THE ASPIRATIONAL SOCIALISM OF SATURNINO BRAGA

The elections of 1985 were, astonishingly, the first democratic mayoral elections in the city's history. For four centuries, ruling powers had appointed executive officeholders in Rio. Cariocas finally had their chance to elect someone to fulfill the interests of popular citizens, and they elected Saturnino Braga—a choice most would come to regret. The PDT's nomination of a Saturnino Braga and his running mate, vice-mayoral candidate Jó Resende, surprised many party loyalists. Braga was a PDT senator but was not a dyed-in-the-wool *brizolista*. He had served as a senator for the moderate opposition through much of the dictatorship and joined the PMDB upon its foundation. He left that party because of his distaste for Chagas Freitas and turned to Brizola's PDT for lack of any better option. For Brizola, the choice of Braga as a mayoral candidate promised to appeal to the moderate sectors of the university-educated middle class. Jó Resende, for his part, had built a strong base of support through his militancy in the middle-class association movement and was also close to the nucleus of the Rio de Janeiro branch of the PT. He was not officially a member of the PT but clearly had that party's support. By nominating him for vice-mayor, Brizola could secure the alliance of the PT at least through the elections.

Brokering this deal required the services of another master political tactician, Herbert de Souza, better known to all as Betinho. Like Brizola, Betinho was a former radical exile. Upon return to Brazil, he and two colleagues had founded the pioneering policy think-tank Ibase, the Instituto Brasileiro de Análise Social e Estatística (Brazilian Institute of Social and Statistical Analysis). Betinho was a beloved figure on the carioca left, influential in both the PDT and the PT and capable of articulating their approximation. In mid-1985, Brizola met with Betinho, Saturnino Braga, and Jô Resende at Ibase's Botafogo offices, a few blocks from the Santa Marta favela. In a closed-door meeting, they hammered out the basis for an alliance. Resende would affiliate with the PDT in return for the promise that he be able to use his position as vice-mayor to strengthen ties between municipal government and the neighborhood associations. Saturnino Braga would be Brizola's candidate but, if elected, would be free to make his own choices as mayor.

The Braga-Resende ticket, dreamed up by Brizola and brokered by Betinho, amounted to the temporary alliance of the PDT and the PT. As an electoral strategy, it was brilliant: Braga and Resende trounced the field in the November election, garnering 40 percent of the vote in an election by plurality, while their closest competitors took less than 20 percent. As a governing coalition, it would prove more fragile. All four men considered themselves socialists but they understood that ideology in different ways, and those differences would ultimately weaken their alliance. Brizola wanted to build a party reminiscent of Western European Socialist parties, but with the Brazilian flair of *socialismo moreno*. For him, socialist reform could only come through messy and at times unsavory parliamentary politics, guided by a strong, pragmatic party. Betinho believed in the tentacular Gramscian occupation of available spaces in a way that burrowed deeper into Brazilian society than party politics and would eventually make profound transformation inevitable. Resende was focused on bringing the middle-class and favela federations further into local government as the guarantors of urban reform. Braga was the wild card in this hand: in theory, his understanding of the necessity of building a Socialist party on a Western European model did not differ radically from that of Brizola's. In practice, however, he could not hide his disdain for the populism of the PDT. No one was sure what he would do as mayor.

Tensions began to emerge even before Braga officially took office, when he irked PDT members by appointing cabinet secretaries from other parties. He claimed to base his choices only on skill, not on party affiliation, an assurance that left PDT loyalists both insulted and rejected. He further roiled the waters with his decision to stamp the slogan Prefeitura Socialista do Rio de Janeiro (Socialist Municipal Government of Rio de Janeiro) on all official documents and publicity. This aspirational identification pleased almost no one: PDT supporters resented its procrustean limitations, opposition leaders interpreted it as an affront, and marxists dismissed it as a superficial flourish. César Maia, a cabinet minister in Brizola's state administration, went to the heart of the matter: "the Municipal Government has too few resources to be socialist, despite its pretensions."[1]

Maia, an economist with an intimate knowledge of municipal funding, knew whereof he spoke. All of Brazil's major cities faced budgetary challenges in the late 1980s, but Rio's problems were particularly grave. The "fusion" of Guanabara and Rio de Janeiro in 1975 had transferred strong obligations for social services to Rio's municipal government. Brizola's reforms placed further strains on the city budget, as the governor transferred budgetary responsibility for many of the new CIEPs from state to city accounts.

Braga refused to let budget constraints stand in the way. He announced plans to hire nearly three thousand teachers and service workers to staff the CIEPs and other schools, and he raised municipal taxes and fees to finance these expenditures. This move outraged voters and angered President Sarney, who had recently announced his own plan for combating hyperinflation. Rising international interest rates were multiplying Brazil's foreign debt, leading to devaluation of Brazilian currency. Monthly inflation in the double digits meant that Brazilians needed to recalculate prices and wages constantly, disrupting investment and planning at every level. Early in 1986, Sarney announced a bold plan to issue a new currency, the cruzado, while freezing wages and taxes. Braga's new municipal taxes and fees flew in the face of Sarney's freeze. Sarney promptly struck back by rejecting Braga's bid to issue municipal bonds, exacerbating Rio's budget woes.[2]

Braga viewed these as the inevitable trials to be faced in order to forge a socialist government in the crucible of conflict: "Within my first month in office . . . it was clear to me that, rejecting the option of mediocre continuity, I would have to confront very probably in some moment of my mandate a grave financial crisis. . . . I had to be bold and risk, or give up and denounce. I opted for the risk of crisis without hesitation." Braga would soon have greater crisis than he had bargained for.[3]

In the meantime, the mayor sought to prove that he was a man of the people by circulating throughout the city and pressing the flesh. During his campaign, he had drawn attention from the press with his morning jogs, an activity previously unknown among Rio's politicians. As mayor, he replaced these morning jogs with "socialist jogs up the hills," as he described his visits to numerous favelas. He eschewed the customary chauffeured town car of executive officeholders in favor of a *fusca*, a Brazilian-manufactured Volkswagen beetle, which he drove himself. But Braga lacked both Brizola's charisma and his sense of humor. "O fusca do Saturnino," Saturnino's beetle, became the object of political satire. It was difficult to escape the sense that Braga was trying too hard.

ESCADINHA AND THE COMANDO VERMELHO

Rio had other problems. The day before Braga's inauguration, José Carlos dos Reis Encina, a notorious drug trafficker better known as Escadinha, escaped from the Ilha Grande State Penitentiary. The escape was both spectacular and scandalously easy. As Escadinha strolled the prison grounds, a helicopter approached. At the helm was a pilot either bribed or threatened by one of Escadinha's accomplices, in the passenger seat. The helicopter hovered low, Escadinha ran to it, his accomplice pulled him up, and the craft took off before guards had any time to react.[4]

Escadinha was, along with Dênis da Rocinha, the most prominent of the new model *dono do morro*. He hailed from Juramento, a large favela in on Rio's north side, and was beloved by its residents for his largesse. His nickname, meaning "the little ladder," supposedly had its origins in a bad haircut he had received as a child. It became the syncopated refrain of numerous popular sambas written in the trafficker's honor. Whereas Saturnino Braga struggled in vain to win a place in the people's heart, Escadinha seemed to achieve it effortlessly.[5]

Escadinha had escaped from Ilha Grande's island prison previously, by rowboat, in 1983. He had returned to Juramento, lived and trafficked more ostentatiously than ever, and was captured again in 1985. His Ilha Grande experience had acquainted him with the Falange Vermelho, or Red Phalanx, a gang started in that prison a decade earlier. Ilha Grande's notorious facility had blended the dictatorship's political prisoners with common thieves, such as bank robbers and muggers. By the early 1970s, the political prisoners had instructed the bank robbers in the strategies of organizing, training, and disciplining revolutionary factions composed of autonomous cells, and the bank robbers had instructed the political prisoners in the arts of illegal fundraising.[6]

Through most of the 1970s, the Falange Vermelho was a small prison gang that funded its control over Ilha Grande's black-market economy through extramural actions such as bank heists and auto thefts carried out by former prisoners and allies. The organization had first come to the attention of most cariocas with a spectacular 1981 shootout between a single Falange Vermelho member and hundreds of policemen in a middle-class housing complex, where the fugitive had been gathering information for a series of bank strikes. But the Falange Vermelho followed the money. By the mid-1980s the money was in cocaine, and the cocaine trade moved through Rio's favelas. The Ilha Grande Prison became a meeting ground for aspiring favela traffickers such as Escadinha and an established criminal network, one that would give the rising donos do morro new access to weaponry and logistical support. As the network expanded, it took on a name more suitable to its enlarged ambitions: the Comando Vermelho, or Red Command.[7]

Brizola recognized that Ilha Grande was an outmoded facility and had previously appealed to the federal government for funding to construct a new, maximum-security state penitentiary, to no avail. By 1985, the Comando Vermelho was all but running the prison while tolerating the presence of the warden and guards. Escadinha's escape was a cakewalk, one of several high-profile escapes that year.

Over the early months of 1986, while Saturnino Braga conducted his "socialist jogs" up Rio's hillsides, Escadinha was also making the rounds of Rio favelas—attending a barbecue in Juramento, meeting friends in Jacarezinho, negotiating with allies in Providência. He was on the lam but far from lying low. These competing tours laid bare the contrast in strategies for addressing the favelas between that of the Socialist government of Rio de Janeiro and that of the Comando Vermelho. Saturnino Braga tried to persuade favela residents of his good intentions with earnest discussion. Escadinha did it with personal favors. One Jornal do Brasil reporter concluded that Escadinha's approach was more successful because it responded directly to the desires of Rio's favela residents. Strikingly, the reporter analyzed Escadinha in light of an academic concept increasingly fashionable in Brazil, British historian Eric Hobsbawm's theory of social banditry. Hobsbawm argued that some well-known criminals cultivated the loyalty and affection of the poor populations that protected them by casting themselves as rebels against political and economic oppression, and by distributing resources to the community. The reporter suggested the theory applied well to Rio's new donos do morro, particularly Escadinha: "In light of Hobsbawm's theory, maybe the trafficker is a typical example of a *primitive rebel*, a kind of Robin Hood, integrated with the community, who robs from the rich to give to the poor, capable of feats like fleeing from Ilha Grande in a helicopter and gaining a reputation for immortality."[8] Within a few years, as trafficker violence became more extreme and took a greater toll on favela populations, such arguments would become increasingly unconvincing. In the mid-1980s, they were common enough to pass as objective reporting in one of Rio's most prominent newspapers.

Escadinha was eventually recaptured midway through 1986 and locked in a prison in downtown Rio de Janeiro, with security redoubled. The recapture failed to dent his popularity. Nor did it prevent him from running drug-trafficking operations on Juramento, a task he carried out through the offices of visitors and released prisoners, integrated into the expanding organizational structure of the Comando Vermelho. While observers debated social banditry, the Comando Vermelho built a far-reaching criminal empire with an aggressive strategy of favela exploitation.

SATURNINO AND JÓ IN THE FAVELAS

Saturnino Braga mapped out an ambitious plan for favela urbanization. In his first months as mayor, he upgraded the municipal census and survey department into a cabinet-level urban planning secretariat. He staffed this secretariat, now known as Iplan, with some of Rio's most enterprising young urbanists. Most of these had been strongly influenced by Carlos Nelson Ferreira dos Santos's favela upgrading projects. They saw both the problems and the advantages of favelas: their lack of infrastructure and security of tenure on one hand, their diversity of function and organic patterns of growth on the other.[9]

In an early mission statement, Iplan's staffers drew attention to the Morro do Pinto, a working-class hilltop neighborhood just north of the Morro da Providência. They pointed out that although the Morro do Pinto shared topographical and architectural features with many favelas, it had the benefit of adequate infrastructure and services and was both economically diverse and well integrated into the surrounding urban fabric. "Walking through the Morro do Pinto, we learn what a well-consolidated favela could be. . . . Its center is well defined. . . . Its narrow principal street ascends to this center, its constructions are solid, sheltering multiple activities, all articulated with a certain mastery and zeal, demonstrating the viability of an ample program of consolidation."[10]

Use of the term "consolidation" marked a new paradigm shift. "Removal: had its brief heyday in the 1960s and its disastrous decline in the 1970s. "Urbanization" had emerged as the term of art among urban planners in the wake of removal's failure; it had the advantage of recognizing and reinforcing the persistence of favelas but continued to imply a policy visited upon the favela, with or without the consent of its residents. "Consolidation" implied a process directed from within and merely facilitated from without. This would gradually become the new ideal of favela planners.

Iplan's technicians wedded the term to another new idea, that of "areas of special social interest." By declaring favelas and other low-income neighborhoods areas of special social interest, Iplan's technicians could eliminate the legal requirement of bringing all housing and infrastructure up to standard municipal codes. They also hoped to use the designation to enable formal titling in favelas without triggering a process of gentrification that would drive out existing residents. To facilitate these goals, Iplan's technicians outlined projects for a host of favelas across the city. These were pioneering ideas that eventually guided flexible, innovative municipal policies toward the favelas. There was only one problem: Iplan had no money. The secretariat had a minimal budget and depended on other state and municipal departments, such as the Department of Works and the Department of Social Development, to carry out its designs. Given the worsening budget crunch, this meant that Iplan's projects remained a beautiful dream and a plan for a subsequent generation.[11]

In the meantime, Braga and Resende hoped to facilitate improved political representation for Rio's favelas by decentralizing administration. The crux of their plan lay in strengthening connections between municipal government and neighborhood associations in both middle-class neighborhoods and favelas. To do so, they increased the number of existing administrative regions, adding four new regions comprising the city's largest favelas: Rocinha, Jacarezinho, the Complexo da Maré, and the Complexo do Alemão. They granted local favela associations the power to veto nominations to staff these positions. This gave individual association officers decisive leverage in choosing new regional administrators, effectively giv-

ing them influence over distribution of resources and hiring for municipal projects.[12]

They also created two new institutions, the Conselho Governo-
Comunidade (Government-Community Council) and Conselho Escola-
Comunidade (School-Community Council). These were modeled after Brizola's Justice Council, meant to connect representatives of organized civil
society directly to key government servants. There were thirty Community-
Government Councils, one for each administrative region in the city, and
each council comprised one representative from local favela associations,
one from middle-class associations, and one from the local chamber of
commerce. The regional administrator was ex-officio president of each
council. Representatives of key municipal cabinet ministries were required
to attend monthly council meetings. The councils did not have direct budgetary authority but presented priorities for local public spending. Braga
and Resende instructed municipal cabinet secretaries to follow these recommendations as closely as possible.[13]

The School-Community Councils were designed on the same model, but
dedicated specifically to questions of local education. Like the Government-
Community Councils, they were granted extensive influence, at least on
paper, holding the power to choose principals of local schools. This gave
association officers veto power over the direction of local schools. Braga
and Resende expected that community support would turn the councils
into vital instruments of participatory government.[14] They were surprised
to find that their efforts were met with the dull echo of popular indiffer-
ence. Few cariocas were eager to spend their evenings wrangling in committee meetings. In the late 1970s, such participation was understood to
be an integral part of the broad process of redemocratization. By 1986,
citizens had other priorities.[15]

The plethora of Government-Community and School-Community
Councils rarely succeeded in raising a quorum for their monthly meetings. Yet the structure of Braga's administration required these councils
to make policy decisions and appoint school administrators. In practice,
this meant that such decisions were left to a few local powerbrokers. Most
dealings between association officers and government officials took place
not in the public council meetings but out of public view. Their relationship became a quasi-contractual exchange of cooperation for control over
resources. One staffer from the Municipal Secretariat for Social Develop-

ment recalls association officers deciding how municipal resources would be invested and who would benefit—choosing, for example, which local residents were permitted to enroll their children in a municipal daycare facility. "The president of the association and the local field agents would say 'We control our daycare center, and the children who may enter here are the children we think should be here. . . . That woman over there, no, she's a gossip.'" When the Development Secretariat's staff insisted on equal access to public facilities, association officers replied, " 'Wait a minute, that is not what we agreed. What we agreed is that you would build this daycare center for us.' And that 'us' meant absolute control."[16] Braga's administration, designed to incorporate these association officers, agreed to concede this control at the local level. As a result, favela residents only had access to municipal improvements if they were in the good graces of their association officers.

THE NUCLEUS FOR SUBDIVISION REGULARIZATION IN ACTION

The subdivisions, as always, present a compelling contrasting case. By the time Braga and Resende took office, the municipal Núcleo de Regularização de Loteamentos (NRL, Nucleus for Subdivision Regularization) was already connecting residents of irregular subdivisions to the state prosecutor's office, the state housing authority, the water and sewer authority, and the municipal works department. Braga's administration brought Iplan technicians into the mix, making it possible for subdivision residents to pursue title regularization and infrastructural improvement at the same time, in mutually reinforcing processes.[17]

By mid-1986, the nucleus was holding weekly meetings with the required attendance of representatives of key municipal departments. Like the Community-Government Council meetings, these called for extensive participation from community representatives. In this case, though, participation fulfilled the municipal administration's goal of directing resources in a way that responded effectively to community needs.[18] Subdivision residents bought into the nucleus, literally and figuratively. Within the first few months of Braga's administration, residents in thirty-seven subdivisions had ceased making mortgage payments to their irregular real-estate developers, depositing them instead into public accounts in the state bank. The state prosecutor's office backed this transfer, ensuring that irregular developers could not initiate proceedings against individual homeowners. The nucleus supplied account books for each household, ensuring that monthly payments would be registered with the notary for property registration. As a result, continued monthly payments to the nucleus plan facilitated individual title regularization, demonstrating consistent occupation and equity in the property.[19]

Most of the irregular developers were in flagrant violation of municipal, state, and federal laws and had already made substantial profits. As a result, few contested these proceedings. In some cases, the nucleus brought criminal charges against irregular developers. Although Nucleus lawyers recognized that these suits were unlikely to lead to conviction and imprisonment, they invested in them in an attempt to deter future irregular development.[20] In the meantime, the mortgage payments made by subdivision residents to the nucleus plan enabled greater funding for infrastructural improvements in the subdivisions. The NRL's achievements were incremental, but this gradual nature itself proved to be an advantage: the agency flew beneath the radar of local politics and never became controversial. As a result, it continued to function, modestly but successfully, throughout Braga's administration and beyond, with little variation.

The nucleus's approach required municipal and state government to commit to both upgrading and regularization and gave subdivision residents incentives to participate in those processes. The nucleus intervened between corrupt developers and residents and guaranteed those residents the right to remain in their homes and work toward regularization. Individual residents, as a result, had both the capacity and the incentive to participate in the nucleus regularization process. In the favelas, no similar incentives were offered to individual residents. Instead, city government worked solely through the associations. The officers of these associations had strong incentives to work with municipal administrators in distributing resources and local jobs, but none to regularize property. Gradual regularization of the subdivisions—in terms of property title, infrastructure, and political representation—presented a clear contrast with the perpetuation of the favelas as territories of exception.

The subdivisions also proved less vulnerable than the favelas to criminal turf monopolization. In part this was because of their location; most were in the featureless expanses of the west side, far from middle-class cocaine consumers and the port area of downtown Rio. They were not enticing targets for takeover by drug traffickers. But it was also because of their resolute ordinariness. They were never distinct from the surrounding fabric of the city and over time became indistinguishable from neighboring regular developments. They constituted the majority of the city's west side, rather than islands of difference. They had no boundaries to patrol, no identifiable turf to monopolize.

The irregular subdivisions were not magically transformed into thriving democratic precincts characterized by healthy civic participation. The titans of the numbers racket cultivated a network of corrupt police and city council members on the city's west side and in the Baixada Fluminense, just north of municipal boundaries. This corruption, marked by its own sporadic violence, undermined the rule of law and political representation. Nevertheless, gradual regularization made these conditions less persistent and pronounced than they were in the favelas. Elite cariocas continued to turn up their noses at the mere mention of western districts such as Santa Cruz and Campo Grande, home to most of the city's irregular subdivisions. That disdain, however, was in part a reaction to the unspectacular nature of life in these parts. The subdivisions — slowly tilting toward regularity and gradually becoming more prosperous — were apparently just as boring, in the eyes of the well-to-do, as any lumpen district. By the late 1980s, many residents of violent south side favelas would have jumped at the chance for such boredom.

THE GUBERNATORIAL ELECTIONS OF 1986

Brizola nominated his vice-governor and secretary of education, Darcy Ribeiro, as the PDT's candidate for governor of Rio State in 1986. In contrast to the wide-open 1982 contest, it was clear that only two candidates had a viable chance: Ribeiro and Wellington Moreira Franco, the runner-up in 1982. Moreira Franco had a new party affiliation, running for the PMDB, taking advantage of that party's strength in the interior of the state and its alliance with President José Sarney at the federal level. He also had a new hairstyle, wearing his shock of white hair below the ears, blown dry in a startling coif. Brizola dubbed him the Gato Angorá, or Angora Cat. The campaign was a study in contrasts. Ribeiro ran as the education candidate, vowing to expand and improve the CIEPs. Moreira Franco ran as the law-and-order candidate, vowing to put an end to urban violence within six months.

Inevitably, the favelas were a key battleground, both for their votes and for their value as the image of everything about the city that needed fixing—although the two candidates had diametrically opposed visions of how to do that. Neither candidate had Brizola's touch when it came to persuading favela residents. Attempting to bolster Ribeiro's campaign, Jó Resende vouched that Moreira Franco would not even be able to campaign in the favelas, because their residents would block him at the entrance. The assertion was particularly inept. It appeared to recognize and endorse an increasing turf control on the part of favela-based trafficking crews. This was the "law of the hill" Bezerra da Silva alluded to in the samba that serves as an epigraph to this chapter; those who did not have the respect of local traffickers would have to pay a toll to go up or down. Resende seemed to be encouraging the new donos do morro to keep Moreira Franco out.

This suggestion handed Moreira Franco the perfect press opportunity: availing himself of the old Chagas Freitas machine, he arranged a campaign visit to Juramento itself. Ironically, he needed Escadinha's permission to do so. The imprisoned trafficker, interviewed from his new confines, assured reporters that he had sent word to the hill to ensure Moreira's safety—there was little doubt that Escadinha was still the most important authority in Juramento. The candidate's visit went smoothly, indicating that the donos do morro really did not care which politician was elected as long as their territorial control remained unthreatened.[21]

Resende was right about one thing: favela leaders were beginning to use restricted access as a tool for political negotiation. He was wrong, though, about the results of this restriction, as it did not translate into support for Darcy Ribeiro. In Rocinha, Maria Helena Pereira da Silva negotiated with Moreira Franco's brother for a series of projects in the favela in return for access to Rocinha. In the words of the director of a community school in the favela, "To enter here in Rocinha, Moreira Franco had to promise to support the school, in addition to giving four houses to the community. And there could be no other result: Rocinha voted for him in force." In practice, Dênis and his crew were the ones with the power to restrict access, but the favela leaders used the threat of that power to extract short-term investment.[22]

The Angora Cat won the November elections decisively, beating Ribeiro by more than a million votes. Moreira Franco's election immediately endangered all of Brizola's reforms. Brizola quickly moved to reassert his influence over Saturnino Braga in order to rescue his project at the municipal level. Moreira Franco, for his part, needed to figure out how to make good on his far-fetched campaign promise to put an end to urban violence in six months.

UP THE HILL WITH GUNS BLAZING

The new governor promptly sacked Nazareth Cerqueira and Nilo Batista from their posts as military and civil police chiefs and brought back aggressive policing in Rio's favelas. Typical of this initiative was Emir Larangeira, a tough-talking anti-brizolista cop who liked to described no-nonsense lawmen like himself as *fodões*, or "big fuckers," a role he contrasted to soft bureaucrats that he denominated *bundões*, or "big buttocks." He was Nazareth Cerqueira's opposite in almost every way. Larangeira was white, Nazareth Cerqueira black. Larangeira favored militarized incursions, Nazareth Cerqueira community policing. Larangeira played pickup soccer with his men, Nazareth Cerqueira played one-on-one basketball with Nilo Batista. Both were authors and both had climbed from impoverished backgrounds to positions of influence, but even here they differed: Emir Larangeira wrote violent cop thrillers — thinly veiled, autobiographical novels. Nazareth Cerqueira wrote dry treatises on police reform. Emir Larangeira characterized his success as the just reward of a fighter. Nazareth Cerqueira characterized his as the serendipitous result of opportunities denied to most poor, black children. Moreira Franco showed where he stood by demoting Nazareth Cerqueira and naming Larangeira chief of Rio's Ninth Battalion, responsible for policing the extensive favelas in Rio's northeast quadrant. There could have been no clearer indication of a radical transition in policing strategy.[23]

Despite these measures, Moreira was no more able than his predecessor to resolve the split within the police forces. Many officers had sincerely adopted the reforms championed by Nazareth Cerqueira, and they had risen through the ranks during Brizola's administration. Jorge da Silva, one of Nazareth Cerqueira's most prominent junior officers, was a black officer who had been born and raised in the Alemão favela on Rio's north side. Silva was an advocate of Nazareth Cerqueira's strategy and an irreproachable commander. As governor, Moreira Franco had the power to remove the military police chief, but he could not fire Jorge da Silva and other officers who had internalized Nazareth Cerqueira's methods. Even new Battalion commanders such as Larangeira could not easily replace figures like Jorge da Silva without provoking further unrest. In consequence, a fundamental rift over the nature of effective policing widened within Rio's police force.[24]

Moreira Franco had better luck winning the support of federal authorities. Sarney immediately passed on resources long denied to Brizola, including funding for construction of a new maximum-security prison in Bangu, on Rio's west side. Escadinha, the facility's first resident, moved there in advance of its official inauguration a year later.[25] Moreira Franco's police could also rely on federal assistance in tracking down fugitive suspects. In mid-July 1987, they scored their first major victory: they arrested Dênis da Rocinha. He had been hiding out in a luxury hotel in Florianópolis, hundreds of miles south of Rio.[26]

His arrest sent shockwaves through Rocinha. Over the next several weeks, Maria Helena Pereira, president of Rocinha's most important association, made increasingly vitriolic denunciations of police abuse; Dênis's comrades-in-arms warned of an impending explosion of social unrest. Fulfilling their threats, one month to the day after Dênis's arrest, thousands of the favela's residents descended the hill in protest against his imprisonment, prompting the favela's businesses to shut their doors. When military police tried to disperse the protesters, residents threw stones at the officers and barricaded the highway at the foot of the hill. The protest blocked the tunnel connecting the chic south side neighborhoods of Leblon and São Conrado, cutting off the main artery between central Rio and the middle-class district of Barra da Tijuca. Commuters trapped in the tunnel eventually abandoned their cars and walked out, backing up traffic for miles. This being Rio, the protesters eventually turned the event into a party. Rocinha's residents played samba and soccer on the closed highway and chanted Dênis's name in exultation. The police stood by until nightfall, then struck back with vengeance, beating and arresting anyone unlucky enough to be caught in the streets.

As chants of "Dênis, Dênis!" resounded in the background, Maria Helena Pereira da Silva contended that the real motivation for the protest lay in police violence against favela residents in general. Fellow community leaders suggested that if Dênis had been on hand, he could have avoided the confrontation, probably by paying off the police: "He would have been able to negotiate and control everyone, including the police." They described the protest as one manifestation of a larger conflict: "It is a path of class struggle, because the population demonstrated that it is losing its

FIG. 4.1. Rocinha residents protesting the arrest of Dênis da Rocinha, 1987. The protest shut down the highway and the Túnel Zuzu Angel, bringing rush hour traffic to a halt. Police bide their time as residents man the barricades. Photograph by Luiz Bittencourt, CPDoc JB.

FIG. 4.2. Rocinha residents descend the hill en masse and throw rocks and bottles at police, 1987. This central commercial strip, evidence of Rocinha's economic dynamism, shut down during the protest. This deference, borne out of self-protection, soon became a ritual demand of drug traffickers organizing similar manifestations. Photograph by Luiz Bittencourt, CPDoc JB.

fear of confronting the police." There was some truth to all these observations: police abuse of favela residents was growing more intense, Dênis probably could have stopped the protest at a word, and the deliberation confrontation of the police by protesters showed a dramatic change in tone in favela activism. These contentions notwithstanding, it was clear that this was a popular manifestation directed by drug traffickers for their own benefit. What community leaders left unsaid—they were in no position to say it—was that favelados may have gained the freedom to criticize the police but they had lost the freedom to criticize traffickers.[27]

The new military police spokesman responded to these allegations by calling attention to Pereira da Silva's alleged connections to Dênis and vowed to take the necessary steps to impose order on the favela.[28] The implication was that if favela residents were willing to defend the traffickers, the police would not hesitate to inflict retribution on those residents; they would all be treated like criminals.

The Rocinha protest and its repression marked the beginning of a new stage in city politics. Favela associations had led protests against the imprisonment of local traffickers before, as in the Pavão-Pavãozinho protest of 1985. The Rocinha manifestation, however, was more than a protest of Dênis's arrest. It was a demonstration of the political costs to be incurred for interfering with the drug traffic, an indication that the traffickers could shut down an entire quadrant of the city. The indiscriminate, violent repression of the protest demonstrated that Nazareth Cerqueira's policies of community policing and tolerance for nonviolent crime had been decisively shelved. Both the protest and the repression amounted to an emphatic statement of the separation of favela and city.

Two weeks later, another spectacular conflict erupted, this one triggered by battles between rival factions of a drug gang in Santa Marta. Former partners Zaca and Cabeludo split in a violent feud, culminating in a well-publicized, eight-day battle for terrain.[29] The "Santa Marta War," as it became known, synthesized important transitions in the nature of Rio's drug trade, the policing of that trade, and media coverage of both. Zaca was a migrant from the northeastern state of Paraíba and a former military policeman expelled from the force for his involvement in crime. He kept a low profile and avoided inconveniencing the favela's older residents. Cabeludo, or Hairy, was a rebel nicknamed for his flowing locks, who had entered the drug trade as an avid consumer before taking over the hill's primary *boca de fumo*, or point of sale. He invested heavily in expanding the

FIG. 4.3. After dark, Moreira Franco's police struck back, 1987. Similar scenes, unthinkable in middle-class Rio de Janeiro, became a constant feature of favela life. Photograph by Luiz Morier, CPDoc JB.

market by hiring Rio's most famous sambistas to play at all-night parties in Santa Marta's *quadra*, a concrete plaza used as a sports court, rehearsal space for the local samba school, and entertainment venue. He distributed generous quantities of free samples to partygoers, and sought out violent conflict with the police and rivals, cultivating the adoration of the youngest drug traffickers, the scouts and delivery boys known as *olheiros*, lookers, and *aviões*, airplanes. These junior members of the crew, often as young as twelve, would become the next generation of donos do morro. Cabeludo gave two new wrinkles to the dono do morro phenomenon: the will to seek violence in order to establish his reputation and the interest of publicizing those feats both within Santa Marta and in the rest of the city. He became the first of Rio's new donos with a media spokesman. He sent one of his young lieutenants to tell reporters his version of the ongoing struggle, spinning a tale of Cabeludo's self-sacrificing protection of the favela's marginalized residents, describing the dono do morro as a social bandit.[30]

Moreira Franco's police held their fire for several days, an uncharacteristic restraint that suggested that as long as drug traffickers were only shooting at each other, the police saw no need to intervene. Rio's newspapers and television stations disseminated shocking images of gun-wielding adolescents locked in a battle for control of the hill. Santa Marta's residents continued to come and go throughout the struggle, keeping their heads down and adopting a posture of strategic neutrality, avoiding traffickers, police, and reporters where possible. Only after a week of sporadic gunfire did the police occupy Santa Marta, in a botched operation that enabled both Zaca and Cabeludo to flee. The police held the hill temporarily but soon withdrew, and Santa Marta's drug traffic was only briefly interrupted. Zaca soon returned to the hill and established control. Cabeludo himself was killed in an attempted stickup months later. But the death-defying, flamboyant young soldiers he had mentored later carried out vengeance in his memory, seizing Santa Marta with the support of the Comando Vermelho.[31]

The "Santa Marta War" and conflicts like it fueled the Comando Vermelho's growth. Internal disputes within a favela's trafficking crew, or disputes between adjacent favelas — as in Cantagalo and Pavão-Pavãozinho — led enterprising traffickers to ally with the Comando Vermelho in order to acquire superior weapons and reinforcements. Alliance with the network also enabled leading traffickers such as Escadinha and Dênis to continue to run their operations from jail, through intermediaries in the network. The network's expansion inevitably generated internal tensions as varying donos competed for primacy. Escadinha and a group of allies ultimately split with the Comando Vermelho, beginning a rival faction, the Amigos dos Amigos (Friends of Friends) — a name that alluded to the mutual protection strategy of linked commanders with no clear hierarchy. Like the Comando Vermelho, the Amigos dos Amigos sought to escalate violence in order to persuade local crews of the wisdom of seeking its alliances. Turf battles between the Comando Vermelho, the Amigos dos Amigos, and subsequent splinter factions and rival groups became cyclical and self-sustaining.

The interventions of Moreira Franco's aggressive police only exacerbated this violence. Although the new governor criticized Brizola for allegedly telling police to stay out of favelas, he did no better than his predecessor in establishing reliable policing in these areas. Instead, precinct commanders such as Emir Larangeira treated the favelas as enemy territory, to be invaded with maximum prejudice when necessary. Moreira Franco undertook no serious effort to combat police corruption, and many officers accepted generous payments from drug traffickers. The traffickers understood these payments to be the cost of doing business. When covert

FIG. 4.4. A masked member of Cabeludo's gang points to coverage of the Santa Marta War in the newspaper, 1987. The image, taken during a lull in the action, captures the circularity of spectacular violence. Young traffickers stepped up violence in part to guarantee the street credibility that came with media coverage. Two younger children gaze up at the traffickers. Within a few years, nearly all of Cabeludo's soldiers had died in subsequent conflicts. Photograph by Chiquito Chaves, CPDoc JB.

FIG. 4.5. Police occupation of Santa Marta, 1987. The police sent to work on the front lines of Rio's turf wars were mostly young and poorly trained. The construction here—with older stone topped by newer brick, and netting extended to protect against risk of falling rocks— shows the constantly changing nature of favela architecture, always a work in progress. The phrase *vende-se*, for sale, is partly visible behind the police, reminding us that turf wars did not stop the informal real-estate market. Photograph by Olavo Rufino, CPDoc JB.

negotiations broke down, rogue police often kidnapped traffickers, freeing them only after a ransom had been paid. Arrest without warrant and extra-judicial violence became more common than they ever had been under the military dictatorship.

TAKING THE ASSOCIATIONS

The consequences of growing trafficker strength for the favela associations were disastrous. As was so often the case, Rocinha's experience was pre-figurative. Dênis's imprisonment set off power struggles on the hill be-tween rival claimants to serve as lieutenant for the jailed leader. Within weeks, Maria Helena Pereira was killed in her own home. The death, which was never investigated, signaled that association presidents now served at the pleasure of local crime lords — a message delivered repeatedly in years to come.

Favela manifestations against police interference with the drug trade multiplied. Taken at face value, these were popular actions denouncing real police abuses, of which there was no shortage. But in many cases, local traffickers directly instructed association officers to lead these protests. In May 1986, for example, association officers from Providência led a protest in front of the governor's palace, accusing police of entrapment, violence, and extortion at the local drug bazaar. The favela residents provided vehicle numbers of officers they alleged to be stealing money and marijuana from traffickers, a specificity of denunciation of police malfeasance unimagin-able only a few years earlier. Still there was no mistaking the underlying message: the governor should call off his dogs and leave the favela alone.[32]

In some favelas, traffickers took direct control of associations. In an April 1987 operation in the Morro do Sereno, for example, police arrested the association president along with several other members of the local crew after finding them with hundreds of packets of cocaine and mari-juana, along with an impressive arsenal of weapons. The Morro do Sereno was not far from Juramento and was part of Escadinha's sphere of influ-ence. The arrest strongly suggested that the association president was part of Escadinha's network.[33]

The value of leverage over the association corresponded directly to the value of the local drug trade. In consequence, the associations most vul-nerable to criminal infiltration were not those in the poorest and most iso-lated favelas. On the contrary, the more integrated a favela was to broader networks of commerce and political power, the more likely its association leaders were to feel pressure from local traficantes.

Mangueira was home to a legendary samba school that attracted visitors from across the city to its weekend parties, including scores of international tourists bused in from south side hotels, making it one of the most lucrative trafficking operations in Rio. In order to protect that trade, Mangueira's traffickers moved early to establish decisive leverage over the local association. In June 1987, police raided Mangueira to arrest dono do morro Beato Salu, a key Comando Vermelho leader. The action was typical of Moreira Franco's administration: when heavily armed police entered the favela, local teenagers began throwing rocks at them. The police fired back indiscriminately, wounding several children before capturing the trafficker. Several days later, Mangueira's association president led a protest against the police, shutting down the road at Mangueira's base. The president, sticking to the script of social banditry that was already becoming standard, emphasized the contrast between the police and Beato Salu: "While the police come in shooting everyone, he helped out the people."[34]

By the following year, another trafficker was running operations on Mangueira while Beato Salu did time. When police returned to Mangueira in search of the new leading trafficker, they asked the association president to open a locked office in the association building for them. They found three thousand packets of marijuana, four grenades, several semiautomatic weapons, bundles of cash, and stolen stereo equipment. They promptly arrested the association president, who insisted that he had no idea that the room—adjacent to the association headquarters and built with municipal funding for a local health post—had become a warehouse for drug traffickers. He was soon released from jail and immediately held a press conference with allies from the favela federation, insisting that he was a legitimate community leader with no links to the drug trade. Representatives of the Municipal Social Development Secretariat participated in the conference, demonstrating a clear rift between Saturnino Braga's city government and that of Moreira Franco at the state level. The participation of city officials showed how completely the Secretariat of Social Development had pinned its own mission on collaboration with association officers, opting to defend those officers even when compelling evidence suggested their cooperation with drug trafficking factions.[35]

Rio's police were by no means above planting incriminating evidence, but they had no capacity to plant a room full of drugs, weapons, and stolen merchandise in a prominent building in the heart of a densely populated favela. Instead, the claims to innocence made by Mangueira's association president rested on the contention that he had no idea what was going on next door to his office, within the Mangueira association building. The circumstances of the arrest made clear that Mangueira's traffickers took whatever they needed for their operations, under cover of community representation. Yet city government continued to work through Mangueira's favela association for the next decade and beyond.

Santa Marta, adjacent to upscale residential neighborhoods, was also well located for serving middle-class cocaine consumption. Not surprisingly, local traffickers moved to take over its association, driving out the Eco Group that had made Santa Marta's association one of the most vital and participatory in the city. Late in 1988, in the first association elections after the Santa Marta War, the Eco Group was given the strong message that it was time to step down. Several residents told Itamar Silva in advance that they could not vote for the Eco ticket: "I really like you, but the *tráfico* is going to present a ticket, and there is a threat." Losing the election was undoubtedly the best thing for Silva's personal safety. Following the vote, some residents told him, "I didn't vote for you, because I like you too much."[36]

José Custódio da Silva, better known as Zé Castelo, the winning candidate for association president, was a bar owner and beverage distributor closely allied with Zaca. He also cultivated connections with the PDT and city government. As association president, he became a political front for Zaca, helping to protect the traffic from the police and to monitor the loyalties of local residents. When the soldiers of the fallen Cabeludo returned and seized Santa Marta in 1991, they murdered Zé Castelo, his wife, and his secretary and drove surviving members of their family from the hill. His former vice-president assumed the presidency and immediately allied with the new dono, but was soon assassinated himself.[37] The Santa Marta episodes demonstrated that the new generation of traffickers not only wanted control over the association, they would not hesitate to expel or eliminate anyone who protested.

Santa Marta's tragic case also showed that neither highly effective local leaders, nor solid connections to academic and government institutions, posed serious obstacles to criminal takeover. When the traffickers moved to assert their influence, they exploited every opportunity and brooked no opposition; *chegaram pra valer*, "they came to make it count," in carioca parlance. Looking back on this transition years later, Itamar Silva was typically insightful: "The Resident's Association began to have a direct interlocution with the state. It became very clear that it was a space that had strength, and that the *tráfico* was going to contend for that space, one way or another. From one side, it would undermine it, from the other, it would try to co-opt it, and in other places, it would take over completely, it would assume power openly and appoint people to those spaces." Silva's language is strikingly reminiscent of the Gramscian theory of "occupying spaces" that had informed the Pastoral movement a decade earlier. As his analysis suggests, the perverse genius of the traffickers was to hijack and distort the communitarian mobilization that had once given Santa Marta so much hope.[38]

Over the remainder of the 1980s, the model of trafficker infiltration in favela associations spread from the most lucrative outposts to other regions of the city. The north side favela complex of Acari had three neighborhood associations, and by the early 1990s all three were controlled by local traffickers. The local dono, Cy do Acari, was imprisoned in the late 1980s but continued to run trafficking operations in the favela complex through intermediaries. His crew chiefs moved decisively to control local associations. In one instance, the crew chief's brother served as vice-president of the association. In another, the crew chief's father was treasurer of the association. In this same association, the president's daughter was married to the brother of the local crew chief. In another case, the crew chief appointed his mother-in-law as accountant of the local association; the association found that this arrangement made it considerably easier to collect monthly dues. In all of these cases, association officers also took on the duties of paying protection money to corrupt police, a process so routinized that it had its own designated location at one entrance to the favela, akin to an ATM for corrupt police.[39]

Growing trafficker influence over associations was by no means the result of an organized conspiracy. It was instead the result of a series of logical responses to the changing political context. This influence took various forms across the city; in the most notorious cases, the link was direct and unmistakable, and in other cases, the local crew granted relative autonomy to the association as long as its officers made no attempt to infringe on its operations. Only one kind of relationship was impossible: direct denunciation of local traffickers. Association officers, even where they maintained functional autonomy, were prohibited from making any complaint about drug traffickers. This was an unwritten but universally acknowledged element of the *lei do morro*, or law of the hill, described by Bezerra da Silva in the samba used in the epigraph to this chapter.

As this model spread across the city, community leaders in the favela of Rio das Pedras deliberately created a countermodel, organizing a defense militia to frighten away or eliminate prospective drug traffickers. The same cohort that controlled the association was known to command the militia and governed with unquestioned authority. Those deemed undesirable were driven from the favela or eliminated. This countermodel, however, was far from the kind of communitarian mobilization envisioned by the Pastoral. Instead, it quickly became an alternative form of turf monopolization, characterized by intimidation and rent-seeking that paralleled similar trends in favelas where the drug traffic held sway. To begin, the Rio das Pedras association demanded unusually high monthly dues and was vigilant in collecting, making it clear that the militia would back up this requirement with force if necessary. Dues for local business owners were even higher. The association also became the semiofficial real-estate developer in the community, overseeing lucrative expansion into new subareas. Furthermore, it took aggressive steps to silence any dissent regarding these practices. As one resident put it, "Only the troublemakers disappear." Although the Rio das Pedras association was not a front for drug trafficking, in other ways its attenuation of the meaning of local democracy was just as severe as that exercised in favelas such as Santa Marta.[40]

By the end of the 1980s, the Rio das Pedras model had begun to spread to nearby favelas. As the decade drew to a close, the immediate prospects for favela residents appeared to be subjection to the violent and turbulent control of the traffickers—constantly at war with the police and each other—or to the menacing authority of the nascent militias.

THE ELEPHANT ON THE HILL

Although drug trafficker control over favela associations must have been apparent to those paying attention, it went largely unremarked in polite society. The police denounced trafficker influence, but the police were not considered reliable interlocutors. Their dismissal of association officers was often difficult to distinguish from disdain for favela residents in general. Few other politicians and civil servants risked drawing attention to the phenomenon: the political costs were too high. In a radio interview in July 1987, Moreira Franco revealed that favela association officers were pressuring him to suspend repression of drug trafficking. This seemed to be an inadvertent reference, however, as the governor avoided following up on it. Weeks later, Moreira Franco's brother, Nelson—the state secretary of social advancement, responsible for most state-level overtures to Rio's favelas, and an administrator who had forged a productive relationship with Rocinha's association—argued precisely the opposite, claiming that the associations served as a bulwark against drug trafficking and should be strengthened.[41]

Municipal civil servants echoed Nelson Moreira Franco's position—not a surprise, given vice-mayor Jó Resende's deep links to the neighborhood association movement. In a prominent interview in the Rio daily O Globo, Sérgio Andrea, Braga's new municipal secretary for social development and himself a former officer of the Botafogo association, suggested that the traffickers were "a kind of leadership that formed with the omission of public power" but were not true leaders. "Leaders are those who act in the associations," he argued, and suggested that only increased government cooperation with the associations could serve as a counterweight to the patronage distributed by the leading traffickers. Andrea further argued that favela traffickers were mere low-level opportunists who should not be confused with the powerful criminals masterminding the drug traffic from more august locations. "Where is the upper echelon of the traffic?" he asked rhetorically, suggesting it was not to be found in places like Juramento.[42]

Andrea's argument typified an emerging rhetoric that attributed trafficker control of favela turf to the "absence of the state" from favelas, and excused favela traffickers as minor players in a hemispheric drug trade. As one policy paper described it, "The favela drug traffickers are only the poor arm of the real traffickers, and the real traffickers do not live in the favelas."[43] Both claims were false. There were favelas where the state was nearly absent, but these were not the favelas targeted first by the drug traffic. Instead, the favelas taken over soonest and most viciously were those with the greatest connections to city and state government, such as Pavão-Pavãozinho, Rocinha, Mangueira, and Santa Marta, because they also happened to be the favelas with the most lucrative drug trade. And although the vast majority of favela traffickers were low-level pawns, figures such as Escadinha and Cy do Acari played decisive roles directing that trade. They were not tools of outside agents, but powerful criminal operators, with extensive national and international networks of support.

Despite its demonstrably false nature, the rhetoric of the absence of the state became increasingly common because it was politically convenient. It served all participants in favela politics, except for those who had no voice. Civil servants used this rhetoric to suggest that they knew the secret for undermining traffic control and it was simple: merely strengthen state presence. This was the one point on which Saturnino Braga and Moreira Franco could agree: "In spite of a few divergences, State and Municipality seem to have found the recipe to combat the political influence of the drug trafficking gangs. . . . The diagnosis emerged from observing that the traffickers carry out works or develop projects benefiting the community. And the recipe is very simple: strengthen the residents' associations and combat the clientelism of the *bandidos*."[44] The traffickers, unfortunately, were already two steps ahead of this strategy, having taken over the associations and integrated themselves into the city's clientelist networks. Nonetheless, admitting that would have thrown a wrench into city and state administrative strategies, making the city ungovernable. For association officers, the rhetoric of the absence of the state provided a way to shift responsibility for local problems to outside forces and to justify their strategy of using the association as a conduit for state and municipal resources. For the traffickers, the rhetoric enabled them to cast themselves as defenders of neglected communities.

The rhetoric of state absence was closely related to the rhetoric of social causes, which attributed all urban violence to the economic marginalization of the poor. At one level, these rhetorical strategies contradicted one another, as blaming turf monopolization on the absence of the state focused on politics and policy, whereas attributing crime solely to social causes focused on inequality and discrimination. In practice, however, political figures combined these rhetorical strategies, suggesting that the right kind of political intervention in the favelas could magically resolve inequality. In a visit in 1988 to one north side favela, for example, Jó Resende faced questions about how he intended to cope with rising crime and urban violence. He responded, "People have asked what we are going to do about security and I respond that we are already doing it. We are building schools to protect our children and take them away from the wrong turns that lead to violence."[45]

Lula (at the time still officially known as Luís Inácio da Silva) employed similar rhetoric during a visit in 1988 to Rocinha and Santa Marta, in the early stages of his campaign for the 1989 presidential election. He dismissed the police as unprepared and unnecessarily combative—certainly true—and remarked, "How cretinous of government officials to speak of the rise in criminality without taking into account the misery in which favelados live?"[46] This sentiment became a theme of carioca politics through the next decade. Again, such rhetoric was pointedly disingenuous, offering only the most vague long-term solutions to rising urban violence. All the same, it enabled politicians to avoid acknowledging that their favela visits depended on prior approval from traffickers.

Many public figures described the new donos do morro as social bandits who served as valued leaders of their communities. Political scientist Vânia Bambirra, a founding member of the PDT and Brizola adviser, argued, "The bandido in general is an individual who distinguishes himself with his high intellectual capacity and with his innate qualities of leadership, who in a more just society might have been a scientist or a political leader."[47] Editorialists for the left-wing newspaper O Povo na Rua went further, arguing that leading traffickers contributed to "solidarity on the hill" by repressing petty crime and paying for medicine.[48]

At the same time, the rhetoric of social banditry was more than matched by an opposing trend, particularly prevalent in newspaper and television depictions, that treated favelas as the source of urban violence, a scourge on the city. This coverage tended to take at face value the claims of drug traffickers and corrupt association officers to speak on behalf of the favela, accepting them as representative of all favela residents. Lost in both the disingenuous rhetoric of social ills and the sensationalist depiction of urban violence was any serious consideration of the violence perpetrated by traffickers on residents of the favela themselves. Favela residents could not speak publicly of this violence; the law of the hill prohibited that. Their putative representatives in the favela associations, often in fear for their own lives, had strong motivations to avoid the topic. Policymakers, in turn, had no strong incentive to bring it up on their own, given the difficulty of providing any solution. As a result, when the municipal council hosted a seminar in 1989 on "violence in the favelas," the speakers carefully limited themselves to discussing police violence. Violence perpetrated by traffickers against favela residents became the elephant on the hill that no one wished to mention.[49]

One intriguing example of this phenomenon comes from a documentary film entitled Duas semanas no morro (Two weeks on the hill), chronicling a fortnight in the life of Santa Marta. Director Eduardo Coutinho shot the film before the "Santa Marta War," but editing was completed and the film released in the aftermath of that conflict. In striking contrast to the treatment of the cocaine-addled gunmen and preteen gangsters that characterized newspaper and television coverage of the conflict, *Duas semanas no morro* emphasized the dignity of hardworking favela residents and the integrity of community leaders.[50]

In one scene, a handsome and charismatic teenager discusses his aspirations to become a professional graphic designer. The film does not reveal that the teenager, Márcio Amaro de Oliveira, was a low-level member of Cabeludo's crew — something most people in the small favela of Santa Marta knew. By the time the documentary came out, he had been detained and released twice for involvement in drug trafficking, and had participated in the epic gunfights with Zaca's forces. In the early 1990s, Oliveira, by then better known as Marcinho VP, became the dono of Santa Marta, perpetrator of multiple homicides, veteran of dozens of battles, and Rio's most wanted man.[51]

There are two ways to read Marcinho VP's appearance in Coutinho's film. The first is that when the film crew visited Santa Marta in 1986, Marcinho was a rambunctious teenager with great potential, in the process of being shunted into a short life of violent crime by the foreclosure of other opportunities. The film captured that potential before it could be snuffed out. The other is that by avoiding any coverage of the teenager's involvement in the drug trade, and the costs of that drug trade for the residents of Santa Marta, the film omits as much as it reveals about the nature of life in the community. These two readings are equally persuasive and complementary. Coutinho's film, designed as a counterweight to sensationalist depictions of favela violence, offers only half the picture.

By the late 1980s, public debate on favelas and drug trafficking was divided between these two extremes. On the Right were figures such as Emir Larangeira, who advocated a scorched-earth strategy for destroying traffickers, accepting collateral casualties as part of the cost of doing business. On the Left were figures like Jó Resende, who responded to questions about urban violence with answers about primary schools. Few public figures sought a middle ground.

Anthropologist Alba Zaluar was the most prominent exception. Zaluar's book *A máquina e a revolta* (The machine and the rebellion), published in 1985, investigated the survival strategies of the urban poor and working class in Cidade de Deus in the early 1980s, including analysis of the local drug traf-

FIG 4.6. A police commander prepares to meet the community of Santa Marta, 1987, Chiquito Chaves, CPDoc JB. This officer, shown armed with a double-gauge shotgun, a semiautomatic rifle, and a tear-gas canister, typified Moreira Franco's police. Like the young traffickers they set out to combat, the police used the theatrical display of weaponry to emphasize their own *disposição*, or readiness to do battle.

fic. Zaluar showed that the traffickers were not social bandits, that they brutally enforced hierarchy, and that conflicts between them took a heavy toll on local residents. She also showed that neighborhood associations in Cidade de Deus observed boundaries established by feuding traffickers, in turn reinforcing those boundaries, helping to demarcate turf.[52] Following publication of A *máquina e a revolta*, Zaluar deepened her research on favela traffickers, balancing an empathetic depiction of their constrained options with recognition of their pernicious influence. This work, along with that of a handful of other pioneers, helped to set the agenda for reconsiderations of favela violence in the mid-1990s and beyond.[53] In the late 1980s, however, Zaluar was rowing against the tide. In the meantime, state and city government continued to work through the favela associations, even as drug traffickers used those associations for their own ends.

The rapid expansion of drug-trafficking networks and the more covert expansion of the militias took place against a backdrop of demographic growth, economic crisis, and natural disaster. The failure of One Plot Per Family, the absence of any public popular housing construction, and the continued annual arrival of tens of thousands of migrants from rural Brazil resulted in continuing favela expansion. Iplan estimated that Rocinha alone grew 50 percent between 1980 and 1987. This growth complicated attempts to expand infrastructural and social services to favelas. Iplan's projects for managed favela consolidation were often outdated before any ground was broken.[54]

Sarney's economic plan functioned through 1986 and then collapsed in 1987. Hyperinflation returned with a vengeance, reaching greater rates in 1987 than it ever had before Sarney's election. Simultaneous currency devaluation and expanding demand for services strained Saturnino Braga's municipal budget, laying waste to his vision for socialist government. He tried in vain to cut city workers and close the CIEP construction factory, but was forced to retreat by fierce resistance from PDT council members, who demanded instead that he scrap his Community-Government Councils and grant the PDT control over city payrolls. At an impasse, Saturnino Braga walked out on the PDT, formally breaking with the party in July 1987, cutting his ties to Brizola.

Rarely has the mayor of a big city been so disdainful of the coalition that brought him to power. The maneuver left Braga with no base of parliamentary support. Brizola was furious and insisted that all PDT members immediately leave municipal employment. Most rank-and-file workers, such as favela agents in the Secretariat for Social Development, stayed put. Higher-ranking civil servants hoping for future PDT favors, however, could not risk alienating Brizola, and quit their jobs. The subsequent walkout left Braga's administration in tatters.[55] As for Brizola, the walkout might have satisfied his ego but left him marginalized from both city and state government. The Brizola reforms, deprived of strong supporters at either level of government, withered on the vine.

Braga's break with the PDT failed to endear him to President Sarney. His appeal for federal financial assistance was denied. Sarney also refused Braga permission to contract new international loans or to issue municipal bonds, leaving him with no way to raise the funds necessary to pay for his municipal commitments. As 1987 drew to a close, Braga was politically isolated, all of his bold initiatives beginning to come undone. Then things got really bad.

Heavy rains in February 1988 brought flooding in the lowlands of the north side and triggered landslides on hillside favelas. Cantagalo, Santa Marta, and Mangueira were all hit hard. Thousands of cariocas were displaced. Resende led the municipal government's response, orchestrating disaster relief and temporary housing, working closely with local leaders to ascertain the damage and direct resources to the neediest. The urgent response to the floods temporarily awakened the collaboration between grassroots social organization and municipal administration Resende had dreamed of. With no way to sustain this collaboration, however, the short-term achievements of flood relief became the medium-term problems of a penurious administration. Flood relief proved to be both the high point and the breaking point for the experiment in participatory government.

Resende housed most of the displaced flood and landslide victims in CIEPs, whose underutilized spaces—well equipped with ample showers and kitchens—seemed perfect for the purpose. The floods struck during summer vacation, and there was no immediate obstacle to using the CIEPs to house the homeless; indeed, it seemed to fulfill Brizola's vision for the schools as community centers and as a means for promoting social welfare. When February wore into March and April, though, the city had no place to move the displaced residents. As most of the city's schools resumed their activities, the affected CIEPs were stuck in neutral. A few of their teachers attempted to work around the temporary residents, or incorporate them into the pedagogy, but many simply declined to show up as long as their classrooms were being used for housing. The measure turned into one more hindrance to the successful education of Rio's poor.[56]

The flood response efforts further strained the municipal budget. Braga declared a state of municipal emergency on February 22, 1988, allowing him temporarily to override federal controls on deficit spending. Yet emergency expenditures only made meeting annual budget goals less likely. Defying federal proscriptions, Braga contracted short-term loans at crippling interest rates from private banks. Servicing the private debt left him unable to pay interest on outstanding loans from the Central Bank of Brazil and the State Bank of Rio de Janeiro. In August, the Central Bank blocked municipal accounts. Next, the State Bank refused to advance payroll funds, leaving Braga unable to pay municipal workers or interest on private loans. Facing the inevitable, on September 15, 1988, Braga officially declared municipal bankruptcy.[57]

Once it became clear they would not be paid, municipal workers walked off the job. Schools shut down, public hospitals reduced their services to minimal life support, streetlights went dark and daycare centers closed. The Municipal Secretariat for Social Development, the outpost of favela residents in government and provider of most city resources to favelas, shut down its field operations and all but shut its doors entirely. By the calendar, Braga's Socialist Municipal Administration still had three and a half months left in office. In reality, it was already over.

SIGNS OF EXHAUSTION

Moreira Franco's security strategy was reaching a simultaneous impasse. From one standpoint, that strategy had been remarkably efficient. Early in his administration, Moreira Franco had made a list of the twenty most powerful drug traffickers in the city and pledged to capture them. By early 1988, most had been arrested or killed in confrontations with the police. Moreira Franco did not hesitate to seize credit for taking the battle to the streets in an effort to wipe out the traffic. But from a pragmatic standpoint that strategy had been remarkably ineffective. Incarcerated traffickers continued to control their turf from prison, where they strengthened their alliances and coordinated strategy. Younger aspirants to power quickly emerged to take their place in the management of local operations.

Unlike their elders, the younger traffickers did not accumulate power through the gradual cultivation of alliances on the hill; they won it suddenly, in battle. In consequence, they were more rash and combative, and less durable. A trafficker named Bolado briefly prevailed in the skirmishes following Dênis's arrest and claimed preeminence in Rocinha, in effect claiming the privilege of serving as Dênis's local deputy. Following the new trend of press outreach pioneered in the Santa Marta conflict, he promptly gave an interview to reporters from the *Jornal do Brasil*, posing with his Israeli machine gun. Within weeks, he was killed by a rival.

In May 1988, Bolado's successor, Ednaldo de Souza, better known as Naldo, celebrated his own rise to power by posing for photographers from *Veja* magazine on a Rocinha rooftop and firing his machine gun into the air. Naldo and his soldiers invoked the rhetoric of social banditry, explaining to reporters that they represented the community and claiming that they were the new face of a social revolution that would sweep Brazil. The *Veja* article relaying their claims, however, noted that only weekly payoffs to corrupt police enabled Naldo and his soldiers to cling to power. Even this sensationalist coverage made it clear that Moreira Franco's security strategy was not so much eliminating Dênises as it was manufacturing Bolados and Naldos.[58]

Like Saturnino Braga, Moreira Franco appealed for federal assistance, asking Sarney for direct federal involvement in securing Rio's favelas. Sarney was willing to provide funding for a new prison complex but wanted nothing to do with policing the favelas. With direct presidential elections finally scheduled for 1989, no one in the federal government wanted to risk involvement in disastrous hillside battles in Rio. Moreira Franco soldiered on, sending his police to occupy Rocinha, briefly stifling the drug traffic. As in Santa Marta, police occupation was only temporary. By the close of 1988 everything was back to normal, or what was now accepted as normal: teenagers toting machine guns paid off police in order to keep selling cocaine to middle-class consumers while the remainder of the favela's population stepped gingerly in order to avoid offending them.

The Pastoral das Favelas, already weakened by the "paid *mutirão*" controversy of 1985, finally ran out steam entirely. Archibishop Sales had authorized the creation of the Pastoral das Favelas because he agreed with Father Ítalo Coelho that favela removal was an outrage, but he had never shared the Pastoral's commitment to radical social change. By 1985, removal was no longer an urgent threat, and Sales declined to authorize the Pastoral's application for another Ford Foundation grant. This shut down the Pastoral's juridical wing.

Eliana Athayde promptly created an NGO, naming it the Bento Rubião Foundation in honor of her former colleague, who had recently died of a sudden illness. Athayde applied for and received Ford Foundation support for the new organization, which carried on the Pastoral's legal work under a new name. The loss of the juridical wing robbed the Pastoral of much of its energy and influence, leaving field agents scattered throughout the city's favelas largely on their own. Archbishop Sales, keeping step with a papal turn against liberation theology, became increasingly critical of their work, reminding pastoral agents to focus on spiritual matters and avoid political controversy. By 1987, rousing pastoral seminars condemning police violence, hosted by the archbishop, were decidedly a thing of the past. By the end of 1988, as the city struggled through municipal bankruptcy and its consequences, most of the Pastoral das Favelas veterans who had led the surge a decade earlier had left the organization.

The favela federation's decline was equally marked. Both Governor Brizola and Vice-Mayor Resende had sought to incorporate that federation into their administrative structures, but those initiatives had foundered on the shoals of partisan conflict and drowned in the rising waters of fiscal crisis. In the process, the federation had lost both its connections to everyday favela life and its bid for greater political relevance. Individual association officers, increasingly subject to the control of traffickers or militias, largely opted out of the federation.

AS THIS DEEPENING turf control suggests, Rio's real bankruptcy was not fiscal but political. In November 1988, Marcello Alencar—Brizola's protégé—won elections to succeed Saturnino Braga, assuming office early in 1989. The day Saturnino Braga left office, enactment of new federal laws began to deliver greater shares of tax revenue to municipal government. With more money coming in and the cooperation of a PDT-controlled city council, Alencar quickly pulled the city out of fiscal bankruptcy. He paid municipal workers, and they returned to work. City government resumed operations, in its fashion.

Rio's political problems were more enduring, particularly regarding favela policy. The organizations that had shaped favela mobilization in the late 1970s and early 1980s, the Pastoral das Favelas and the favela federation, were depleted—pale shadows of their former selves. Brizola's socialismo moreno, Saturnino Braga's participatory Socialist Municipal Government, and Moreira Franco's gun-slinging rough justice had all been tested and found wanting. Yet with no viable new ideas forthcoming, cariocas seemed condemned to keep tinkering with the approaches of the past decade, looking for a combination that might see them through the next crisis.

The cyclical nature of Rio's political crisis was difficult to escape. Marcello Alencar reactivated the Municipal Secretariat of Social Development and resumed use of that Secretariat to funnel resources through favela associations. These resources were far from generous; they remained uneven and contingent in comparison with standard investment in public infrastructure and services in middle-class neighborhoods. That very contingency reinforced a politics of exception to the rule. Public spending on favelas was sequestered in a different category and sent through separate channels, already known to be subject to the influence of criminal interest groups. This was the crux of the matter: the problem did not lie in the nature of favela associations, which had previously served as the vanguard of democratization. The problem lay in the incorporation of criminal turf control into the operations of municipal government. Moreira Franco, meanwhile, carried on with his own strategy of hunting the leading donos do morro with extreme prejudice. This amounted to paying the traffickers with one hand while shooting at them with the other. Trafficker bribery of corrupt police completed the circle. The involvement of off-duty police in militias was another manifestation of this closed circuit. In effect, city and state government invested in maintaining favelas separate and vulnerable. Government administration exacerbated favela turf wars, rather than resolving them.

A CIEP in the Favela Rubens Vaz was symbolic of the city's political paralysis. Construction of the school was completed in final months of Brizola's administration. Municipal government was responsible for inaugurating and staffing the school, but Saturnino Braga never found the funds to do so. Moreira Franco—who scuttled further CIEP construction and cut funding for the program—was not willing to help, leaving the school an empty shell. In the wake of the 1988 floods, several families moved in. By the time Marcello Alencar took office, thirty families were living in the abandoned building, in desperate poverty. To make matters worse, the school sat in a no man's land running along the border of several favelas in the Complexo da Maré. When conflicts heated up between trafficking crews in rival areas within this favela complex, the schoolyard became a battleground. Residents of the abandoned CIEP were caught in the crossfire, literally and figuratively.

The school became a prominent example of an emerging phenomenon: it was the favela of the favela. Improved structural conditions and services in central areas of major favelas, results of the Brizola years, contrasted strongly with disadvantaged subareas, usually of more recent and peripheral settlement. The abandoned CIEP had the same kind of relationship to the Complexo de Maré as the Complexo de Maré had to the city at large; it was where the least fortunate were consigned to live. Municipal and state governments washed their hands of the problem. For years, the families holed up in the abandoned school languished in the no man's land of failed social and security policies, caught between rival gangs, waiting for resolution.

THE UNRAVELING

A violência da favela começou a
    descer pro asfalto
Homicídio, sequestro, assalto
Quem deveria dar a proteção
Invade a favela de fuzil na mão
	("*The violence of the favela begins to
	    descend to the asphalt*
	Homicide, kidnapping, robbery
	Those who should give protection
	Invade the favela with rifle in hand")

— MV BILL, "Soldado de Morro" (song), 1998.

Things got worse before they could get better. How could they not? There were no instant solutions forthcoming, and none of the problems had magically disappeared. Hyperinflation, unemployment, cocaine trafficking, corrupt and abusive police—all persisted. For the next several years, state and municipal civil servants behaved like zombies, scripted to carry out the same predictable actions repeatedly while the world rushed by and away from them.

There were glimmers of hope as the 1980s drew to a close, but none that promised change any time soon. During the Constitutional Assembly of 1988, delegates from Rio de Janeiro successfully pushed for inclusion of mechanisms for urban reform in the final document. Specifically, the Constitution of 1988 included provisions guaranteeing the right to housing and requiring urban property to serve a "social function." The document granted rights of adverse possession to residents who could show ten years of uncontested occupancy and gave municipal governments the power to alter building and zoning codes based on "special social interest." The constitution itself resolved nothing, but it gave both citizens and municipal governments new tools to use in guaranteeing a place in the city for the urban poor.

The presidential campaign of 1989 held out high hopes initially, but these were soon dashed. Brizola and Lula, both viable candidates, promised to put the full weight of federal government behind thoroughgoing social reform. Lula surprisingly edged out Brizola in the first round, finishing in the top two along with northeastern regional oligarch Fernando Collor de Mello. Brizola checked his impatience with Lula's PT long enough to support the fellow leftist in the second round. Even the combined forces of Lula and Brizola, however, could not match the powerful media campaign, backed by the influential Globo empire, that swept Collor to victory. The new president made clear from the outset that he had no interest in taking on Rio de Janeiro's problems. There was no use looking to the federal government; Rio would not be saved from above.

Violence within Rio continued to escalate. By the end of his term in office at the close of 1990, Moreira Franco's campaign promise to put an end to urban violence in six months became a punch line of local politics. It became impossible to ignore his administration's failure to contain the Comando Vermelho and rival networks. The new constitution precluded Moreira Franco from running for a second term, but he would not have stood a chance in any case. The failure of his security policy, the peg on which he hoped to hang his administration, made it impossible for him to anoint a successor. Instead, Rio's citizens turned to another familiar candidate: Leonel Brizola won the gubernatorial elections of 1990 easily, returning to office early in 1991.

Brizola's return symbolized the essence of Rio's politics in the 1990s. They amounted to a remix of hits from the 1980s, this time without the hopeful swelling of the orchestra in the background. Criminal turf monopolization in Rio's favelas deepened, with local crews arrogating the powers to control circulation and shut down local commerce. Drug trafficking networks expanded from the favelas with the most lucrative markets to hundreds of locations throughout the city, linked in competing networks. The militias responded in turn, expanding steadily through the city's west side. Criminal networks—both traffickers and militias— became integrated further in city and state politics, through local associations and direct support for corrupt officeholders.

Although the associations continued to function as conduits for municipal funding, no one looked to them anymore as agents of change. Instead, new NGOs assumed that mantle. The NGOs had nothing, however, to guarantee their safe passage besides good intentions and delicate diplomacy, and they worked within the prevailing political bargain rather than confronting it. They denounced police violence but could not risk doing the same for criminal turf monopolization. Security policies swung wildly between militarized incursions that treated favelas as enemy territory and community policing that failed to undermine criminal networks. The cumulative result of these factors was the reinforcement of the understanding of favelas as zones of exception, outside the rule of law and expectations of rights that applied elsewhere in the city.

As Rio's violent 1990s have been investigated in detail elsewhere, this chapter will present only an overview of that unraveling, concentrating on the reasons new attempts at reform inevitably ran into old obstacles to change, failing to bridge the gap between favela and city.

A CITY AT ODDS WITH ITSELF

The result of the gubernatorial elections of 1990 was the same as in 1982, but the context and expectations had changed greatly. This time around, participation in the campaign and election was desultory instead of exuberant. Beyond the die-hard brizolistas, few expected a new Brizola administration to resolve Rio's problems. The governor's own expectations were unclear. His presidential ambitions delayed, he needed to craft a credible administration in Rio to lay the groundwork for another national campaign in 1994. He began by reviving many of the key projects from his first administration.

Rather than attempting another massive titling project, Brizola picked up where he had left off in education and security. He restarted construction of new CIEPs and restored full levels of funding for the existing schools. This did not immediately resolve the issue of the squatter-occupied CIEP in Nova Holanda, which fell between the cracks of municipal and state administration for another three years, but it did expand enrollment in functioning CIEPs, without addressing other shortcomings of the model.

Brizola also brought back Nazareth Cerqueira, this time as secretary of security, with authority over both military and civil police. Nazareth Cerqueira had changed more than Brizola. His vision for Rio's police remained much the same, though his strategy for pursuing that vision was less radical. He took greater pains to persuade officers of the wisdom of community policing and nonviolent crime prevention, skirting the senior commanders that had obstructed his reforms and working directly with younger officers where possible. And he recognized that community policing could itself become so diluted or corrupted that it created more problems than it solved. More than a change in unit structure, Rio's police needed a change in culture, and Nazareth Cerqueira now understood that change could not be achieved overnight. This time around, he moved more cautiously.

Nazareth Cerqueira took steps to smoke out, dismiss, and prosecute corrupt officers. He was greatly hampered in this both by widespread acceptance of illegal payoffs within the officer corps and by the deeply rooted problems of the Brazilian judiciary. Brazil's courts had historically been structured in ways that practically guaranteed that wealthy and well-connected defendants would be exonerated and that poor defendants would face incarceration in degrading, unsafe conditions even before sentencing. The military dictatorship, which had relied on military police as the unrestrained advance guard in enforcing order, had exacerbated these problems. Nazareth Cerqueira had the power to dismiss low-ranking officers from the force and did so whenever evidence supported this action. But it was nearly impossible to prosecute and convict higher-ranking officers for corruption or abuse of force.

Several battalions had embraced the confrontational strategies of the Moreira Franco administration and were loath to abandon them, particularly Emir Larangeira's Ninth, on the city's far north side. Larangeira himself stepped down as battalion commander in 1990 to run successfully for state deputy, elected, as he described it, "by his comrades in the Military Police and numerous friends." Nonetheless, his methods remained in force in the Ninth. As a legislator, Larangeira became another obstacle to Nazareth Cerqueira's reforms, criticizing proceedings against officers accused of malfeasance. Although Nazareth Cerqueira inspired a cohort of younger officers who would eventually lead the way toward deeper reform, in the short term he was unable to rein in police violence.[1]

A few statistics reveal the parameters. In 1982 there were twenty-three homicides per 100,000 residents in the metropolitan region of Rio de Janeiro. That number rose to thirty-three in 1985, to forty-six in 1988, and sixty-three in 1991. It finally peaked at seventy-three in 1994. Anything above 30 per 100,000 is generally considered intolerably high by international standards. (By way of comparison, New York City's rate in the late

1980s was thirty, a period considered one of the most violent in the city's history. By 2006 it had fallen to six.) Rio's homicide rates in this period climbed steadily no matter who was governor; the indices continued to rise precipitously under both Brizola's community policing and Moreira Franco's aggressive crackdown. Looking specifically at the cohort at greatest risk—males from fifteen to nineteen years old—in 1990, for every 100,000 of these youths, 190 were killed in a shooting, a rate that remained consistent throughout the 1990s. Rio's mortality rates for young men were higher than those in any active war zone.[2]

Several notorious episodes of the early 1990s reveal more about the period than the raw numbers. In July 1990, eleven residents of Acari were kidnapped by a group of armed men identifying themselves as police. The favelados, including several suspects of theft, had previously informed friends that they were the targets of police threats and extortion. They had taken refuge at a cabin outside the city, where the gunmen tracked them, beat them, demanded money, and took them prisoner. None was ever seen again. The sole surviving witness—the grandmother of one of the victims, who had fled into the woods when the gunmen arrived—implicated the police. Mothers of several of the victims began a campaign for justice, demanding investigation of extortion and abuse in the military police's Ninth Battalion, responsible for policing Acari. State prosecutors investigated but did not successfully prosecute any officer, nor offer a coherent explanation of the episode. One of the mothers was also subsequently assassinated, with strong indications of police participation in her death. The "mothers of Acari," as they became known, never got any answers, much less justice.[3]

In the summer of 1992, teenagers from Vigário Geral and other north side favelas initiated several melees on Ipanema beach. Journalists labeled these events *arrastões*, or dragnets, for the way that dozens of teenagers simultaneously swept up the waterfront stealing cash, cameras, and watches from beachgoers. It was clear from the outset that these events were more terrifying than lucrative. Depending on one's perspective, they were either a manifestation of rage and resentment or a celebration of anarchy and impunity. Compared to the bloodshed of frequent engagements between drug gangs and police, the arrastões were relatively mild. Their theatricality, however, brought extensive attention and their very futility symbolized a city where the rule of law had fundamentally eroded. The arrastões triggered calls for a crackdown on favela youth gone astray, mostly issued by middle-class cariocas, complicating Nazareth Cerqueira's efforts to restrain police violence.[4]

More damaging to the collective carioca psyche were the events of 1993. In late July that year, police assassinated eight homeless youths — ranging in age from eleven to eighteen — where they had been sleeping, outside the Candelária Church in downtown Rio. The breezeways fronting office buildings across from the church were a popular spot for homeless cariocas; as many as sixty were sleeping there on the night of the massacre. The police and accomplices simply opened fire, killing victims randomly. Nazareth Cerqueira acted swiftly to discover and prosecute the perpetrators. Still, only three gunmen were convicted, despite clear indications that several more were involved.

Only a month later, Rio hit bottom. On the August 28, 1993, traffickers in Vigário Geral killed four off-duty military policemen from the Ninth Battalion, reportedly after their customary arrangements for buying police protection had broken down. The following day, a team of several dozen hooded gunmen descended on the favela, moving from house to house and assassinating residents — an act of indiscriminate, collective vengeance exacted from the favela at large. In contrast to the hillside favelas of the south side, Vigário Geral is an expanse of one- and two-story buildings in the low-lying north side flatlands. The main entrance is a *passarela*, or pedestrian bridge across the adjacent Avenida Brasil, a major highway. A pedestrian on the bridge can survey the entire favela, and this was where corrupt police would customarily meet traffickers for payment. Beyond the pedestrian bridge, there is only one other exit from Vigário Geral, easily blocked by a single squad car. For the gunmen on that August night, it was like a closed shooting gallery.

Twenty-one residents were killed, none with any link to the drug traffic. Survivors displayed the corpses in two lines of open coffins in Vigário Geral's plaza, the bloody and contorted bodies a horrific testament to Rio's state of disorder. Newspapers and magazines around the world published grisly photographs of the coffins, making Rio, at least temporarily, the symbolic world capital of urban violence.

Nazareth Cerqueira acted swiftly, expelling dozens of suspects from the force and initiating prosecutions. Thirty-three officers were initially accused of participating in the massacre, but the prosecution was plagued by dubious testimony, sloppy forensics, and forged evidence. A second round of investigations resulted in formal accusations of more than a dozen additional officers. Only a handful of officers were convicted for participating in the massacre and most of those secured release from prison while they appealed their sentences, a process that can take well over a decade in Brazil. Only one officer remained in jail for more than a few years.[5]

The Vigário Geral massacre made clear that neither Brizola nor Nazareth Cerqueira had control over Rio's police, or any means of guaranteeing the civil rights of favela residents. In the wake of the massacre, no one looked to the favela association for help. Since the late 1980s Vigário Geral's association had functioned at the pleasure of the local trafficking crew. The association president had lobbied state government to keep military police out of the community, in practice leaving traffickers to establish authority. For several years, the traffickers maintained that autonomy through payoffs to the police. When that system broke down, residents—rather than the leading traffickers, who had taken refuge elsewhere—were left to pay the price. The massacre was the brutal consequence of the forces set in motion a decade earlier—a failed structure of local political representation, compounded by internal conflict and corruption in the police force subjected local residents first to violent turf control and then to brutal police retribution.[6]

THE NGO WAVE AND THE EVOLUTION OF THE DRUG TRAFFIC

The Vigário Geral massacre also revealed that no solutions were forthcoming from within either municipal or state administration. Nongovernmental organizations arose to do what government could not, attempting to bolster the citizenship of Rio's unprotected classes. The new NGOs were more disciplined and focused offspring of the grassroots movements of the late 1970s, but lacked their transformative agenda and ability to inspire broad participation. Vigário Geral itself became ground zero for the NGO wave. Social service organizations had been active in Rio's favelas for decades, and the closure of the Pastoral das Favelas' judicial wing and inauguration of the Bento Rubião Foundation in 1986 had marked the first sign of an impending transition from grassroots mobilization to targeted NGO action. The reactions to the Vigário Geral massacre then focused and hastened this transition.

Several influential NGOs sprang directly from Vigário Geral or from partnerships between Vigário Geral activists and outsiders forged in the wake of the massacre. The most influential of these were Afro-Reggae, the

Casa da Paz, and Viva Rio. Prior to the massacre, *Afro-Reggae* had been a newsletter on favela youth culture published sporadically by a few Vigário Geral residents. Afterward, it began organizing youth culture activities to draw teenagers away from drug trafficking. Afro-Reggae's leaders looked to outside partners to support and publicize these initiatives. By the early 2000s, Afro-Reggae had grown into a massive NGO with dozens of corporate sponsorships, organizing youth culture programs in favelas across Rio, partnering in projects in other Brazilian cities, and sending performance groups around the world.[7]

Casa da Paz had an equally promising takeoff though more turbulent growth. Local activists founded the institution in partnership with an influential group of outsiders, including Betinho of Ibase and Rubém César Fernandes, director of the Instituto Sociológico do Estudo da Religião (ISER, the Sociological Institute for the Study of Religion). Both Ibase and ISER were think tanks with interests in direct action social services but constrained by the need to maintain an objective and scholarly profile. Even before the Vigário Geral massacre, their leaders had been interested in creating an NGO capable of drawing on Ibase and ISER policy recommendations in the creation of nimble, focused social service projects. Casa da Paz became the first of these, initiated in conjunction with the early growth of Viva Rio, the larger NGO.[8]

The initial structural relationship bore some similarities to that between individual associations and the favela federation in the early 1980s; Casa da Paz was an autonomous local project linked to broader activities across the city, and given greater political projection, by Viva Rio. That similarity was shaped by the understanding of the new favela NGOs as replacements for the decadent associations and their federation. They were intended to revive, in a more focused way, the spirit of favela mobilization of the late 1970s. Not for nothing did Viva Rio describe itself as a "movement," rather than an organization.

In the first few years after the massacre, Casa da Paz ran community education classes and executed well-publicized popular actions to bring media attention to Vigário Geral. By the end of the 1990s, however, Casa da Paz had fallen prey to internal dissent and lost traction in the community.[9] Viva Rio, in contrast, grew into Rio's largest and most prominent NGO, the whale in the midst of a school of fish.

By the end of the 1990s, thousands of NGOs were active in favelas across Rio, ranging from tiny organizations run by two or three local residents to

Viva Rio, run by hundreds of volunteers and paid staff and bringing in millions of dollars in domestic and international financing for dozens of simultaneous projects. The NGO wave brought funding to favelas, opened opportunities for employment and economic and educational advancement, and brought consistent media attention, inhibiting the kind of police abuse that had thrived on anonymity and social invisibility.[10] There were, and are, outstanding favela NGOs that made impressive gains in local healthcare and education. The Centro de Estudos e Ações Solidárias de Maré (CEASM, Center for Study and Solidary Action of Maré), in the Complexo de Maré on Rio's north side, initiated pioneering preparatory courses for college entrance exams and public employment exams, among numerous other projects. The number of local residents winning coveted spots in public universities and white-collar civil service jobs rose dramatically.

In order to carry out their projects, however, NGO organizers, whether they lived in the favelas in which they worked or came from elsewhere, had to submit to the same "law of the hill"; respecting the dominance of the local trafficking crew or militia was accepted as the price of access. NGOs were able to improve public health, education, cultural programming, job training and community outreach. The one thing they were not permitted to do was to challenge trafficker control of territory. Where necessary, the NGOs operated within the new political map of criminal turf monopolization and remained silent about the compromises this required. An internal document from the offices of Viva Rio, written in mid-1994, reveals the nature of this compromise. Viva Rio's directors summarized their early work in Rio's favelas, noting a preference to work with local associations where possible. In Mangueira's case they noted that options were limited, as "the residents' association is weak and at the mercy of the *tráfico*." It was the kind of observation Viva Rio could circulate in an internal memo but could not afford to make in public, at the risk of losing access to the favela.[11]

The traffickers quickly learned to capitalize on NGO strategies. Only in rare cases did traffickers directly take over local NGOs, perhaps because the NGOs were often transitory and had no accepted mediating role with municipal government, making them less inviting targets than the associations. Instead, traffickers used NGO activity to get out their own message. In 1995, Viva Rio organized a march against urban violence through downtown streets, calling the event Reage Rio (React Rio). Viva Rio and allied organizations led 150,000 white-clad citizens in a show of civic concern. Traffickers, however, easily turned the diffuse protest against violence to their own ends. Several *donos* hired buses and sent hundreds of favela residents to the march in order to protest police violence. Their strategy hinged on the prospect that the police could be constrained by popular mobilization. The traffickers themselves felt no such constraint.[12]

Instead, traffickers laid low as long as attention was focused on their neighborhood, then resumed operations. In Vigário Geral, for example, traffickers were back in action by 1994, and they were soon exercising authority over the favela association more strongly than ever before. Turf wars between the local crew and rivals across the highway in the adjacent neighborhood of Parada de Lucas ripped through the region several times in the late 1990s and early 2000s, interrupted only by a short-lived community police operation in 1996–97.[13] Vigário Geral's crew allied with the Comando Vermelho, whereas Parada de Lucas's looked to the rival Terceiro Comando. This dynamic was typical, as similar splits emerged in adjacent favelas in Borel and Chácara do Céu, in Cantagalo and Pavão-Pavãozinho, in Vidigal and Rocinha. In each case, the involvement of the larger networks, engaged in capillary turf struggles throughout the city, guaranteed the perpetuation of local conflict.[14]

During the late 1990s, these criminal networks became the most feared entities in Rio de Janeiro. Their organizational structure made them highly effective and singularly difficult to dismantle. They were hierarchical but flexible and characterized by constant turnover of personnel in the field. Senior commanders such as Escadinha and Dênis organized drug trafficking from prison, marshaling resources to arrange for shipment and distribution of cocaine and weapons. At the same time, local crew chiefs dispersed throughout the city acted with extensive autonomy. When one died in action or was arrested, another quickly took his place. This flexible structure meant that the networks could not guarantee loyalty. Twice in the 1990s, brash young commanders split from the CV, organizing smaller rival factions. This decentralization also meant the networks could not be crushed from the top down; they spread like mushrooms throughout the city.

The style of local crew chiefs changed dramatically. Escadinha and Dênis by no means eschewed violence; each was directly or indirectly responsible for dozens of violent deaths. Their hold on community influence, however, depended as strongly on the distribution of favors and the cultivation of alliances as it did on violence. The generation of traffickers who rose to power in the late 1990s carried violence to new extremes. Patrick Salgado

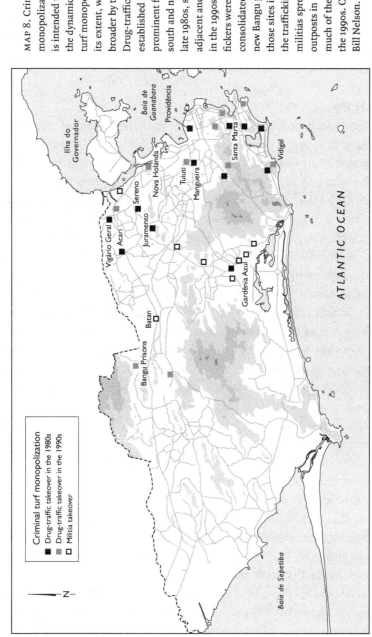

MAP 8. Criminal turf monopolization. This map is intended to show only the dynamics of criminal turf monopolization, not its extent, which was much broader by the mid-1990s. Drug-trafficking networks established strongholds in prominent favelas on the south and north sides by the late 1980s, spreading out to adjacent and nearby locations in the 1990s. As leading traffickers were arrested, they consolidated power inside the new Bangu prisons, turning those sites into a new hub of the trafficking network. The militias spread from initial outposts in the 1980s through much of the city's west side in the 1990s. Cartography by Bill Nelson.

Criminal turf monopolization
■ Drug-traffic takeover in the 1980s
▨ Drug-traffic takeover in the 1990s
□ Militia takeover

—N—

Ilha do Governador

Baía de Guanabara

Providência

Santa Marta

Vidigal

Vigário Geral
Acari
Sereno
Juramento
Nova Holanda
Tuiuti
Mangueira

Gardênia Azul

Batan

Bangu Prisons

ATLANTIC OCEAN

Baía de Sepetiba

Souza Martins, better known as Patrick do Vidigal, gained notoriety for taking his rivals prisoner and cutting off their limbs with a machete. Elias Pereira da Silva, better known as Elias Maluco (Elias the Madman), placed victims in a cylindrical stack of gasoline-soaked automobile tires and set them on fire. Traffickers were joined in competition to commit the most spectacular acts of savagery to terrify local residents, underlings, and rivals and to impress imprisoned superiors.[15]

THE SECURITY PENDULUM

Rio's security forces proved incapable of a coherent and effective response. After the horrors of 1993, calls mounted for federal intervention. Brizola would likely have resisted any federal involvement in state security, but he soon lost any authority over the issue. He stepped down as governor in April 1994, in an ill-fated campaign for president. In contrast to 1989, when he remained a strong contender through the first round, in 1994 Brizola was an "also-ran." The ongoing security crisis in Rio was an insuperable liability. Fernando Henrique Cardoso, buoyed by the success of the anti-inflationary economic plan he had initiated as minister of finance under sitting president Itamar Franco, coasted to victory.

Brizola's renunciation left his vice-governor Nilo Batista the temporary occupant of the governor's chair, and Batista did not have the influence to muster resistance to federal intervention. In October 1994, the army made its move, sending thousands of troops to "occupy" twelve key Rio favelas. Officially, this was a partnership between the army and the state police, but few doubted that both Batista and Nazareth Cerqueira had accepted the terms of the agreement under duress and had no control over the operation.[16]

"Operation Rio," as the army dubbed it, had few lasting consequences other than to demonstrate that the army had no magic solutions. Tanks rolled into favelas and sat obtrusively at key intersections. Heavily armed soldiers demanded identification from schoolchildren and conducted bracing morning calisthenics. The price of cocaine rose temporarily during the operation, indicating a constricted supply. Even so, turf wars between criminal factions continued. Also, these factions continued to exercise the power to shut down local commerce, a prerogative they had taken to exercising whenever a key trafficker was killed in combat. In memorial to the fallen soldier and as a demonstration of their power, they would send out a message to shopkeepers in the surrounding area to shut their doors for the day. Operation Rio proved unable to put an end to the practice. Crime in the metropolitan area actually rose during Operation Rio, an increase that several local scholars attributed to displacement. Army occupation forced traffickers to look further afield and practice different crimes to bring in resources. Operation Rio came to end in February 1995, leaving the city in the same condition it had been six months earlier.[17]

In the meantime, Marcello Alencar managed to avoid Saturnino Braga's fate as mayor and survived his term with enough popular support to win the 1994 gubernatorial election. Upon taking office, he named Nilton Cerqueira his secretary of security. In one of the ironies of common Brazilian family names, Nilton Cerqueira shared the unrelated Nazareth's last name but differed from him in almost every other way. Whereas Nazareth had risen through the police force, Nilton Cerqueira was an army general who had commanded repression of revolutionary guerrilla factions during the dictatorship. Alencar's hope—and Nilton Cerqueira's promise—was that stifling the drug-trafficking networks would be no more challenging than defeating the guerrillas. They were mistaken.

Nilton Cerqueira brought back and intensified the policies of confrontation used in the Moreira Franco administration. He rewarded officers with "bravery bonuses" and "bravery promotions" for aggressive action against traffickers. These incentives could quickly quadruple the pay of a street-level officer and contributed to a sharp rise in violent confrontations and civilian casualties. Under Nilton Cerqueira's direction, Rio's police killed six times as many people as they had under Nazareth Cerqueira, many of these innocent bystanders caught in the crossfire. Between August 1995 and February 1996, the Ninth Battalion alone killed seventy-five civilians. Some cariocas applauded these casualties as an indication of effective policing, but the drug wars raged on unabated. For favela residents, fear of *balas perdidas*, stray bullets, became a constant undercurrent of life in the city.[18]

Although Marcello Alencar had entered carioca politics as Brizola's protégé, his support for Nilton Cerqueira's gunslinging security policy demonstrated a clear break with his former mentor. This was not unusual, as Brizola was the King Lear of Rio's politics; most of the state's prominent politicians owed their start to Brizola, but all turned against him to one degree or another. No case was more curious than that of Anthony Garotinho, a former radio broadcaster from the north of the state of Rio who served as secretary of agriculture in Brizola's second administration. Garotinho ran successfully for governor on the PDT ticket in 1998, promising brizolista reforms, including subsidies for the urban poor and community policing. Garotinho went so far as to hire academic researchers to ghostwrite a security policy paper for him, advocating an end to militarized incursions in favelas.[19] As governor, Garotinho followed up on some of these promises, yet did so in an openly personalist way that made Brizola's own social spending look evenhanded and politically neutral by comparison. Garotinho quickly built his own political machine, separating himself from Brizola.

This break was particularly striking and consequential in the field of public security. Garotinho appointed one of his ghostwriters, the anthropologist Luiz Eduardo Soares, as the sub-secretary of security and charged him with overseeing the community-policing strategy. Soares initiated pilot projects in several favelas, most prominently Cantagalo and Pavão-Pavãozinho.[20] On the surface, Rio's policing strategies swung 180 degrees back in the direction favored by Brizola and Nazareth Cerqueira. In marked contrast to Brizola, however, Garotinho did not even try to carry out deeper police reform. The community police efforts were a façade for politics as usual. When Soares accused senior officers of corruption, the governor found a pretext to fire him. Deprived of police protection and fearing retribution from enemies on the force, Soares soon fled to the United States.[21] Garotinho then limited community policing to the pilot projects, avoiding further reform.

The pilot projects themselves had uneven results. In Cantagalo and Pavão-Pavãozinho, Major Antônio Carballo Blanco, the project's first commander, was a disciple of Nazareth Cerqueira and himself a scholar of best practices in community policing. As long as Carballo Blanco remained in charge, the project succeeded in diminishing violence while breaking down long-standing hostilities between police and local residents.[22] In 2002, his efforts received some support from interim governor Benedita da Silva, who assumed office when Garotinho stepped down to run for the presidency. Benedita da Silva was a longtime resident of the favela Chapéu Mangueira, a few kilometers down the beach from Cantagalo and had gotten her start in politics in that favela's association. In one respect, her ascendancy to the governor's office was the administrative high watermark for the favela movement, the culmination of the practice of seizing political appointments initiated with Brizola's election of 1982. Silva was the first woman, the first black citizen, and the first favela resident to rise to the post of governor. But Silva governed within Garotinho's administrative structure, which allowed for no serious effort to eliminate police corruption. She committed some resources to community policing, but few observers had any illusion that her commitment would endure.[23]

Rosinha Matheus, Garotinho's wife, won the gubernatorial election of 2002, taking office in 2003. Matheus completed the shift back to aggressive police strategies. She replaced Carballo Blanco with a hard-line officer, and local police returned to their truculent ways. Community policing in Cantagalo and Pavão-Pavãozinho, like the remainder of the pilot projects, gradually fizzled.[24]

THE ASSOCIATIONS IN THE 1990S

As Vigário Geral's experience suggested, favela associations continued to suffer the intrusions of the trafficking networks. Association officers who resisted the influence of the traffickers, or whose alliance with one faction left them vulnerable when rivals seized control, paid the consequences. Over the course of the 1990s, favela association president became the riskiest occupation in Rio. In 2002, the Human Rights Commission in Rio's state assembly issued the findings of a special investigation indicating that over the previous decade dozens of favela association officers had been assassinated, and many more forced to leave their communities. Precise figures were impossible to verify, but several notorious cases — along with the rising ferocity of the traffickers — lent credence to these estimates.[25]

In Nova Holanda, for example, Eliana Sousa Silva served three terms as the association president in the 1980s and early 1990s and then stepped down. The next president left both the office and the community suddenly after a shift in local trafficking power. His successor immediately established close relationships to local traffickers and ran the association as a closed shop. In Silva's analysis, "There is a sense . . . in which you can only survive if you have relationships with the tráfico, with those armed groups, so that they understand what you are doing. And lots of people believe that that is the only way to continue. I think that the residents' associations started making concessions within that logic, and that generated very close involvement with those groups. And everything just *degringolou* (disintegrated) from then on."[26] When the ablest and most committed leaders left the associations to work in NGOs, the associations remained in the hands of those willing to compromise with the traffickers or the militias, if not act in their direct service. When turf changed hands, those officers fled or suffered retribution.

Once traffickers exercised control over local associations, they used those associations to expel critics from the favela and distribute employment and resources to allies. In 1999, for example, municipal government hired the private contracting firm EC Engineering for an infrastructural project in Borel. Following standard practice, the contractor hired local workers through the favela association but soon found that local traffickers were controlling the hiring. Unhappy with the workers, the contractor abandoned the project, and the municipal government passed the contract on to a different firm. In the analysis of Borel's association president, "EC Engineering was a Northeastern contractor, and they were not used to the favela."[27] The implication was that firms used to doing business in the favela had grown accustomed to trafficker demands.

Militia-controlled associations exercised even stricter authority over favela residence and employment. Because most militia members were police or firemen, they had greater access to formal political power than the traffickers, and they used that access to cultivate close ties to city and state government. Several key militia leaders won elections for city council and state assembly and used these posts to direct resources to militia-led associations and protect them from juridical interference. The favela association, an instrument of mobilization and unification in the late 1970s, had become an instrument of containment and division.[28]

FAVELA-BAIRRO

César Maia, Rio's mayor in the mid-1990s and again in the early 2000s, was another of Brizola's prodigal sons. He had gotten his start in politics as Brizola's staff economist and eventually broke with Brizola precisely over questions of economy. César Maia was seduced by the siren song of neoliberal reform whereas Brizola remained faithful to socialism—at least in principle—until his death. As mayor, Maia sought to initiate third-way reforms, eliminating open-ended entitlements and creating high-profile, targeted projects that were funded by private and international partners. Key to this strategy was Maia's partnership with the Inter-American Development Bank in creating Favela-Bairro, a project whose name indicated its putative goal: to overcome the differences between favelas and the rest of the city, turning favelas into regular neighborhoods, or *bairros*.[29]

The program invested in upgrading projects in over one hundred favelas. Teams hired by Favela-Bairro crafted sophisticated urban interventions and sought to build community support through the incorporation of popular suggestions and the preference for local employment. Favela-Bairro effectively put into practice many of the initiatives imagined by the underfunded Iplan during the Saturnino Braga administration. Many of its projects were successful interventions in urban space; the program's expanded streets and public plazas were immediately appealing. Yet Favela-Bairro included no tools to bridge the legal gap between favela and city, nor any meaningful commitment to maintenance.[30]

The design of Favela-Bairro, at least in its early stages, strongly reflected the misapprehension of favelas as places where the state was absent. Sérgio Ferraz Magalhães, the architect Maia chose as the key administrator for the program, considered the favelas "degraded by the absence of the Brazilian state" and guided the project to rectify that perceived absence.[31] Favela-Bairro was designed to deliver more state to the favelas, in the form of infrastructure and public employment. The program did not begin to confront the ways in which city and state policies *reinforced* distinctions between favela and bairro.

As a municipally administered program, Favela-Bairro had no power to address issues of security. Consequently, the program had no positive effect on the control of criminal networks over favela territory. On the contrary, by raising the value of that territory, Favela-Bairro may have contributed to the strength of those networks. As one scholar noted, "Trafficker power . . . comes not from state absence, but, rather, from the way that the state is present."[32] In several communities, traffickers quickly took over the pocket plazas created by Favela-Bairro, using them as drug bazaars. Similarly, Favela-Bairro had no control over land titling. The program's stated goal of extending property title to favela residents was merely a rhetorical flourish because the program included no mechanism for titling and did not contribute to any expansion of property title in favelas. Instead, it coincided with rising rates of housing informality and, by making informal real estate more valuable, probably contributed to them. As a series of targeted infrastructural and architectural projects, Favela-Bairro was reasonably successful. It did not and could not address the deeper political separation between favela and bairro.

VIOLENCE AND DEMOCRACY

As Rocinha was to Rio, so Rio was to the rest of Brazil, to Latin America, and indeed to the Global South. The simultaneous expansion of formal democracy and rise of entrenched urban violence in Rio prefigured transitions elsewhere. São Paulo, twice the size of Rio and growing even faster, went through similar convulsions in the late 1980s and through the 1990s. São Paulo's attempt to incorporate the urban poor into participatory democracy was equally fraught. Because of its spatial and topographical differences, characterized by less shoulder-to-shoulder rubbing between rich and poor than Rio, its eruptions of violence tended to attract less media attention. Not always—the massacre of 111 prisoners in Carandiru Prison by São Paulo's state military police in October 1992 was as horrific as the massacres that shook Rio the following year, and they had similar effects on the urban psyche. São Paulo's transition to architecture and lifestyles of urban brutalism was, if anything, more complete than Rio's, as there was no beach culture to soften the city's image.[33]

Transitions in São Paulo, a mere five hours from Rio away by car, were linked closely to those in Rio, in both negative and positive ways. São Paulo's major criminal faction, the Primeiro Comando da Capital (PCC, First Command of the Capital), at first modeled itself on the Comando Vermelho, then allied with it. In the early 2000s the affiliated networks collaborated in distributing drugs and arms and seemed to compete with one another in displays of power, shutting down their respective state capitals through displays of exemplary violence. But the gangs were not the only ones building connections. As in Rio, a generation of São Paulo's scholars turned its attention to the problems of urban violence, and these scholars gradually forged connections to municipal and state government.[34]

Bogotá and Medellín spiraled into endemic violence even more catastrophically than did Rio, their problems compounded by the presence of the dominant cocaine cartels, as well as by the enduring social schisms of unresolved civil war. Again, these challenges gave rise to entire new academic fields, and eventually to new collaborations between academics and policymakers: Colombia's *violentólogos*, or scholars of violence, became world renowned.

Buenos Aires, Mexico City, Caracas, Lima—no major Latin American city was immune to the problems of rising urban violence in the late 1980s and through the 1990s. In most of these cities, this transition accompanied a return from dictatorship to democracy, or an expansion of the practices of formal democracy to include previously excluded classes. Following routes of drugs and arms trafficking, rising violence struck major hemispheric metropoles first. It then spread out to secondary cities—Belo Horizonte, Nuevo Laredo, Managua, Guatemala City. As in Rio's favelas, except on a continental scale, the transition in each city was an epic unique in its details but conforming to encompassing patterns. Homicides climbed as administrations scrambled ineffectually to contain violence while meeting expanding social demands. In all these cities, interest groups with a stake in reproducing cyclical violence found ways to infiltrate government or at least exert strong influence over it, guaranteeing repeated conflict.

Just as there was no single cause for this combination, there has been no single solution. Few cities have even begun to bend the homicide curve. Bogotá was first, followed by São Paulo. In both these cities, by the early 2000s scholars of violence and urban planning had joined forces with policymakers to forge a new generation of reforms. Strategies differed across these cities, but both concentrated on reducing homicides first to make way for combined infrastructural upgrading and expansion of social services. In both, new strategies have propelled and been bolstered by economic growth which, in its turn, has expanded employment opportunities and defused some of the most immediate reasons for discontent.

São Paulo's experiences were most directly relevant for Rio. Beginning in the early 2000s, a network of NGO activists, academics, and policymakers began to craft a loosely connected menu of initiatives to combat police corruption, target preventive policing where it was most needed, and strengthen prison security, reducing the hold of the PCC over state penitentiaries. At the same time, city and state government expanded social services, particularly popular education and job training. These initiatives did not yield immediate improvement; instead, they took hold gradually, slowly turning the tide.

CARIOCAS — AND FAVELA RESIDENTS, in particular — had to wait longer. Yet they did not wait idly. Rising violence and criminal turf control notwithstanding, Rio's favelados seized whatever new opportunities became available in the 1990s and early 2000s. They did so most prominently in education: the first generation of university graduates from the favelas earned their diplomas in the 1980s and early 1990s — figures such as Hélio Oliveira, Itamar Silva, and Eliana Sousa Silva. Over the rest of the 1990s, *favelados universitários* became more common at both private universities and Rio's highly selective public universities.

As always, broader trends shaped individual possibilities. Brizola's educational initiatives, whatever their shortcomings, massively expanded the population of favela residents with the opportunity to earn a high school degree. The military regime, for very different reasons, had supported the expansion of public universities, an expansion carried over into the democratic period.[35] The success of the 1993–94 economic plan in stifling hyperinflation also played a role, facilitating the kind of long-range planning required to fund the slog toward an advanced degree — even attending the free public universities requires deferring short-term earnings. The *favelado doutor*, a favela resident with a PhD — a virtual contradiction in terms before the 1990s — suddenly became a reality.

Broad contextual factors, however, only set the context for the contingencies and sacrifices of individual efforts. An illness in the family, harassment by the police, expulsion by local traffickers — challenges whose risks would be greatly diminished or nonexistent for middle-class cariocas — could derail a promising trajectory. It is ultimately impossible to explain why some individuals found their way to success while many did not, a contrast that anthropologist Janice Perlman describes as "the mystery of mobility."[36] Regardless, the triumph of some favela residents is a reminder that a fixed focus on violence and criminal networks can itself reinforce oversimplified understandings of the favela as separate from the rest of the city. The greatest tragedy of criminal turf control, and its routinization in the functioning of the city, is the way it foreclosed these opportunities for so many more.

Some of the residents who "made it" in the world of formal employment left the favela, moving to formal neighborhoods. Many did not, opting to stay in favelas where they had grown up despite opportunities to live elsewhere. As some favelas prospered or struggled forward whereas others did not, favela architecture and infrastructure differentiated, as well. One of the shared understandings facilitating the communitarian efforts of the late 1970s had been the sense that the residents of any given favela were in it together, that they shared the same challenge in securing possession, water, and electricity. By the mid-1990s, that was clearly no longer the case. Well-serviced central areas, often the targets of Favela-Bairro upgrading projects, contrasted sharply with underserved and more precarious fringes.

This individuality of favelas made them more similar to the formal neighborhoods they abutted, in diversity and aspirations if not in other ways. Despite the distortion of state presence by the criminal networks, despite the spectacular violence of the young traffickers, most favela residents were ultimately not so different from those in nearby formal neighborhoods. They wanted an education, a job, a decent home, and a place to live where they would not be required to defer to capricious gunmen, whether from criminal networks or the police force. São Paulo and Bogotá had begun their transitions. Why not Rio? Perhaps the time had come for a renewed embrace of the ideals that had animated the favela movement—most important, the belief that favela and city could be bridged—but only if that embrace were balanced by sober confrontation of the problems that had prevented realization of that ideal a generation earlier.

Nosso morro é coisa chique	("Our hill is something chic
É favela fashion week	It's favela fashion week
Sobe lá pra você ver	Go up and you will see
Vem ver o que é bom	Come see what is really good
Nosso morro é muita treta	Our hill is very wily
Nossa Gisele Bündchen é preta	Our Gisele Bündchen is black
E ela faz acontecer	And she makes it happen")

—LEANDRO SAPUCAHY, "Favela Fashion Week" (song), 2011.

One of the best-known books about the relationship between favela and city in Rio de Janeiro is *Cidade Partida*, a work from 1994 by journalist Zuenir Ventura.[1] The title can be translated as Broken, Separated, Split, or Fragmented City, depending on one's perception. Based on Ventura's reporting in the wake of the Vigário Geral massacre of 1993, the book implies that favela residents have been fundamentally cut off from the benefits of the formal city. Ventura's work was the most influential of many accounts, some more sensitive than others, making similar arguments.[2]

There were times as I conducted the bulk of the field research for this book in 2004 and 2006 that I came near to thinking that the city was indeed broken, not in the neat way Ventura suggested but in ways that incorporated a kind of dangerous malfunction into the operations of the city itself. Cyclical patterns of violence had become deeply ingrained in security policy and in the constant expansion and retraction of rival gangs.

Less than a decade later, I am sometimes amazed by how well Rio works. Despite the city's inequalities, Rio's poor find ways to improve their own lives and those of their children. Despite high rates of violence, cariocas exude relaxed charm and enjoyment of their city. My own sunnier perspective owes something to fond remembrance of the city, as opposed to daily investigation of its inequities. It owes a good deal to the improving economic and security situation in the city and to the buoyant mood I have encountered among cariocas of all classes upon return visits in recent years. My interviews in 2004 and 2006 frequently elicited despair and confusion; my subjects often looked back on the favela movement of the late 1970s and wondered where Rio had taken a wrong turn. Follow-up interviews in 2010–13 elicited a relieved and often amazed sense of hope. Yet my changing perspective owed most of all to the *way* recent transformations have been achieved, through reclamation of the best ideas of the reformers of the 1980s, while attempting to avoid the mistakes of that period. This has not changed my reading of what *happened* in the 1970s and 1980s, but has changed my perspective on what has been salvaged, retained, and nourished from that period.

It has become commonplace to describe the 1980s as a "lost decade" for Latin America, primarily in reference to the hyperinflation that destroyed savings, drove up unemployment, and halted growth. That perspective, however, ignores the exhilaration of redemocratization and the lessons it bequeathed. As the anthropologist Hermano Vianna has written, "There was a while where I thought the 1980s would pass definitively and irremediably into History as a lost, uptight, reactionary decade. . . . I knew that wasn't true, but who says what gets left for History is true? . . . But the 1980s are back and fulminating. . . . Almost everything truly important in contemporary culture . . . was projected in the 1980s."[3]

One of the last and most affecting interviews I conducted in my research for this book was with Olívia Rodrigues Cavalcante, owner of a *birosca*—a combination market, hardware store, and neighborhood meeting place—in the west side favela of Asa Branca. Dona Olívia spent her childhood in Pará, in the Amazonian North of Brazil. She came to Rio in the early 1980s, when she was fourteen, for a mathematics competition—she was a promising student and won sponsorship for the trip from a local religious organization. She had access neither to higher education nor to employment in Pará, and she decided to stay on in Rio. She found work as a live-in maid and tried to study on the side. By 1988, she had a *companheiro*, or common-law husband, was pregnant, and needed her own place to live. She moved to Asa

Branca when the community was still a small cluster of shacks carved out of a break in the swamp grass of Jacarépaguá, the flatlands of western Rio.[4]

Not long after, she began selling food and drink in the favela, an operation that gradually turned into the dynamic birosca I saw in 2011. Through much of the 1990s, she convinced a neighbor to pedal her two children—the daughter born in 1988 and a son born two years later—to a municipal school three kilometers away, on the back of his bike, because there was no bus. By 2011, the daughter had earned her bachelor's degree in physics from the prestigious Universidade Federal do Rio de Janeiro. Her brother was completing his degree in engineering from the same institution, undeterred by the three-hour bus ride each way to campus. Both were preparing for graduate study. When they were not studying, they ran the store.

Asa Branca itself has changed dramatically in the past two decades. In the early 1990s it was a mosquito-infested network of mud paths. Early in the new millennium, the residents, entirely of their own volition and through their own labor, raised the streets and buildings on reinforced landfill, lifting the community several feet higher. It is now safer from floods and storms, with freshly painted storefronts abutting well-swept streets. Asa Branca is far from paradise; it is still fighting off threats of partial removal and has not escaped the militias operating on the west side. Dona Olívia and her neighbors, however, have built a better life there. Dona Olívia and her family are exceptional because of their unusual talent, diligence, and savvy. But every favela has its Dona Olívias. And for them, the favela has been the only place they could make their way in the city.

As I conducted the first rounds of field interviews for this project in 2004 and 2006, I was struck by the gap between what residents told me on and off record. Off record, they gave specific accounts of police accepting bribes, neighbors drawn into criminal networks, city workers with dubious connections to local traffickers, militia bosses driving out residents who challenged their hold over local commerce. On record, they often gave me sincere but sterile accounts of the enduring stigma faced by favela residents and the pressures of life in zones of recurring violence.

It did not surprise me that residents of violent favelas were not more forthcoming on record. I was familiar with the notorious "law of the hill," the informal code prohibiting favela residents from saying anything critical of the local criminal operators or anything that might invite police scrutiny. I was naive but not that naive; I had no expectation of parachuting into a violent favela and expecting residents to open their hearts to me as soon as I pulled out a digital recorder. Quite the opposite: what surprised me was how much recent acquaintances were eager to share off record, and how carefully they drew the line between private and public speech. There was talking—which was free flowing, candid, and detailed—and there was interviewing, which had the rhythms and digressions of extemporaneous speech but which followed the outline of a previously accepted script. After a few interviews I knew the script and had a good idea of what was coming next. The talking, in contrast, was always fresh and revealing.

This was particularly true among residents of trafficker- or militia-controlled favelas but was also true of city workers and of NGO volunteers. The dividing line was equally clear whether informants were discussing events that had happened the previous week or twenty years earlier. If anything, residents took even greater care when discussing the rise of violent traffickers in the 1980s.

This experience told me two things. First, it showed that the law of silence, like so many other laws in Brazil, was not considered universally binding, but only to be followed in certain circumstances. Brazilians describe behavior that is undertaken only to please foreigners, masking a less attractive reality, as pra inglês ver, for the English to see. In Rio's favelas, however, outsiders are typically called alemão, or German—a disparaging ascription of unknown origin. It became clear that the much-invoked law of silence was a silence pra alemão ouvir, a silence for the German to hear, contrasting strongly with the chatter that marked life off the record.

Second, it showed that I was onto something. The transitions of the 1980s had cut close enough to the bone that their secrets could not be casually sown to the winds. Also, the stories that came off record were so enticing that I felt compelled to look beyond the relative reticence of the official interviews. I jettisoned my plans to make oral history interviews the core of my research and resolved to use my interviews as a source of background knowledge while redoubling efforts in archives and libraries, which turned out to be a rewarding decision. It led me to scores of unpublished master's theses on the new social movements of the early 1980s written by participant observers, fresh with vivid detail and immediate perspectives. I found technical reports on favela upgrading of the last three decades, obscure newsletters circulated among favela activists, and the original plans and outlines of the key reforms of the 1980s—documents I might not have found if I had maintained a focus on oral history.

As important, this allowed me to spend my field visits to varying corners of Rio less as a goal-oriented seeker of specific information and more as a passive recipient of impressions. Anthropologists would no doubt describe this as Ethnography 101. But as I was not writing an ethnography, I did not need exhaustive detail on a single community, leaving me free to take an aleatory path across the length and breadth of the city. It was then that the city opened itself up for me, as cities always do.

In previous experience as a scholar in Rio, my travels had been relatively circumscribed: a MapMyRun GPS record of my previous paths in Greater Rio would have shown a tight cluster of wanderings throughout the entirety of the historic center and the middle-class neighborhoods of the south side with occasional forays to favela samba schools, to the university out near the airport, and to the Ilha de Paquetá—the poinciana-studded municipal beach island in the middle of the Guanabara Bay.

Now I saw different sides of the city; more than simply seeing them, though, I learned to understand their meanings. While walking with a friend through a favela not far from the Fazenda Botafogo metro stop on the deindustrializing north side, we approached what looked to me to be two men repairing a car at a humble auto body shop. Apropos of a conversation we had been having about police corruption, my friend whispered under his breath, "Por exemplo, olha esse dois caras depenando esse carro" (For example, look at those two guys "defeathering" that car). As much as the observation itself, I was fascinated by the verb, the first time I had heard it in this context, which perfectly captured the way the men were stripping the car of chrome, tires, lights, and mirrors.

"And now these police will roll by and take their cut," he continued, referring to a squad car I had not yet seen rolling up behind us. Sure enough, as the squad car pulled to the side of the road, one of the mechanics walked over, removed a thick wad of currency from his belt, leaned into the car, and placed it in the hand of the officer in the passenger seat. The squad car rolled on, driver and passenger barely glancing in our direction. The transaction was at once efficient and brazen. I had studied and analyzed the consequences of police corruption and seen it in action at occasional traffic stops around the city, but it was only then that I realized the palpable presence of that corruption as a continuous affront to the dignity of favela residents.

THE CITY I SAW on my field visits often did not match up with commonly accepted descriptions, or even with the comparatively nuanced understanding I had reached after fifteen years of experience in tidier precincts. In Cidade de Deus, the vast housing project turned favela on the west side made notorious by the movie about its history of drug wars, I found a neighborhood of upwardly mobile homeowners, characterized by *churrascarias*, fast-food franchises, bank agencies, and gas stations. In other words, it looked like most other Brazilian suburbs. Here was the *nova classe c*, the new C class, as Brazilian market surveys referred to consumers climbing out of the working class into the lower middle class. Although this transition has not been smooth and is far from universal in Cidade de Deus, evidence of the economic dynamism behind it is everywhere. As Alba Zaluar showed in the mid-1980s, civil society organizations such as samba *blocos*, or informal parade bands, soccer teams, and local branches of political parties were crucial to organizing life in the area, but were in many cases checked, distorted, or undermined by criminal networks. Although these problems have not been eliminated, they have been mitigated by the diversification of civil society organizations. Church groups, NGOs, and sport leagues jostle for space in Cidade de Deus, in some cases competing, in others allying. Government presence has broadened as well, again in ways that alleviate some problems while merely complicating others, but that in general yield an urban environment characterized by greater opportunities and resources. Cidade de Deus is far from the urban wasteland known in popular portrayals.

Vigário Geral, in contrast, is considered ground zero of the NGO wave, birthplace of several of the city's most prominent NGOs in the 1990s, including Afro Reggae, celebrated locally and internationally for its programs designed to lure teenagers away from the drug trade and limit police violence by drawing the attention of media and government agents. In Vigário Geral, I was surprised to find a neighborhood where fear of local drug traffickers and prospective invasion of rival networks was still palpable, where residents avoided lingering in public spaces and seemed constantly wary of being watched.

These understandings were doubtless shaped by timing. As many researchers have noted, the mood in Rio's favelas changes dramatically in response to the vicissitudes of conflict among criminal networks and between those networks and the police. Residents know that the death or imprisonment of a key trafficker in their favela or an adjacent favela is likely to trigger renewed violence, and they react accordingly. Yet what these impressions showed was that Cidade de Deus in 2006 was both the neighborhood scarred by a long history of criminal violence and home to an upwardly mobile and diversifying population; Vigário Geral in the same year was both the birthplace of enterprising NGOs and a neighborhood that continued to be plagued by criminal networks and a highly constricted economy.

IN 2010, 2011, AND 2013 I returned to the field for shorter visits, sitting down once again with residents I had first interviewed four or five years earlier and renewing my perambulations throughout the city. What changed in the intervening years? A great deal. To begin, the gap between on-record interviews and the off-record conversations shrank. Interview subjects were more willing to go on record about the past and continuing challenges of life in Rio's favelas. In the Morro dos Cabritos, for example, a resident from whom I had learned much of the history of the community in informal conversation, but who had tactfully avoided consenting to a formal interview in 2006, caught up to me on my visit in 2011 and said, "Now let's do that interview."

Why the new openness? Partly this is the result of economic growth driven by international demand for Brazilian commodities and the internal growth of a new middle class. Brazil in general has boomed over much of the past decade, and the state of Rio, in particular, has been buoyed by the profits of burgeoning offshore oil production. Economic growth has led to a rise in formal employment for the first time in decades, a pattern accelerated by investments in preparation for the World Cup in 2014 and the Summer Olympic Games in 2016. In contrast to other recent cycles of growth—the Brazilian "miracle" of the early 1970s, for example, which exacerbated inequality—favela residents have shared some of the benefits of the current boom.

More surprisingly, some of the new sense of openness stems from the favela security strategy implemented since late 2008, a venture known as the Unidades de Polícia Pacificadora (UPPs, Units of Pacifying Police). The UPP strategy, now present in over thirty favelas formerly controlled by traffickers or militias, is coordinated by the state government but depends on federal oversight and involvement. Each UPP begins with a militarized "occupation" intended to drive out criminal networks. Once the phase is deemed successful and complete, a period that has varied from a few days in Morro dos Prazeres to several months in the Complexo do Alemão, militarized occupation gives way to community policing in tandem with investment in social programs.

The UPPs explicitly update the mid-1980s strategies of Colonel Magno Nazareth Cerqueira, implementing them with greater resources and commitment to persuade both police and residents of their viability and permanence. In the mid-1980s, Nazareth Cerqueira's strategies failed because at least half the police were against them, the resources available did not match idealistic aspirations, and few of the key players realized the extent of the dangers posed by new criminal networks. In the updated version, commanders have been more successful in persuading officers to embrace their approach, have proceeded cautiously from one favela to the next—hoping not to overreach their capabilities—and have placed a priority on diminishing armed violence and turf control.

The deliberate retaking of Nazareth Cerqueira's strategies this entails is surprising: as recently as ten years ago, few police spoke openly in admiration of Brizola's secretary of military police. Yet the persistently confrontational approach favored by Nazareth Cerqueira's successors failed catastrophically, leading toward a return to community policing, albeit a return characterized by deep awareness of the flaws in earlier attempts at implementation.

In a March 2011 presentation of the UPP strategy at Washington, D.C.'s Wilson Center, Antônio Roberto Cesário de Sá, subsecretary of public security in the state of Rio, recalled that as a young police recruit in the 1980s he had not seen the relevance of Nazareth Cerqueira's ideas. Only after years of experience of the futility of confrontational security strategies lacking any component of community outreach, both in Rio and elsewhere in Brazil, did Sá embrace Nazareth Cerqueira's vision of crime prevention and community policing. Sá's experience was typical and amounts to a sea change in Rio's state police. The commanders of Emir Larangeira's generation have retired. Many of the new commanders of Sá's generation—recruited in the 1980s, veterans of entrenched urban conflict—have dramatically changed their evaluation of Nazareth Cerqueira's model.

Funding and administrative support for the updated version of that model has proven equally decisive. Whereas Nazareth Cerqueira had only a few officers operating in a vast neighborhood such as Cidade de Deus, the UPP implemented in Cidade de Deus in 2009 counted on scores of offi-.cers, followed by a larger wave of state and city workers. Directives for the UPP require replacing local officers every eighteen months. This constant "recycling" of officers, together with the gradual expansion of the overall program, requires a larger police force. The state government has greatly expanded its police academy to respond to this demand.

Federal involvement and oversight have also been necessary. Whereas the federal government shunned and rejected Nazareth Cerqueira's reforms in the mid-1980s, it has backed the UPPs, committing both funding and federal officers to the program. The federal police corps has been marked by higher standards of professionalism than the state corps, and federal involvement has clearly shaped UPP implementation.

Most important to this transition, perhaps, have been greater efforts to rein in police corruption. Since 2008, scores of police have been arrested or expelled from the force for corruption—including high-ranking officers such as the former chief of civil police. This new willingness to prosecute police corruption fulfills aspirations of Nazareth Cerqueira previously thwarted by resistance within the police corps and judiciary. Although the crackdown on police corruption is not limited to the UPPs, it is a decisive factor in their viability. The confluence of these factors has persuaded most favela residents that the UPPs will not be abandoned under the next state government and may avoid the abuses of power that have plagued previous initiatives.

Like Nazareth Cerqueira's efforts, the UPP strategy is risky and uncertain. A century of tradition in violent policing, particularly ingrained in recent decades, is not easily overturned. The UPPs have succeeded in diminishing violence in and around "pacified" favelas, but criminal networks have by no means disappeared. In July 2011, for example, the former president of the residents' association in the Morro dos Macacos was shot to death by unknown assailants less than one hundred meters from UPP headquarters. The assassination had all the hallmarks of the kind of a *queima de arquivo*, or archive burning, that took the lives of so many association presidents in the midst of the factional drug wars of the 1990s and 2000s.

In April and May of 2013, criminal networks in the Morro dos Macacos and the Complexo de Alemão temporarily shut down local commerce in reprisal against the arrest of powerful traffickers from those neighborhoods. In both cases, the local UPP was not enough to persuade residents that it was safe to defy the mandate of the traffickers. More ominously, UPP officers have been implicated in several cases of police abuse and are suspected in at least one case of disappearance of a favela resident.

As these episodes reveal, the UPPs represent a considerable gamble in a context where police corruption has long been considered standard operating procedure. The greater the number of officers involved, the greater the risk that some will revert to past practices. As the program has expanded from pilot initiatives in small favelas to some of the largest complexes in the city, its weak points have become more evident. Should the UPPs slide into the kinds of habits that marked previous favela "occupations," they could become a new obstacle to the integration of favelas with the rest of the city. Notwithstanding these risks, in its first five years the program has achieved positive results—a relative success that contrasts with previous community policing initiatives in Rio.

A visit to Borel I made in April 2011 brought this home to me. My previous visits to that favela, between 2004 and 2008, had yielded a depressing picture. Twenty years of drug-related conflict had left a generation scarred and reduced by violence. Shootouts were common, and the trafficking crew exerted a stranglehold over local commerce within and on the border of the favela. Borel has one main road winding up its steep hillside, and the local trafficking crew had established its primary point of sale at the first sharp curve in that road. That point of sale also became a de facto checkpoint for the favela; in practice, any outsider who cared to venture further needed a chaperone, a role usually fulfilled by someone from the favela association, acting under the watchful eye of the traffickers. Favela-Bairro investments in the late 1990s had merely expanded and upgraded this point of sale without changing its use, and any improvements were quickly deteriorating by 2006.

The Carrefour hypermarket across from the favela had shut down as a result of the depredations of the local traffickers, exacerbating local unemployment and imposing greater expenses on residents forced to take the bus to markets farther away—a vivid example of the economic consequences of criminal violence. The CIEP at the foot of Borel had a dwindling student population, and its sports court was always deserted; few dared play there at any hour, their fear substantiated by the pockmarked walls of the complex, riddled by stray bullets. Property values in the area were declining rapidly.

Borel's UPP was initiated in June 2010. When I returned in 2011, life in the favela had changed dramatically. Residents congregated in the street and gathered in great numbers in the favela's community center for a meeting on the social projects connected to the UPP. Enrollment at the CIEP had doubled, and students played soccer on its sports court at recess. Formal employment in the area had begun to pick up. For the first time in my experience there, the favela had a tangible air of optimism and conviviality.

The primary point of sale long favored by local traffickers was now a key intersection of the main road and much-traveled footpath. Although local drug trafficking had by no means been eliminated, it no longer dominated public spaces in the favela. Violence had been reduced dramatically. New businesses were starting up, no longer inhibited by the fear of shootouts, temporary shutdowns forced by the criminal network, and the grinding, extralegal taxation of low-level extortion. Property values both within the favela and in adjacent areas rebounded and began to climb again.

It is too soon to tell whether these initial gains can be sustained, withstanding risks of renewed abuse. Given the record of failed initiatives in the recent past, healthy skepticism is warranted. Initial research on the UPPs, carried out in a collaborative effort by researchers from the World Bank and from multiple academic institutions in Rio de Janeiro, suggests that their success or failure in any given favela depends as much on the local history of violence as it does on the UPP strategy itself. In favelas scarred by recent violence of drug-trafficking rivalries, the UPP has been welcomed and supported by local residents. In favelas with a long history of resentment against police violence, residents are skeptical of the UPP, remaining aloof and noncommital about its merits. In favelas that have suffered both trafficker and police violence, like Borel, "perceptions combined strong feelings of relief with strong apprehensions about the future and return of drug traffickers."[5]

Whether the feeling of relief and the improvements it reflects will be sustainable depend largely on the delicate relationship of favela residents to the police. The same World Bank report astutely observes that "while for outsiders . . . the UPP represents an attempt to bring peace to the favelas, for most residents the UPP represents an attempt by the state to pacify the police."[6] Permanently reducing police aggression against favela residents may be the greatest challenge of the UPP, as well as the one most worthy of the legacy of Nazareth Cerqueira.

Unfortunately, the impending World Cup and Olympics place greater strains on the new security strategy and on the improved relationship between favela and city more generally. In the recent past, such mega-events have been marked by preemptive crackdowns on the poor. In a city where this tendency appears deeply ingrained in local security forces and where wealthy investors push the authorities to maintain a sanitary cordon protecting the mega-events, there is ample reason to fear renewed deterioration in police-favela relations.

Notwithstanding these caveats, the UPP has at least temporarily checked the spread of criminal turf monopolization, reversing longstanding trends. One veteran favela activist invokes the oft-cited *direito de ir e vir* to synthesize this transition: "The freedom we have gained is the right to come and go! The tráfico had taken away that freedom!"[7] The greatest risk of the UPP is that, rather than being gradually absorbed into an effective security strategy for the state of Rio de Janeiro, it will be perpetuated as a mode of favela control, reinforcing the separation between favela and formal city. Continued public insistence on transparent prosecution of police abuses is the best, and perhaps only, defense against this potential outcome.

In the meantime, increasing connections between favela and formal city go well beyond the UPP. Cidade de Deus's fortunes, after all, began to improve well before the inauguration of its UPP. Much remains to be desired, particularly in relation to inequality, which remains stubbornly high in Rio, despite declining elsewhere in Brazil. But as employment has risen and opportunities have expanded, favela residents have gotten back some of the pride they had in the late 1970s—not the aggressive posturing of armed traffickers, but the pride in belonging to a place its residents, at least, recognize as a valuable *part of* the city. This often entails putting a unique favela twist on whatever is happening in the rest of Brazil. As Leandro Sapucahy puts it in a samba about favela style, "Our Gisele Bündchen is black," a sentiment that recalls the most hopeful aspects of the *socialismo moreno* of the Brizola years. Sapucahy reminds us that favela exceptionalism can have a positive spin; the favela *is* different from the formal city, of course, and that difference is most apparent in architecture and popular culture, both of which have become sources of favela pride in recent years. The current moment offers the opportunity, for the first time in thirty years, of asserting positive difference while combatting exclusion from the rule of law and the guarantees of civil rights.

This opportunity does not come without risks. The fear of *remoção branca*, or veiled removal—the uprooting of poor favela residents through gentrification of their communities — stirs anew. And forced removal itself has returned to carioca politics. The infrastructural improvements associated with favela upgrading have led to eviction of hundreds of favela families. Elevated tramway projects in Santa Marta, Providência, and the Complexo do Alemão have been the most visible of the infrastructural projects, and each uprooted local residents. Construction of highways and rail lines to facilitate transportation, mostly in preparation for the 2016 Olympics, has drastically increased removals. In theory, each of the evicted families is given indemnification for the value of the home and "social rent" to cover expenses of renting in the area while awaiting more permanent resettlement. In practice, indemnification values have been set artificially low and social rent payments have been unreliable and insufficient. Favela residents in the path of infrastructural projects have been forced into high-stakes negotiation with municipal authorities. Some residents have negotiated successfully and have secured comparable housing, while others have been constrained to accept low indemnifications that leave them few options.

To complicate matters, the new infrastructural projects are in some cases necessary improvements and in others dubious gambles. In the case of the Complexo do Alemão, the aerial tram opened in 2011 marked the first major public investment in over fifteen years in this region of the city and made immediate improvements in local circulation. In Providência, the aerial tramway planned to open in 2014 seems designed more for touristic use than for local residents, and has resulted in significant evictions in a small favela. These variations in objectives and implementation make it difficult to offer a blanket assessment of recent infrastructural projects. Those projects that incorporate the lessons of previous experiments and emphasize dialogue with local residents have a strong possibility of succeeding. Those that repeat previous mistakes will fail, and could fail disastrously.

The impending World Cup in 2014 and the Summer Olympic Games in 2016 intensify these risks. Rio is in the midst of a real-estate boom, a phenomenon that has a way of distorting high-minded social policies. With square footage at a premium and favelas enjoying a new-found tourist chic, dozens of *pousadas*, or bed-and-breakfasts, have opened in south side favelas. Again, these enterprises increase local economic vitality and thicken the connections between favela and city, at the risk of uprooting longtime residents. In addition, larger real-estate developments have endangered favelas in the path of Olympic installations.

These instances of removal and gentrification could turn out to be the tolerable, if painful, costs of economic growth and infrastructural improvement, or they could spiral out of control, blossoming into renewed social disaster. The outcome depends on the democratic process. Here, too, there are some causes for cautious optimism. As this book has made clear, politics in Rio in recent decades has often been marked by entrenched factionalism. Yet it has never been a winner-take-all affair, and favela residents have been far from powerless in its unfolding. They have proven fierce and savvy advocates in defending themselves against prospective eviction associated with upgrading or Olympic development. As Sapucahy observes, the favela is *muita treta*, very wily, in current carioca slang.[8] In mid-2013, favela residents joined fellow citizens from all over the country to take to the streets in a surprising wave of popular mobilization. The protests began with objections to increased public transportation costs and accelerated in response to inept police crackdowns. For favela residents, the protests granted an opportunity to amplify their objections to removal and police abuse, connecting them to broader popular demands. For the first time in a generation, residents of favelas and middle-class neighborhoods found common ground as they protested colossal spending on the Olympics at the expense of social priorities. The vigorous debate about displacement and security policy currently underway is a sign of health, not failure. Favela residents are claiming a greater stake in direct political participation in defining the future of the city than they have since the early 1980s.

In all these ways, Rio de Janeiro has come back around to the best opportunity for breaking down the barriers between favela and city that it has seen in thirty years. The opportunity of the early 1980s was squandered. There is reason to hope that careful revival of the hopes of those years, balanced by sober avoidance of the mistakes, may contribute to more successful initiatives this time around.

What are the lessons of the previous period for current reforms? What does the history of mobilization, reform, reaching the breaking point and unraveling between the late 1970s and the early 1990s reveal about the current prospects for strengthening democracy in Rio's favelas? The spirit of collective action that marked the late 1970s dissipated over the course of the 1980s and 90s, undermined by urban violence and criminal turf control, made less urgent by apparent security of land tenure and the achievement of minimal public services. The loss of that collective spirit has occasionally led some favela residents to idealize the days of mobilization and to suggest that residents, ironically, had more democracy under the late dictatorship than they have enjoyed in the nominally democratic period that ensued. This is not the case: the mobilization of the late 1970s deserves to be honored. It was a grassroots movement of humble people emboldened by a noble purpose, but that should not obscure the real limitations on the citizenship of favela residents in the late dictatorship, when land tenure remained deeply insecure; access to public education, health, and infrastructure was tenuous and partial, and discrimination against favela residents in public spaces and in the employment market was pervasive. In all these matters, the civil rights of favela residents have been greatly strengthened since the end of the dictatorship.

Older residents who lived through the vibrant mobilization of the late 1970s have often longed for a revival of that communitarian spirit. Some hope that the 2013 protests could establish the basis for such a revival. Yet, popular mobilization can neither be sustained indefinitely nor revived in precisely the same guise. The favela association movement of the late 1970s ended the policy of favela removal and brought favela residents into the halls of political power. Inevitably, this led toward institutionalization and routinization. This may have drained some of the enthusiasm from favela politics, but it provided a structure for representation in city and state government. The greater problem was that the institutionalization that unfolded tended not merely to expand the structures of formal representation to include favela residents but to create parallel structures, with their own rules and pathways. Those parallel structures ultimately reproduced the separation of the favela from the formal city.

In order to make lasting improvements, the current movement must avoid this tendency. Successful reform will depend on recognizing that favela residents have both individual rights that must be protected and collective interests, as members of a community, that must be respected. Any nominal protection of individual rights that fails to respect community interests could prove destructive, if it were to lead to rapid displacement. But protection of putative community interests without defense of individual rights has been disastrous. The lessons of the 1980s, finally, suggest that stable frameworks for gradual, steady improvement are likely to yield greater gains than high-profile programs for urgent, radical reform. The greatest threat to gradual improvement is the perpetuation of favelas as zones of legal exception whose residents suffer from reduced access to rights and representation.

IN CHAPTERS 1 AND 2 I presented details of the trajectories of favela leaders of the 1960s through the early 1980s in order to demonstrate the transition from the old guard to the new of favela activism. I would like to close the book with the words of another favela activist, this one of the current generation. Ratão Diniz was born in 1981 and is thus too young to remember most of the events in this book clearly, but he has lived — and continues to live — their consequences in a way that reveals the legacies of the long 1980s. Like Eliana Sousa Silva, Ratão Diniz is from Nova Holanda, part of the sprawling region of favelas known as the Complexo da Maré, and he grew up participating in the social programs and NGOs that Sousa Silva and her peers pioneered in that favela. It was in these programs, more so than in the CIEP he attended, that Diniz honed his academic and political skills, and he speaks of Sousa Silva and her generation with deep respect for their transformative work in the favela. He usually has his laptop with him and is abreast of the latest graphics programming and social-networking platforms. He is, as well, a deft negotiator of opportunities, keenly aware of new programs that might enable him to bring resources and interlocutors to Maré. His hip-hop attire and prominent piercings might suggest a reluctance to cultivate connections to authorities, but this notion is quickly belied by his outgoing, candid, and unpretentious nature. He appears equally comfortable talking with local kids about the latest funk and with academics about the persistence of preindustrial popular cultural practices in the favela.

His formative experience came in the School for Popular Photographers, a program run by the Observatório das Favelas, or Favela Observatory, one of Maré's most enterprising NGOs. The School for Popular Photographers — itself part of a larger program known as Images of the People — trains favela residents in photography, bringing in celebrated journalistic and art photographers to teach their technique. Diniz is one of the program's most illustrious graduates, and also now one of its teachers. He has photographed and exhibited his images throughout Brazil and internationally. Along with his colleagues, he has published a compelling book of photographs, revealing the rapid transitions in favela life in the early twenty-first century. He is constantly working, but his work is a nonstop combination of his passion for photography, his gregarious networking, and his commitment to drawing attention to the struggles of Brazil's working poor.

He is the consummate wired activist. In contrast to the previous generation of activists, who mobilized neighbors through the face-to-face construction of local alliances, Diniz opts for incisive communication with a wide array of allies and contacts. He is a networker rather than a movement builder, a difference with advantages and disadvantages. He is not perceived as a rising political figure in the way that Sousa Silva was when she was first elected as Nova Holanda's association president. The improvements he brings are incremental and small scale rather than vast and far reaching. But he can call on local and global allies with a tweet, an ability that might seem trivial but one that has enabled him to bring new resources to the School for Popular Photographers, attract media attention to Maré, and connect his students to opportunities throughout the city. His activism is pragmatic and optimistic. It is the approach that the moment demands, suited to reap its potential benefits and defend against its risks. In keeping with that personality, his estimate of the legacies of the long 1980s, though careful, is generally positive. "That was when all of this," he says, taking in Maré's vast reaches with a sweeping hand, "became permanent, part of the city that no one could take away. Since then, favelados might get beaten down, we might suffer from violence. But no one can tell us we don't have the right to live in this city."

INTRODUCTION

1. Paulo Roberto Muniz, author interview, April 2011.

2. Eliana Athayde, author interview, March 2006. Rubião and Athayde were both assistants to esteemed advocate Heráclito Fontoura Sobral Pinto, who served as head counsel in the Vidigal case. Rubião and Athayde played a more prominent role in mobilization on the hill and in the subsequent development of the Pastoral das Favelas. On Sobral Pinto, see John W. F. Dulles, *Resisting Brazil's Military Regime: An Account of the Battles of Sobral Pinto* (Austin: University of Texas Press, 2007).

3. Arquivo Pastoral das Favelas (hereafter, APF), Vidigal, caixa 1, pasta 1, "Documentos referentes a remoção." The APF's records pertaining to Vidigal contain extensive documentation revealing a series of achievements and setbacks on the path toward this judicial recognition in mid-1978. These documents make clear that civil servants (judge, prosecutor, and expert witnesses from the state's geographic division) were strongly divided on Vidigal's future; that other private claimants—in addition to putative landowner Yvette Palumbo—had also filed suit requesting removal of favelados; and that only community mobilization and persistent efforts by the Pastoral's lawyers forestalled removal.

4. For a general overview of favela removals in this period, followed by close investigation of one case, see Mário Sérgio Brum, "Cidade Alta: História, memória e estigma de favela num conjunto habitacional de Rio de Janeiro," Ph.D. diss., (Universidade Federal Fluminense, 2011). For a complementary case, see Janice Perlman, *Favela: Four Decades of Living on the Edge in Rio de Janeiro* (New York: Oxford University Press, 2010).

5. Some observers have argued that Brizola was not really a socialist, but an old-school populist in socialist's clothing. That is as may be. He described himself as a socialist and the party manifesto for the PDT, his new party, explicitly identified the party as socialist. In addition to serving as vice president of the Socialist International for fourteen years, he was Honorary President of that body at the time of

his death in 2004. His resumé supports his self-identification as a socialist. The party he founded, however, was one of several competing socialist parties in Brazil in the 1980s. Therefore I describe his self-identification with a lower-case rather than a capital "s." Throughout the book, I use lowercase to describe socialist and communist ideology, and uppercase to refer to specific entities or institutions, such as the Brazilian Communist Party and Saturnino Braga's "Prefeitura Socialista," or Socialist Municipal Government. For an insightful collection of essays on Brizola, see Marieta de Moraes Ferreira, ed. *A força do povo: Brizola e o Rio de Janeiro* (Rio de Janeiro: ALERJ, 2008). For analysis of Brizola's base, see João Trajano Sento-Sé, *Brizolismo: Estetização da política e carisma* (Rio de Janeiro: Fundação Getúlio Vargas, 1999).

6. For Saturnino Braga's own perspective on these goals, see Roberto Saturnino Braga, *Governo-comunidade: Socialismo no Rio* (Rio de Janeiro: Paz e Terra, 1989). Note: Saturnino Braga's bona fides as a socialist are similar to those of Brizola: throughout the 1980s, he self-identified as a socialist, described his administration as the Prefeitura Socialista, or Socialist Municipal Government and attempted to implement explicitly socialist policies. I am taking him at his word.

7. Muniz, interview, April 2011.

8. Marcelo Monteiro, "Paraíso Cobiçado," *Favela Tem Memória*, July 5, 2004, http://www.favelatemmemoria.com.br/publique/cgi/cgilua.exe/sys/start.htm ?sid=4&infoid=77&from_info_index=6, accessed on May 23, 2103. "O prefeito e o Vidigal," *Luta Democrática*, December 29, 1977; "Favelados do Vidigal entram na justiça contra remoção," *A Notícia*, December 28, 1977, 3.

9. Muniz, interview, April 2011. APF, Vidigal, caixa 1, pasta 1, "Documentos referentes a remoção."

10. "Fundação remove mais três famílias do Vidigal mas só duas vão para Antares," *Jornal do Brasil*, January 12, 1978, 16; "Favelados do Vidigal entram na justiça contra remoção."

11. Muniz, interview, April 2011.

12. Regarding Tamoio's connections to Rio's real-estate sector, see the interview with urban planner Pedro Teixeira Soares in Américo Freira and Lúcia Lippi Oliveira, eds., *Capítulos da memória do urbanismo carioca* (Rio de Janeiro: Fundação Getúlio Vargas, 2002).

13. For further analysis of this point, see Bryan McCann, "The Political History of Rio de Janeiro's Favelas: Recent Works," *Latin American Research Review* 41, no. 3 (2006): 149–162.

14. The literature on urban violence in Rio is vast and multifaceted. For particularly insightful work researched and written during the peak years of violence, see Michel Misse, "Malandros, marginais e vagabundos: Acumulação social da violência no Rio de Janeiro," Ph.D. diss., (IUPERJ, 1999). See also Luiz Eduardo Soares, ed. *Violência e política no Rio de Janeiro* (Rio de Janeiro: Relume Dumará, 1996).

15. On Rio's *milícias* see, for example, Alba Zaluar and Isabel Siqueira Conceição, "Favelas sob o controle das milícias: Que paz?" *São Paulo em Perspectiva* 21 (2007): 89–101.

16. For an influential journalistic account of the Vigário Geral massacre, its context, and its consequences, see Zuenir Ventura, *Cidade partida* (São Paulo: Companhia das Letras, 1994).

17. Mário Sérgio Brum, "Entrevista: Eliana Sousa Silva," Interview, (Rio de Janeiro: Laboratório de História Oral e Imagem, Universidade Federal Fluminense, 2005).

18. For pathbreaking analysis of similar phenomena in São Paulo, see Teresa Caldeira, *City of Walls: Crime, Segregation and Citizenship in São Paulo* (Berkeley: University of California Press, 2000). For insightful journalistic coverage of the beach conflicts of the early 1990s, see the opening chapters of Ventura, *Cidade partida*.

19. See, in particular, Enrique Desmond Arias, *Drugs and Democracy in Rio De Janeiro: Trafficking, Social Networks, and Public Security* (Chapel Hill: University of North Carolina Press, 2006); Marcos Alvito, *As cores de Acari: Uma favela carioca* (Rio de Janeiro: FGV, 2001); Luiz Eduardo Soares, *Meu casaco de general: Quinhentos dias no front da segurança pública em Rio de Janeiro* (São Paulo: Companhia das Letras, 2000); and Alba Zaluar, *Condomínio do Diabo* (Rio de Janeiro: UERJ, 1996).

CHAPTER ONE. THE BIG PICTURE

1. Lícia Valladares's analysis of the "invention of the favela" explores the evolving construction of the favela as distinct and different, including the unintentional role of social scientists in reifying the category of favela. See Lícia do Prado Valladares, *A invenção da favela: Do mito de origem a Favela.com* (Rio de Janeiro: Editora FGV, 2005).

2. Bryan McCann, "Troubled Oasis: The Intertwining Histories of the Morro dos Cabritos and Bairro Peixoto," in *Cities from Scratch: Poverty and Informality in Urban Latin America*, ed. Brodwyn Fischer, Bryan McCann, and Javier Auyero (Durham, NC: Duke University Press), forthcoming.

3. Maria Lais Pereira da Silva, *Favelas cariocas, 1930–1964* (Rio de Janeiro: Contraponto, 2005).

4. "Instruções para revisão do trabalho da base organizacional geográfica," Instituto Brasileiro de Geografia e Estatística (IBGE), Rio de Janeiro, 2000, 14.

5. For influential journalistic usage of this term, including a chapter on Rocinha, see Robert Neuwirth, *Shadow Cities: A Billion Squatters, A New Urban World* (New York: Routledge, 2005). For the early history of informal real-estate markets in Rio's favelas, see Brodwyn Fischer, *A Poverty of Rights: Citizenship and Inequality in Twentieth-Century Rio de Janeiro* (Palo Alto: Stanford University Press, 2008).

6. Favelas are also not generally "arrival cities" — in the sense of peripheral

urban neighborhoods home to recent migrants from rural areas—in the formulation of Doug Saunders. In favelas such as Santa Marta and Borel, many families have lived in the same place for four generations, their populations far more stable than those of adjacent middle-class neighborhoods. Saunders's description of arrival cities applies more closely to Rio's irregular subdivisions than to its favelas. Doug Saunders, *Arrival Cities: How the Largest Migration in History Is Reshaping our World* (New York: Pantheon, 2011).

7. For an overview of the juridical history of favelas, see Rafael Soares Gonçalves, "A política, o direito e as favelas do Rio de Janeiro: Um breve olhar histórico," *Urbana: Revista Eletrônica do Centro Interdisciplinar de Estudos da Cidade* 1, no. 1 (2006): 1–23.

8. Chico Buarque, "Estação derradeira," song, Marola Edições Musicais, Rio de Janeiro (1987).

9. Valladares, *A invenção da favela*; Lícia Valladares, "Social Science Representations of Favelas in Rio de Janeiro: A Historical Perspective," *Lanic Etext Collection*, LLILAS Visiting Resource Professor Papers, lanic.utexas.edu/project.etext/llilas /vrp/valladares.pdf, accessed on May 23, 2013.

10. For a comprehensive overview, see Marcelo Baumann Burgos, "Dos parques proletários ao Favela-Bairro: As políticas públicas nas favelas do Rio de Janeiro," in *Um século de favela*, ed. Alba Zaluar and Marcos Alvito (Rio de Janeiro: Fundação Getúlio Vargas, 2003), 25–60.

11. For analysis of the "urgency of now" in favela politics and its unintended consequences, see Brodwyn Fischer, "A Century in the Present Tense: Crisis, Politics and the Intellectual History of Brazil's Informal Cities," in *Cities from Scratch: Poverty and Informality in Urban Latin America*, ed. Brodwyn Fischer, Bryan McCann, and Javier Auyero (Durham, NC: Duke University Press), forthcoming.

12. Carlos Nelson Ferreira dos Santos, *Movimentos urbanos no Rio de Janeiro* (Rio de Janeiro: Zahar, 1981).

13. Gilda Blank, "Experiência de urbanização de favela." In *Habitação em Questão*, edited by Lícia do Prado Valladares, 93–120, Rio de Janeiro: Zahar, 1980.

14. Carlos Nelson Ferreira dos Santos, *Processo de Crescimento e ocupação da periferia* (Rio de Janeiro: IBAM, 1982), unpaginated. For analysis of mobilization in irregular subdivisions, see Luciana Corrêa do Lago, "O movimento dos loteamentos do Rio de Janeiro," M.A. thesis, (Universidade Federal do Rio de Janeiro, 1990). For analysis of regularization in subdivisions, see Michael G. Donovan, "At the Doors of Legality: Planners, Favelados and the Titling of Urban Brazil," Ph.D. diss., (University of California, Berkeley, 2007).

15. This is, admittedly, an oversimplification describing a general pattern of irregular subdivisions founded between the 1950s and the 1980s. There are exceptions to this general rule. Equally important, this incorporation has not been achieved without considerable political struggle, as detailed in chapter 3.

16. Luiz César de Queiroz Ribeiro and Luciana Lago, "The Favela/(Formal) Neighborhood Contrast in the Social Space of Rio de Janeiro," DISP, no. 147 (April 2001): 39–47.

17. Emílio Duhau, "The Informal City: An Enduring Slum or a Progressive Habitat," in Cities from Scratch: Poverty and Informality in Urban Latin America, ed. Bryan McCann and Javier Auyero Brodwyn Fischer (Durham, NC: Duke University Press), forthcoming.

18. Lícia Valladares, Passa-se uma casa: análise do programa de remoção de favelas do Rio de Janeiro (Rio de Janeiro: Zahar, 1978).

19. Mário Sérgio Brum, "Cidade Alta: História, memória e estigma de favela num conjunto habitacional de Rio de Janeiro," Ph.D. diss., (Universidade Federal Fluminense, 2011).

20. Paulo Lins, Cidade de Deus (São Paulo: Companhia das Letras, 2002). For pathbreaking analysis of the "favelization" of a prominent housing project and its meanings, see Brum, "Cidade Alta." Bezerra da Silva prominently mentions both Cidade de Deus and its crosstown contemporary Cidade Alta, for example. Sérgio Fernandes and Pedro Butina, "Saudação às Favelas" (1985).

21. This idea is Brodwyn Fischer's. She develops it in depth in Fischer, Poverty of Rights. See in particular 7–11, 216–21. See also Olívia Maria da Cunha Gomes and Flávio dos Santos, Quase cidadão: Histórias e antropologias da pós emancipação no Brasil (Rio de Janeiro: Fundação Getúlio Vargas, 2007).

22. Variation across favelas is so apparent that it is risky to generalize about the general racial composition of favelas. Brazilian census data on race has historically been ambiguous, and not geographically specific enough to evaluate favela demographics precisely. Researching in the late 1960s and early 1970s, American anthropologist Janice Perlman found that favela populations were approximately one-third black, nearly one-half white and the remainder mulato, a term that was commonly used but was not part of the official census and that has since declined in popularity. (The census offered the category of pardo, or brown, for mixed-race Brazilians, but the term pardo, in contrast, was almost never used in everyday life. Moreno is now more commonly used than either mulato or pardo, but pardo remains the relevant census category.) Perlman found that "nearly all" black cariocas lived in favelas in the early 1970s. That has changed dramatically: Rio's black population is dispersed far more widely, and favela demographics no longer differ dramatically from those of many irregular subdivisions or working-class formal neighborhoods. Janice Perlman, The Myth of Marginality: Urban Poverty and Politics in Rio de Janeiro (Berkeley: University of California Press, 1976), 58–59.

23. For extensive treatments of race in the favelas, see Robin Sheriff, Dreaming Equality (New Brunswick, NJ: Rutgers University Press, 2001); and Donna Goldstein, Laughter out of Place: Race, Class, Violence and Sexuality in a Rio Shantytown (Berkeley: University of California Press, 2003).

24. For particularly insightful discussion of this history, see the interview with Santa Marta community leader Itamar Silva in Dulce Chaves Pandolfi and Mário Grynszpan, ed. *A favela fala* (Rio de Janeiro: Fundação Getúlio Vargas, 2003).

25. "Projetos para revitalização e reurbanização da Rua Nelson Mandela," Working Paper, Rio de Janeiro: Instituto ComÁfrica, 2004).

26. Christina Vital Regina Novaes, Cristiane Ramalho, Manuel Ribeiro, and Rita de Cássia, "O galo e o pavão," *Comunicações do ISER* 58, no. 22 (2003): 5–49; "Polícia acha armas e drogas na casa de Tom Zé," *O Globo*, July 7, 1985, 14. The "Tom Zé" in question was Antônio José Ferreira of Pavão-Pavãozinho (no relation to the composer of the same name). The article provides details on the growth of drug trafficking in both Cantagalo and Pavão, and its connections to increasing hostilities between the two favelas.

27. The rhetoric of the "rights to the city" came into the favela movement via the work of French sociologist Henri Lefebvre. As analyzed in subsequent chapters, many of the leaders of the favela movement were well versed in social theory, particularly theories of urban mobilization. For Lefebvre's original work, see Henri Lefebvre, *Le Droit à la ville* (Paris: Editions du Seuil, 1968). For more recent analysis of the "rights to the city" and Rio's favelas, see Rafael Soares Gonçalves, "Le Droit, la politique et l'évolution des faveas à Rio de Janeiro: La precarité juridique du discours officiel," in *Ville visible, ville invisible: La jeune recherche urbaine en Europe*, ed. J. Boisonnade (Paris: Harmattan, 2008), 37–63.

28. Mário Sérgio Brum, "Entrevista: Eliana Sousa Silva," Interview, (Rio de Janeiro: Laboratório de História Oral e Imagem, Universidade Federal Fluminense, 2005).

29. Brum, "Entrevista: Eliana Sousa Silva."

30. For analysis of the struggle against traditional forms of patronage in the favela movement, see Robert Gay, *Popular Organization and Democracy in Rio de Janeiro: A Tale of Two Favelas* (Philadelphia: Temple University Press, 1994). For the evolution of patronage despite that movement and the compelling logic of negotiating within the framework of patronage, see Robert Gay, "The Broker and the Thief: A Parable (Reflections on Popular Politics in Brazil)," *Luso-Brazilian Review* 36, no. 1 (1999): 49–70.

31. For early analysis of the local political influence of drug traffickers in Rio's favelas, see Alba Zaluar, *A máquina e a revolta* (São Paulo: Editora Brasiliense, 1985). For subsequent investigation of this issue, see Elizabeth Leeds, "Cocaine and Parallel Polities in the Brazilian Urban Periphery. Constraints on Local-level Democratization," *Latin American Research Review* 31, no. 3 (1996): 47–83; Enrique Desmond Arias, *Drugs and Democracy in Rio de Janeiro: Trafficking, Social Networks, and Public Security* (Chapel Hill: University of North Carolina Press, 2006); Robert Gay, "Toward Uncivil Society: Causes and Consequences of Violence in Rio de Janeiro," in *Violent Democracies in Latin America*, ed. Enrique Desmond Arias and Daniel M. Gold-

stein, 201–225 (Durham, NC: Duke University Press, 2010). On militia influence over favela associations, with close investigation of the paradigmatic case of Rio das Pedras, see Marcelo Bauman Burgos, ed. *A utopia da comunidade* (Rio de Janeiro: PUC-Rio, 2002). For a more general treatment, see Alba Zaluar and Isabel Siqueira Conceição, "Favelas sob o controle das milícias: Que paz?" *São Paulo em Perspectiva* 21(2007): 89–101.

32. On the gleefully unruly nature of the PDT and *brizolistas* more generally, see João Trajano Sento-Sé, *Brizolismo: Estetização da política e carisma* (Rio de Janeiro: Fundação Getúlio Vargas, 1999).

33. On São Paulo, see Teresa Caldeira, *City of Walls: Crime, Segregation and Citizenship in São Paulo* (Berkeley: University of California Press, 2000). See also James Holston, *Insurgent Citizenship: Disjunctions of Democracy and Modernity in Brazil* (Princeton, NJ: Princeton University Press, 2008).

34. For rich analysis of this phenomenon across Latin America, see Enrique Desmond Arias and Daniel M. Goldstein, ed., *Violent Democracies in Latin America* (Durham, NC: Duke University Press, 2010).

35. Cristina Buarque de Hollanda, *Polícia e direitos humanos: Política de segurança pública no primeiro governo brizola* (Rio de Janeiro: Revan, 2005). See also Leonel Brizola, "Instaurou-se a crise," *Jornal do Brasil*, August 30, 1987.

36. Hollanda, *Polícia e direitos humanos*, esp. 135–40.

37. Hernando de Soto, *The Mystery of Capital: Why Capitalism Triumphs in the West and Fails Everywhere Else* (New York: Basic Books, 2000). De Soto bases his arguments on his own experience in urbanization projects in Lima, but he overemphasizes the importance of titling to the success of projects that depended on multiple variables. Subsequent projects that delivered title without simultaneous investment in material upgrading failed to make a significant improvement in the welfare of the neighborhoods in question. See, for example, Martim O. Smolka and Laura Mullahy, ed., *Perspectivas urbanas: Temas críticos en políticas de suelo en América Latina* (Cambridge, MA: Lincoln Institute of Land Policy, 2007).

38. In Rio informal property has offered investment opportunities as lucrative as formal real estate, both to individual residents and absentee landlords. See, for example, the articles collected in Pedro Abramo, ed., *A cidade da informalidade* (Rio de Janeiro: Sette Letras, 2003).

39. Sonia Oliveira, "Associação de moradores: Formatos diferenciados de participação política e representação de interesses," M.A. thesis, (IUPERJ, 1988).

CHAPTER TWO. MOBILIZATION

1. "Morro dos Cabritos tem lavanderia comunitária," *O Dia*, November 10, 1982, 10.

2. In August 1982, for example, Chagas Freitas had funded installation of

twenty-eight water spigots in Rocinha. Jorge Leite, a municipal councilman and part of the Chagas Freitas machine, celebrated the inauguration. Leite was as savvy a favela populist as Chagas Freitas himself, and remained a key figure in local politics through the 1990s. "Rocinha ganha 28 bicas de agua," *O Globo*, August 2, 1982, 7.

3. "Projeto Cidadão no Borel," *O Dia*, August 2, 1982, 10.

4. Bryan McCann, "Troubled Oasis: The Intertwining Histories of the Morro dos Cabritos and Bairro Peixoto," in *Cities from Scratch: Poverty and Informality in Urban Latin America*, ed. Brodwyn Fischer, Bryan McCann, and Javier Auyero (Durham, NC: Duke University Press), forthcoming.

5. José Luís Pires, *Minhas Verdades: Histórias e pensamento de um negro favelado* (Rio de Janeiro: Refluxus, 2004).

6. For background on transformations in Brazil's seminaries in the mid-twentieth century, see Kenneth Serbin, *Needs of the Heart: A Social and Cultural History of Brazil's Clergy and Seminaries* (Notre Dame, IN: University of Notre Dame Press, 2006); 144–200 and Marcelo Monteiro, "Igreja Social Clube," *Favela Tem Memória*, 2004.

7. The idea of a mutirão for favela improvements had emerged in the early 1960s, during the brief tenure of pioneering urbanist José Arthur Rios as secretary of social services in Carlos Lacerda's Guanabara gubernatorial administration. Rios barely had time to launch his "Operação Mutirão" before he was forced out by powerful representatives of the real-estate sector within Lacerda's cabinet, leaving Lacerda's endorsement of favela removal unchecked. But Rios's goals and terminology returned in Cabritos in the late 1970s. Lucia Lippi and Marly Motta, "José Arthur Rios: Depoimento," in *Capítulos da memória do urbanismo carioca*, ed. Américo Freire and Lúcia Lippi Oliveira (Rio de Janeiro: Folha Seca, 2002), 62–77.

8. Pires, *Minhas Verdades*. Arquivo do Pastoral das Favelas (hereafter, APF), "Cartilha do morador, o que é Pastoral das Favelas," 1994.

9. Because Sales eventually pulled the plug on the Pastoral das Favelas and other liberation theology initiatives within his archdiocese, he has often been dismissed as a conservative or, worse, a collaborator of the military regime. However, Sales played a key role both in resisting favela removal and in sheltering political refugees, choosing to challenge the military dictatorship on the basis of moral failings rather than ideological offenses. For an example of Sales's thought on favela reform, see his opinion piece, Dom Eugênio Sales, "Urbanização das favelas," *Jornal do Brasil*, June 13, 1981, 11. For a brief summary of Sales's position regarding the dictatorship, see Mauro de Bias, "O Bispo Vermelho?" *Revista de História*, July 10, 2012. For the standard version of the Pastoral das Favelas association statute, see APF, "Estatuto da Associação de Moradores Canto da Sabiá," in *Associação de Moradores* (Rio de Janeiro, 1994).

10. For a detailed explanation of the struggle against removal and the plan for

cooperative housing in Cabritos, see Arquivo Geral da Cidade do Rio de Janeiro (hereafter, AGC), "Morro dos Cabritos," in *Rio de Janeiro, 4 Favelas: Rocinha, Morro dos Cabritos, Maré* (Rotterdam, Netherlands: Bouwcentrum International Education, 1982).

11. Marcus André BC de Melo, "Políticas públicas e habitação popular: Continuidade e ruptura, 1979–1988," *Revista de Administração Municipal* 36, no. 191 (April/June 1989): 44–59.

12. AGC, "Morro dos Cabritos."

13. Eliana Athayde, author interview, March 2006.

14. Marcelo Monteiro, "Um papa no morro," *Favela Tem Memória*, September 9, 2003, http://www.favelatemmemoria.com.br/publique/cgi/cgilua.exe/sys/start .htm?sid=4&infoid=41&from_info_index=6, accessed on May 23, 2013.

15. AnaCris Bittencourt, "Entrevista: Irineu Guimarães," *Democracia Viva* 35, June 2007, 68.

16. As one MR-8 directive put it, "It is necessary to stimulate vigorously rapid growth in the popular field of the struggle against the dictatorship." MR-8, *Resoluções políticas do Segundo Congresso do MR-8* (São Paulo: Quilombo, 1980), 49.

17. Eladir Fátima Nascimento dos Santos, "Tecendo redes: Narrativas sobre a FAFERJ," in *VII Encontro Regional Sudeste de História Oral* (Rio de Janeiro: FIOCRUZ, 2007), 1–17.

18. Santos, "Tecendo Redes: Narrativas Sobre a FAFERJ."

19. This narrative of the first FAFERJ split draws on analysis by Eli Diniz and Mário Brum. Eli Diniz, *Voto e máquina política: Patronagem e clientelismo no Rio de Janeiro* (Rio de Janeiro: Paz e Terra, 1982), 144–60; Mário Sérgio Brum, "O povo acredita na gente: Rupturas e continuidades no movimento comunitário das favelas cariocas nas décadas de 1980 e 1990," M.A. thesis, (Universidade Federal Fluminense, 2006).

20. Eli Diniz, *Voto e máquina política*, 154.

21. Diniz, *Voto e máquina política*, 154–55.

22. Diniz, *Voto e máquina política*, 145.

23. APF, "Estatutos de Associações de Moradores," in *Associações de Moradores, pasta (folder)*1 (1979–80).

24. APF, "Carta de Jonas Rodrigues a A. Silva," in Relatórios Diversos, pasta 1 (1981). Santos, "Tecendo redes."

25. APF, "Carta de Jonas Rodrigues a A. Silva"; MR-8, *Resoluções políticas do Segundo Congresso do MR-8*.

26. APF, "FAFERJ, diversos," in *Associações de Moradores*, pasta 1 (1981).

27. On the Pastoral das Favelas's Ford Foundation funding, see APF, "Ford Foundation to Pastoral das Favelas," in *Projetos*, pasta 1 (1981). The letter of funding grants US$150,000 over the course of two years and stipulates that the funding

"may not be used to attempt to influence legislation or the outcome of any public election." In theory, the Ford Foundation grant was for the Pastoral's judicial wing; in practice there was no distinction between the judicial wing and the Pastoral's initiatives in founding and advising new favela associations.

28. For rich analysis of the historical evolution of land law and exclusion in Brazil, see James Holston, *Insurgent Citizenship: Disjunctions of Democracy and Modernity in Brazil* (Princeton, NJ: Princeton University Press, 2008), 136–42. Chap. 4 of Holston's work treats usucapião and restricted access to landowning in detail.

29. The APF contains separate files on the legal proceedings concerning dozens of favelas, almost all of them initiated in 1979–80 by the same four lawyers, Athayde most prominently. See, for example, APF, "Documentos diversos, seção judiciária," in Guararapes (1980).

30. The advocacy by the Pastoral das Favelas of a five-year standard for urban adverse possession played a decisive role in the ratification of a clause to this effect in the Constitution of 1988, a clause later strengthened in the Statute of the City of 2001 and incorporated as an amendment to the constitution. Allies in São Paulo and Recife joined them in pushing this legal agenda. But Archibishop Sales, prompted by the Pastoral lawyers, was the first moderate leader of national prestige to advocate the five-year adverse possession as a necessary approach to Brazil's growing housing crisis among the urban poor. Sales, "Urbanização das favelas."

31. None of the cases I located in the APF contains a legal claim for expropriation based on usucapião. Regarding the practical difficulties of filing claims based on adverse possession in favelas, see Rose Compans, "A regularização fundiária de favelas no estado do Rio de Janeiro," *Revista Rio de Janeiro* 9 (January/April 2003): 48–49.

32. Santa Marta is also widely known as Dona Marta. Until the 1990s, most residents insisted on the name Santa Marta, whereas most outsiders referred to the favela as Dona Marta. In recent years, however, the name Santa Marta has become generally accepted, with the exception of the favela's evangelical community, whose members refer to the favela as Dona Marta.

33. Adair Rocha, *Cidade Cerzida: A costura da cidadania no Morro Santa Marta* (Rio de Janeiro: Museu da República, 2005). See also Caco Barcellos, *Abusado: O dono do Morro Dona Marta* (São Paulo: Record, 2004).

34. This biographical sketch of Itamar Silva is pulled from the following sources: AnaCris Bittencourt, "Entrevista: Itamar Silva," *Democracia Viva* 42 (2009): 36–51; Itamar Silva, "Depoimento: Itamar Silva," in *A Favela fala: Depoimentos ao* CPDOC, ed. Dulce Chaves Pandolfi and Mário Grynszpan, 299–360 (Rio de Janeiro: FGV, 2003); Itamar Silva, "Depoimento: Itamar Silva," in *Morar na Metrópole: Ensaios sobre habitação popular no Rio de Janeiro*, ed. IPLAN (Rio de Janeiro: IPLAN, 1988), 54–60.

35. Bittencourt, "Entrevista: Itamar Silva," 44. Silva insists that he was only an ally, never an official "agent," of the Pastoral das Favelas. This is true, and it echoes careful qualifications made by Eliana Souza Silva—another young favela leader— about links to the Pastoral. But there were relatively few official Pastoral agents: most participants, such as both Itamar and Eliana Silva, were informally linked to the Pastoral but clearly recognized as part of the Pastoral cohort within FAFERJ and in local associations. Internal Pastoral das Favelas communications consistently referred to both Itamar Silva and Eliana Souza Silva as key leaders of that cohort.

36. Silva, "Depoimento: Itamar Silva," 311–14.

37. Carlos Nelson Ferreira dos Santos, "Velhas novidades nos modos de urbanização Brasileira," in Habitação em questão, ed. Lícia Valladares (Rio de Janeiro: Zahar, 1979), 41.

38. For population figures, as well as keen analysis of the political strategies Nova Iguaçu's loteamentos, see Scott Mainwaring, "Grass Roots Popular Movements and the Struggle for Democracy: Nova Iguaçu, 1974–1985," in Working Papers (South Bend, IN: Kellog Institute, Notre Dame University, 1985), vol. 52, 1–48; and Carlos Nelson Ferreira dos Santos, O processo de crescimento e ocupação da periferia (Rio de Janeiro: IBAM, 1982), 123.

39. For general background on the difficult relationship between church and state in the latter stages of the dictatorship, see Ken Serbin, Secret Dialogues: Church-State Relations, Torture and Social Justice in Authoritarian Brazil (Pittsburgh: University of Pittsburgh Press, 2000), 219–32. For specific analysis of Hypólito's connections to the MAB, see Leda Lúcia Queiroz, "Movimentos sociais urbanos: O Movimento Amigos de Bairro de Nova Iguaçu," M.A. thesis, (Universidade Federal do Rio de Janeiro, 1981), 136.

40. For further detail on the growth of the MAB, see Queiroz, "Movimentos sociais urbanos"; and Vera Lúcia Pedra Clímaco Mendes, "Tanta gente sem terra e tanta terra sem gente: Movimento do Mutirão de Nova Aurora, 1979–1995," M.A. thesis, (Universidade Federal do Rio de Janeiro, 2006). See also Mainwaring, "Grass Roots Popular Movements and the Struggle for Democracy," 14–17.

41. Federal Law 6.766/79 established 125 square meters as the minimum lot size for single-family homes, but gave municipal governments the power to grant title and provide services to existing smaller lots. Luciana Corrêa do Lago, "O movimento dos loteamentos do Rio de Janeiro," M.A. thesis, (Universidade Federal do Rio de Janeiro, 1990).

42. The lower-middle-class neighborhood of Catumbi mobilized in the early 1970s in response to development threats, but Catumbi's struggle did not find echoes in a broader middle-class movement until 1979–80. For details on Catumbi's struggle, see Mark Kehren, "Tunnel Vision: Urban Renewal in Rio de Janeiro, 1960–1975," Ph.D. diss., (University of Maryland, 2006), 247–54.

43. Centro de Pesquisa e Documentação da Fundação Getúlio Vargas (hereafter, CPDOC-FGV), "Depoimento: Jó Rezende," in História contemporânea do Brasil (Rio de Janeiro: CPDOC-FGV/ALERJ, 2001 [1999]), 16. Jó Resende's name is alternately spelled Jô Rezende, and all possible combinations of these variations. I have chosen the most common spelling for the main text, and cite sources by the spelling they use.

44. Arquivo Público do Estado do Rio de Janeiro (hereafter, APERJ), "Vivemos um momento ainda inicial de reanimação . . . ," in Ação popular e movimentos de bairro (1979). Ângela Borba donated both her papers and those of her deceased husband, Jair Ferreira de Sá, to the APERJ. Documents in both these personal collections (Fundos JFS and AB in the APERJ system) reveal their extensive activities in a range of middle-class associations in the late 1970s.

45. APERJ, "Objetivos políticos gerais do trabalho do bairro," in Ação popular e os movimentos de bairro.

46. APERJ, "Vivemos um momento ainda inicial de reanimação."

47. For Porfírio's own reflections on these events, see Pedro Porfirio, O poder da rua (Rio de Janeiro: Vozes, 1981). For an influential example of the Jornal do Brasil's coverage, see Carlos Drummond de Andrade, "A boca do túnel," Jornal do Brasil, October 11, 1977.

48. For Porfírio's account of this path, see Porfírio, O poder da rua. For a more caustic assessment of Porfírio's political strategies, see CPDOC-FGV, "Carta de Herbert de Souza para Pedro Porfirio Sampaio," in HS.1981.05.00 ib/t (1989); and CPDOC-FGV, "Carta de Herbert de Souza para Marcello Alencar," in HS.1981.05.00 ib/t (1989).

49. APERJ, "Infiltração de grupos esquerdistas em favelas e Associações de bairros," in Comunismo, pasta 155 (1979). See also APERJ, "Projeto de pissertação," comunismo, pasta 158, Douglas Cerqueira Gonçalves (MR-8), October 18, 1982. On collaboration and competition between the MR-8 and the APML in one favela association, see Mauro Amoroso, "Caminhos do lembrar: A construção e os usos políticos da memória no morro do Borel" Ph.D. diss., Fundação Getúlio Vargas–Centro de Pesquisa e Documentação de História Contemporânea do Brasil, 2012).

50. On the importance of human rights activism in forcing redemocratization, see James N. Green, We Cannot Remain Silent: Opposition to the Brazilian Military Dictatorship in the United States (Durham, NC: Duke University Press, 2010).

51. Belisa Ribeiro, Bomba no Riocentro (Rio de Janeiro: Codecri, 1982).

52. APERJ, "Tribuna da Imprensa, 'A Direita Investe contra FAMERJ e as Associações,'" in Departamento Geral de Investigações Especiais (DGIE), Geral e Administração, pasta 293-A (1981); APERJ, "Carta enviada ao delegado do Departamento de Ordem Política e Social," in DGIE, Geral e Administração, pasta 293-A (1981).

53. Marly Silva da Motta, Américo Freire, and Carlos Eduardo Sarmento, A política carioca em quatro tempos (Rio de Janeiro: FGV, 2004), 66.

54. For details on Chagas Freitas's use of the planning agency for the metropolitan region, see Linda Maria de Pontes Gondim, "Planners in the Face of Power: The Case of the Metropolitan Region of Rio de Janeiro, Brazil," Ph.D. diss., (Cornell University, Ithaca, NY, 1986).

55. Francisco de Mello Franco, "Depoimento," in *Capítulos da memória do urbanismo carioca*, ed. Américo Freire and Lúcia Lippi Oliveira (Rio de Janeiro: Folha Seca, 2002), 190–201; Carlos Eduardo Sarmento, ed., *Chagas Freitas: Perfil político* (Rio de Janeiro: FGV, 1999), 205–23.

56. CPDOC-FGV, "Carta de Clóvis Brigagão para Herbert de Souza," in HS e/c C. Brigagão, (1979); Leonel Brizola et al., "Carta de Lisboa," Manifesto, http://www.pdtsp.org.br/index.php?option=com_content&task=view&id=474&Itemid=66, accessed on May 23, 2013.

57. Bittencourt, "Entrevista: Irineu Guimarães," 70. On the internal divisions within the PMDB, see Sarmento, *Chagas Freitas*.

58. Margaret Keck, *The Worker's Party and Democratization in Brazil* (New Haven, CT: Yale University Press, 1992), 47–49, 97–98.

59. Amaury de Souza, Olavo Brasil de Lima Junior, and Marcus Figueiredo, "Brizola e as eleições de 1982 no Rio de Janeiro," *Estudos* (1985): 20–22.

60. CPDOC-FGV, "Depoimento: Lysâneas Maciel," in *História contemporânea do Brasil* (Rio de Janeiro: CPDOC, 2003 [1998]), 31–34.

61. Figueiredo, "Brizola e as Eleições de 1982 no Rio de Janeiro," 22.

62. Carlos Eduardo Sarmento, "Entre o carisma e a rotina: As eleições de 1982 e o primeiro governo," in *A força do povo: Brizola e o Rio de Janeiro*, ed. Marieta de Moraes Ferreira (Rio de Janeiro: FGV, 1982), 52–59; Figueiredo, "Brizola e as Eleições de 1982 no Rio de Janeiro," 24–27.

63. "Propaganda política do PDT," *Jornal do Brasil*, November 14, 1982.

64. Darcy Ribeiro, *Espaço Democrático* 1, no. 16 (June 1–7, 1984): 1–12. Also cited in Cristina Buarque de Hollanda, *Polícia e direitos humanos: Política de segurança pública no primeiro governo brizola* (Rio de Janeiro: Revan, 2005), 68.

65. Nelson do Valle e Silva and Gláucio Ary Dillon Soares, "O charme discreto do socialismo moreno," *Dados: Revista de Ciências Sociais* 28, no. 2 (1985): 253–73; Hollanda, *Polícia e direitos humanos*, 57–58. For investigation of Nascimento's importance as a black intellectual and activist, see Paulina Alberto, *Terms of Inclusion: Black Intellectuals in Twentieth-Century Brazil* (Chapel Hill: University of North Carolina Press, 2011).

66. João Trajano Sento-Sé, *Brizolismo: Estetização da política e carisma* (Rio de Janeiro: FGV, 1999), 164.

67. CPDOC-FGV, "Depoimento: Jó Rezende," 19.

68. Gilberto Rodriguez, "Depoimento," in *A construção de um estado: A fusão em debate*, ed. Marly Motta and Carlos Eduardo Sarmento (Rio de Janeiro: FGV, 2001), 227.

69. Gilberto Rodriguez, "Depoimento," 227; Paulo Henrique Amorim and Maria Helena Passos, Plim Plim: A peleja de Brizola contra a fraude eleitoral (São Paulo: Conrad Livros, 2005).

70. For an account of the balloting controversy that gives firm credence to the brizolista allegations, see Passos, Plim Plim.

71. CPDOC-FGV, "Depoimento: Lysâneas Maciel," 35.

CHAPTER THREE. REFORM

1. Rodolfo Moraes, "Intervenções governamentais sobre movimentos de invasões de terrenos urbanos: Estudo de casos no município do Rio de Janeiro em 1983, M.A. thesis, Escola Brasileira de Administração Pública," Fundação Getúlio Vargas, 1988); Américo Freire, "Novo sindicalismo e movimentos sociais," in A força do povo: Brizola e o Rio de Janeiro, ed. Marieta de Moraes Ferreira (Rio de Janeiro: FGV, 2008), 141–49.

2. Bairro Barcellos was an irregular subdivision that became surrounded and ultimately engulfed by and indistinguishable from the favela. Whereas many subdivisions on Rio's west side made a slow transition from informality to formality, Bairro Barcellos became more entrenched in the informal sphere. The area's advantageous location did spur it toward consolidation and diversification well ahead of the rest of the favela. By 1983, Bairro Barcellos was the gateway to Rio's largest favela and an inviting target for the PDT.

3. Edu Casaes, "De olho na política," Depoimento, Viva Rio, http://www.favela temmemoria.com.br/publique/cgi/cgilua.exe/sys/start.htm?infoid=122&tpl=print erview&sid=2, accessed 28 May, 2013; José Martins de Oliveira, "Depoimento: José Martins de Oliveira," in A Favela fala: Depoimentos ao CPDOC, ed. Dulce Chaves Pandolfi and Mário Grynszpan (Rio de Janeiro: FGV, 2003), 41–43.

4. "Brizola inicia obras em morro e pede cooperação," O Globo, October 5, 1983; Itamar Silva, "Depoimento: Itamar Silva," in A Favela fala: Depoimentos ao CPDOC, ed. Dulce Chaves Pandolfi and Mário Grynszpan (Rio de Janeiro: FGV, 2003), 338–39.

5. Hélio de Oliveira, "Depoimento: Hélio de Oliveira," in A Favela fala: Depoimentos ao CPDOC, ed. Dulce Chaves Pandolfi and Mário Grynszpan (Rio de Janeiro: FGV, 2003), 257–59.

6. Walter Pereira, "Depoimento: Walter Pereira," in A Favela fala: Depoimentos ao CPDOC, ed. Dulce Chaves Pandolfi and Mário Grynszpan (Rio de Janeiro: FGV, 2003), 278–85.

7. Silva, "Depoimento: Itamar Silva."; Mário Sérgio Brum, "Entrevista: Eliana Sousa Silva," Interview, (Rio de Janeiro: Laboratório de História Oral e Imagem, Universidade Federal Fluminense, 2005).

8. Porfírio initially cut Project Mutirão from 500 to 150 favelas, inspiring the

pastoral cohort to stage protests outside the governor's office and to push for stronger defense of the project within FAFERJ. These developments isolated the pastoral cohort from other favela leaders, ultimately leading to their withdrawal from the favela federation. Mário Sérgio Brum, "O povo acredita na gente: Rupturas e continuidades no movimento comunitário das favelas cariocas nas décadas de 1980 e 1990" (Universidade Federal Fluminense, 2006), 119–33; Arquivo do Pastoral das Favelas (hereafter, APF), Codeprom Manifesto, Relatórios Diversos, April 1985.

9. When sociologist Robert Gay probes this ambiguity in a series of publications analyzing the attempt in the 1980s to replace old-school clientelism with participatory government, he moves toward a larger view of the difficulty of transcending clientelism in a political context marked by corruption and violence. Gay's analysis suggests that clientelist practices were so deeply embedded in Rio's political structure that efforts to eradicate them not only faced long odds, but themselves led to new manifestations of clientelism. In this context, relatively forthright exchange of votes for services often brought both greater benefits and greater leverage to the urban poor. Robert Gay, *Popular Organization and Democracy in Rio de Janeiro: A Tale of Two Favelas* (Philadelphia: Temple University Press, 1994); Gay, "The Broker and the Thief: A Parable (Reflections on Popular Politics in Brazil)," *Luso-Brazilian Review* 36, no. 1 (1999): 49–70; Gay, "The Even More Difficult Transition from Clientelism to Citizenship: Lessons from Brazil," in *Out of the Shadows: Political Action and the Informal Economy in Latin America*, ed. Patricia Fernandez-Kelly and John Shefner (State College: Penn State University Press, 2006), 195–218.

10. "Caó promete 1 milhão de lotes em 5 anos," *Última Hora*, October 20, 1983.

11. Rose Compans, "A regularização fundiária de favelas no Estado do Rio de Janeiro," *Revista Rio de Janeiro* 9 (January/April 2003): 41–53.

12. Adair Rocha, Cecilia Minayo, Vitor Valla, and Eliana Athayde, *Favelas e as organizações comunitárias* (Rio de Janeiro: Centro da Defesa dos Direitos Humanos Bento Rubião, 1994), 71.

13. Walther Jacintho Soares, "Nova política para as favelas," *Jornal do Brasil*, January 8, 1984.

14. "Chapéu Mangueira," *Favelão* 3, no. 18 (January 1985): 4.

15. "Resoluções do IV Congresso da FAFERJ," *Favelão* 3, no. 18 (January 1985): 5.

16. "Estado compra Borel e dá lotes a favelados," *Jornal do Brasil*, May 27, 1984, 13; Maria Silvia Muylaert de Araujo, "Possibilidades e limites de uma política pública habitacional: O programa 'Cada Família Um Lote'," M.A. thesis, (Universidade Federal do Rio de Janeiro, 1988), 77.

17. Araujo, "Possibilidades e limites de uma política pública habitacional," 88; Maria Silvia Muylaert de Araújo, "Regularização fundiária de favelas: Imóveis alugados. O caso do programa 'Cada Família Um Lote' no Rio de Janeiro," *Revista de Administração Municipal* 3, no. 195 (1990): 26–35.

18. Maria Silvia Muylaert de Araújo, "Actors' Strategies in a Case Study Favela: Rio das Pedras in Rio de Janeiro," Report no. 1549, (Rotterdam: Institute for Housing Studies, 1990). See also Sonia Oliveira, "Associação de moradores: Formatos diferenciados de participação política e representação de interesses," M.A. thesis, (IUPERJ, 1988). For analysis of similar events in Jacarezinho, see Rafael Soares Gonçalves, "A política, o direito e as favelas do Rio de Janeiro: Um breve olhar histórico," *Urbana: Revista Eletrônica do Centro Interdisciplinar de Estudos da Cidade* 1, no. 1 (2006): 14.

19. Araujo, "Possibilidades e limites de uma política pública habitacional," 52.

20. Araujo, "Possibilidades e limites de uma política pública habitacional," 52–53; Gonçalves, "A política, O direito e as favelas do Rio de Janeiro," 14.

21. Moraes, "Intervenções governamentais sobre movimentos de invasões de terrenos urbanos."

22. Michael G. Donovan, "At the Doors of Legality: Planners, Favelados and the Titling of Urban Brazil," Ph.D. diss., (University of California, Berkeley, 2007); Rafael Soares Gonçalves, "O debate jurídico em torno da urbanização de favelas no Rio de Janeiro," *Revista Internacional de Direito e Cidadania* 2 (October 2008): 139–48.

23. Maria Laís Pereira da Silva, *Avaliação do programa de eletrificação de interesse social*, 4 vols. (Rio de Janeiro: IBAM, 1985), vol. 1.

24. Maria Laís Pereira da Silva, *Avaliação do programa de eletrificação de interesse social*, 3:3–21.

25. Silva, *Avaliação do programa de Eletrificação de Interesse Social*, 3:23.

26. Silva, *Avaliação do Programa de Eletrificação de Interesse Social*, 1:30.

27. Berta Treiger and Eliane Faerstein, "Efeitos de um projeto de urbanização de favela nas atividades locais de geração de renda: O caso Pavão-Pavãozinho," *Revista de Administração Municipal* 35, no. 187 (April–June 1988): 38–50; Bruno Aragão Bastos, "O Povo Unido Jamais Será Vencido: História do Morro da Formiga," Monografia,(Universidade Federal Fluminense, 2008), 40–44.

28. These semipublic vocational programs were run by government agencies but funded by mandated employer contributions. For analysis, see Barbara Weinstein, *For Social Peace in Brazil: Industrialists and the Remaking of the Working Class in São Paulo, 1920–1964* (Chapel Hill: University of North Carolina Press, 1997).

29. Darcy Ribeiro, *Nossa escola é uma calamidade* (Rio de Janeiro: Salamandra Editora, 1984).

30. For material on Ribeiro's academic following, see Mércio Pereira Gomes, *Darcy Ribeiro* (São Paulo: Ícone Editora, 2000). For Ribeiro's general interpretation of Brazil, steeped in dependency theory, see Darcy Ribeiro, *O povo brasileiro: A formação e o sentido do Brasil* (São Paulo: Companhia das Letras, 1995). For Ribeiro's understanding of race, see Darcy Ribeiro, *Mestiço é que é bom* (Rio de Janeiro: Editora Revan, 1996). For Ribeiro's interpretation of Rio's educational needs early in the Brizola administration, see Ribeiro, *Nossa escola é uma calamidade*.

31. Helena Bomeny, "Salvar pela escola: Programa Especial de Educação," in A força do povo: Brizola e o Rio de Janeiro, ed. Marieta de Moraes Ferreira (Rio de Janeiro: FGV-CPDOC, (2008), 101–2.

32. Darcy Ribeiro, O livro dos CIEPS (Rio de Janeiro: Bloch Editora, 1986).

33. "Juiz condena Brizola por CIEPS na beira da estrada," O Globo, July 18, 1986; Ribeiro, O livro dos CIEPS, 14–17, 48.

34. Oscar Niemeyer, "CIEPS na concepção do seu arquiteto," Diário Oficial, Caderno Especial de Educação (1985):3.

35. Bomeny, "Salvar Pela Escola," 107–8.

36. For further details on the initial group of students in the Tancredo Neves CIEP, see the retrospective series published in O Globo in 2006, for example, Selma Schmidt, "André," O Globo, June 2, 2006; and Selma Schmidt, "José," O Globo, June 1, 2006.

37. "Impasse no Andaraí: CIEP ou área de lazer," O Globo, Februrary 4, 1986.

38. Ribeiro, O livro dos CIEPS, 137–38; Ana Chrystina Venancio Mignot, "CIEP— Centro Integrado de Educação Pública: Alternativa para a qualidade do ensino ou nova investida do populismo na educação," Em Aberto 8, no. 44 (December 1989): 45–63.

39. Bomeny, "Salvar pela escola," 108–10; Freire, "Novo sindicalismo e movimentos sociais," 138–40.

40. Mignot, "CIEP," 52–61.

41. "Apadrinhamento em CIEPS leva Brizola à irritação," Jornal do Brasil, April 10, 1986, 7.

42. "Cai por terra a promessa de Brizola de construir 500 Cieps até o fim do mandato," O Globo, January 25, 1987; Lígia Mefano, author interview, September 2006.

43. In Domingues's own assessment, his greatest achievement as secretary of security lay not in achieving any clear result in public security, but in securing funding to buy six hundred police cars. Centro de Pesquisa e Documentação da Fundação Getúlio Vargas (hereafter, CPDOC-FGV), "Depoimento: Osvaldo Inácio Domingues," Depoimento, (Rio de Janeiro: CPDOC, 2001 [1999]), 12–19.

44. Vivian Zampa and Mariana Mello, "Entrevista: Coronel Ubiratan de Oliveira Ângelo," in Sonho de uma polícia didadã: Coronel Carlos Magno Nazareth Cerqueira, ed. Ana Beatriz Leal, Íbis Silva Pereira, and Oswaldo Munteal Filho (Rio de Janeiro: UERJ, 2011), 107.

45. Carlos Magno Nazareth Cerqueira, "Discurso de despedida da primeira gestão," in Sonho de uma polícia cidadã: Coronel Carlos Magno Nazareth Cerqueira, ed. Ana Beatriz Leal, Íbis Silva Pereira, and Oswaldo Munteal Filho (Rio de Janeiro: UERJ, 2011 [1986]), 159.

46. Zampa and Mello, "Entrevista," 107.

47. Leonel Brizola, "Instaurou-se a crise," Jornal do Brasil, August 30, 1987, 7.

48. Zampa and Mello, "Entrevista," 110.

49. Conselho de Justiça, Segurança Pública e Direitos Humanos, Decreto número 6.635, April 13, 1983.

50. Cristina Buarque de Hollanda, *Polícia e direitos humanos: Política de segurança pública no primeiro governo Brizola* (Rio de Janeiro: Revan, 2005), 90.

51. Hollanda, *Polícia e direitos humanos*, 98–99.

52. Cerqueira, "Discurso de despedida da primeira gestão," 163.

53. José Augusto de Souza Rodrigues, "Imagens da ordem e da violência na cidade do Rio de Janeiro," M.A. thesis, (IUPERJ, 1993), 113.

54. "A polícia militar e as comunidades," *Favelão* 3, no. 18 (January 1985): 9.

55. "Violência," *Favelão* 2, no. 15 (1984): 8.

56. "A polícia militar e as comunidades."

57. Helena Duque, Regina Barreiros and Vera Perfeito, "Violência não tem fim nas classes mais necessitadas," *Jornal do Brasil*, August 3, 1986, 22.

58. CPDOC-FGV, "Depoimento: Osvaldo Inácio Domingues," 20–22.

59. Vivan Zampa e Bruna Belchior, "Entrevista: Coronel Sérgio Antunes Barbosa," in *Sonho de uma polícia cidadã: Coronel Carlos Magno Nazareth Cerqueira*, ed. Ana Beatriz Leal, Íbis Silva Pereira, and Oswaldo Munteal Filho (Rio de Janeiro: UERJ, 2011), 66.

60. Alba Zaluar, *A máquina e a evolta* (São Paulo: Editora Brasiliense, 1985).

61. Quoted in Hollanda, *Polícia e direitos humanos*, 118.

62. Bruna Belchior and Marieta Pinheiro de Carvalho, "Entrevista: Mina Seinfeld de Carakushansky," in *Sonho de uma polícia cidadã: Coronel Carlos Magno Nazareth Cerqueira*, ed. Ana Beatriz Leal, Íbis Silva Pereira, and Oswaldo Munteal Filho (Rio de Janeiro: UERJ, 2011), 94–95.

63. Carlos Magno Nazareth Cerqueira, *O futuro de uma ilusão: O sonho de uma nova política* (Rio de Janeiro: Editora Freitas Bastos, 2001), 49–50.

64. Ana Maria Brasileiro and Nanci Valadares, "A Rocinha, o Laboriaux e outras estórias," *Revista de Administração Municipal* 30, no. 167 (April–June 1983): 72–81.; "Mais um caso de invasão de terrenos na Rocinha," *O Globo*, January 19, 1984, Barra 1; "Prefeito: Loteamento na Rocinha é ilegal," *Jornal do Brasil*, May 26, 1984, 12.

65. Marcelo Monteiro, "DNA das Urnas," *Favela Tem Memória*, July 7, 2004, http://www.favelatemmemoria.com.br/publique/cgi/cgilua.exe/sys/start.htm?infoid=101&sid=4&from_info_index=1, accessed on May 23, 2013.

66. João Trajano Sento-Sé, Ignácio Cano, Andréia Marinho, "Efeitos humanitários dos conflitos entre facções do tráfico de drogas numa comunidade do Rio de Janeiro," in *Laboratório de análise da violência* (Rio de Janeiro: UERJ, 2006), 5–7; "Rocinha: Polícia procurava mulher e encontrou Jorge Charuto," *O Dia*, March 26, 1984, 10.

67. "Rocinha cai no samba para comemorar a posse de Maria Helena," *O Globo*, October 11, 1984.

68. Lygia Segala, author interview, June 2006.

69. "O dia a dia da Rocinha: Uma cidade de contrastes," *O Globo*, January 27, 1985, Grande Rio, 1.

70. "O novo dia a dia de Maria Helena," *O Globo*, November 1, 1984, Barra 1; "[Quarenta] 40 assassinatos e crianças no crime organizado Dos Tóxicos," *Jornal dos Sports*, March 8, 1985, 7; João Trajano Sento-Sé, "Efeitos humanitários dos conflitos entre facções do tráfico de drogas numa comunidade do Rio de Janeiro," 21; "Líderes da Rocinha reafirmam queixa contra violência," *Jornal do Brasil*, August 19, 1987, Cidade, 12b.

71. James Patrick Freeman, "Face to Face but Worlds Apart: The Geography of Class in the Public Space of Rio de Janeiro," Ph.D. diss., (University of California, Berkeley, 2002), 159–60.

72. Manoel Ribeiro, "O morro: Territórios, espaços e pertencimentos," in *O galo e o pavão*, ed. Regina Novaes and Marilena Cunha, (Rio de Janeiro: ISER, 2003), 45–49.

73. Mefano, interview, September 2006.

74. "Governador vai a Ipanema e toma posse do Panorama," *Jornal do Brasil*, February 3, 1984, 5.

75. Treiger and Faerstein, "Efeitos de um projeto de urbanização de favela nas atividades locais de geração de renda," 40–43.

76. Treiger and Faerstein, "Efeitos de um projeto de urbanização de favela nas atividades locais de geração de renda," 43–48.

77. Pavão association president Dionísio was replaced several months afterward by a new president, Sebastião Teodoro, but Teodoro did not change the association's strategic relationships. For further details on the negotiations post mudslide between state and municipal government and the Pavão-Pavãozinho association, see APF, "Grande Tragédia: Pavão-Pavãozinho," pasta 1 (1983–84). For the comments on the relative protection offered by the association and the military police, see the untitled newspaper clipping from *O Globo*, December 30, 1983, included in the same folder of documents.

78. Silva worked with 254 local composers on these sambas, including Genaro Soalheiro, Walter Coragem, and Pedro Butina. These otherwise unheralded cowriters often used pseudonyms in order to protect themselves from police persecution. As a result, Silva's sambas can be understood as a collective account of the changing drug traffic. See Claudia Neiva de Matos, "Bezerra da Silva: Singular e plural," *Ipotesi* 15, no. 2 (July/December 2011): 99–114.

79. J. Paulo da Silva, "Tóxico leva PM a cercar de novo Pavão e Pavãozinho," *Jornal do Brasil*, July 7, 1985, 21.

80. Silva and Oliveira's complete findings are available in the four-volume report; see esp. Silva, *Avaliação do programa de eletrificação de interesse social*, 1. For a capsule version, see María Laís Pereira da Silva and Isabel Cristina Eiras de Oliveira, "Eletrificação de favelas," *Revista de Administração Municipal* 33, no. 179 (April–June 1986): 6–17.

81. Treiger and Faerstein, "Efeitos de um projeto de urbanização de favela nas atividades locais de geração de renda," 43–49.

CHAPTER FOUR. THE BREAKING POINT

1. "Pedetista não vê socialismo," *Jornal do Brasil*, January 15, 1986, 8; Marcelo Baumann Burgos, M.A. thesis, "A Falência da prefeitura do Rio de Janeiro" (UFRJ, 1992), 65.

2. Braga skirted the limitations of the Plano Cruzado (Cruzado Plan) on tax increases by raising the units in which taxes and fees were calculated, rather than the taxes themselves, a distinction without a difference. Burgos, "A falência da prefeitura do Rio de Janeiro," 4:5; Roberto Saturnino Braga, *Governo-comunidade: Socialismo no Rio* (Rio de Janeiro: Paz e Terra, 1989), 41.

3. Braga, *Governo-Comunidade*.

4. Escadinha's escape has been widely recounted. For an extensive review of journalistic coverage, see Alexandre Magno González de Lacerda, "Hegemonia e resistência: Imprensa, violência e cultura popular," M.A. thesis, (UFF, 2009), 19–31.

5. For biographical detail on Escadinha, see *Extra* newspaper's series "Uma vida de crimes e fugas," *Extra*, April 5, 2009, http://extra.globo.com/casos-de-policia/escadinhauma-vida-crimes-fugas-399692.html, accessed 28 May 2013.

6. Carlos Amorim and Eduardo Campos Coelho, "Da Falange Vermelha a Escadinha: O poder nas prisões," *Presença* 11(January 1988): 106–14.

7. Ben Penglase, "The Bastard Child of the Dictatorship: The Comando Vermelho and the Birth of 'Narco-Culture' in Rio de Janeiro," *Luso-Brazilian Review* 45:1 (February 2008): 118–45.

8. Israel Tabak, "Pobreza e repulsa à ação policial fazem a marginalidade do Juramento," *Jornal do Brasil*, January 5, 1986, 12.

9. Flávio Ferreira, Paulo Fernando Cavallieri, Marcia Coutinho, Fani Baratz, and Yolanda Villela, *Quatro estudos* (Rio de Janeiro: Prefeitura da Cidade do Rio de Janeiro, 1986).

10. Ferreira et al., *Quatro estudos*, 14.

11. Iplan was most successful in this regard in the technical work that underpinned new zoning codes through most of Rio's south zone. The middle-class neighborhood associations, such as the one in Cosme Velho that had given Jó

Resende his entrance into municipal politics, had many of their demands met through new municipal restrictions on growth in older neighborhoods.

12. Braga, *Governo-Comunidade*, 42–43; Centro de Pesquisa e Documentação da Fundação Getúlio Vargas (hereafter, CPDOC-FGV), "Depoimento: Jó Rezende," in *História contemporânea do Brasil* (Rio de Janeiro: CPDOC-FGV, 2001 [1999]); José Martins de Oliveira, "Depoimento: José Martins de Oliveira," in *A Favela fala: Depoimentos ao CPDOC*, ed. Dulce Chaves Pandolfi and Mário Grynszpan (Rio de Janeiro: FGV, 2003), 42–45.

13. Braga, *Governo-Comunidade*.

14. Braga, *Governo-Comunidade*, 51.

15. Braga, *Governo-Comunidade*, 51; CPDOC-FGV, "Depoimento: Jó Rezende."

16. Mário Sérgio Brum, "O povo acredita na gente: Rupturas e continuidades no movimento comunitário das favelas cariocas nas décadas de 1980 e 1990," M.A. thesis, (Universidade Federal Fluminense, 2006), 126–27.

17. Márcia Coutinho, "Regularização de Loteamentos," in *Quatro estudos*, ed. Flávio Ferreira, Paulo Fernando Cavallieri, Marcia Coutinho, Fani Baratz, and Yolanda Villela (Rio de Janeiro: Prefeitura da Cidade do Rio de Janeiro, 1986), 39–55; Luciana Corrêa do Lago, "O movimento dos loteamentos do Rio de Janeiro," M.A. thesis, (Universidade Federal do Rio de Janeiro, 1990).

18. Michael G. Donovan, "At the Doors of Legality: Planners, Favelados and the Titling of Urban Brazil," Ph.D. diss., (University of California, Berkeley, 2007), 230–50.

19. Coutinho, "Regularização de loteamentos," 42.

20. Coutinho, "Regularização de loteamentos," 44–48.

21. Carlos Amorim, *Comando Vermelho: A história secreta do crime organizado* (São Paulo: Editora Record, 1993), 143–44.

22. Francisca Medeiros Pirozi, "Depoimento: Francisca Medeiros Pirozi," in *A Favela fala: Depoimentos ao CPDOC*, ed. Dulce Chaves Pandolfi and Mário Grynszpan (Rio de Janeiro: FGV, 2003), 61.

23. Emir Larangeira's works are self-published and available on his website, emirlarangeira.com.br. For his own self-contrast with Nazareth Cerqueira, see Emir Larangeira, "A Facção," in *Polêmicas* (Rio de Janeiro: emirlarangeira.com.br, 1995, accessed May 23, 2013), 3–5.

24. Jorge da Silva, *Controle da criminalidade e segurança pública* (Rio de Janeiro: Forense, 1990).

25. Amorim, *Comando Vermelho*, 146.

26. "Traficante de droga preso no Sul é um dos maiores do Rio," *Jornal do Brasil*, July 19, 1987, 30.

27. Emir Sader, "A polícia é um caso de polícia," *Teoria e Debate* (December 1, 1987). Television news footage of the Rocinha protest is available on YouTube. See

also "Em 1987: Rocinha desce para o asfalto e causa tumulto em São Conrado," access July 28, 2011, www.youtube.com/watch?v=kC3p8EEZodw.

28. "Líderes da Rocinha reafirmam queixa contra violência," Jornal do Brasil, August 19, 1987, Cidade, 12b.

29. Zaca's full name was Zacarías Gonçalves Rosa, and Cabeludo's was Emílson dos Santos Fumero, but they were known on the hill and in the city beyond by their nicknames.

30. The Santa Marta War was covered extensively in all of Brazil's major newspapers, particularly the Jornal do Brasil and O Dia. For a more extensive investigation of the conflict, see Caco Barcellos, Abusado: O Dono do morro Dona Marta (São Paulo: Record, 2004), 66–118. For brief but insightful analysis by a foreign journalist, see Alma Guillermoprieto, Samba (New York: Random House, 1990), 8–11.

31. Barcellos, Abusado, 123, 69–80.

32. Arquivo do Pastoral das Favelas (hereafter, APF), "Morro da Providência protesta contra a PM, acusando-a de mortes," in Recortes de Jornais, pasta 3 (1986).

33. "Polícia prende traficantes de entorpecentes," Jornal do Brasil, April 20, 1987, 3; APF, "Líder comunitário é preso por tráfico," in Recortes de Jornais, pasta 3 (1987).

34. APF, "Morro prepara protesto público contra polícia," in Recortes de Jornais, pasta 1 (1987).

35. "Polícia soltou o dirigente comunitário de Mangueira," O Dia, June 8, 1988, 10.

36. Itamar Silva, "Depoimento: Itamar Silva," in A Favela fala: Depoimentos ao CPDOC, ed. Dulce Chaves Pandolfi and Mário Grynszpan (Rio de Janeiro: FGV, 2003), 317–19.

37. Silva, "Depoimento: Itamar Silva," 318–19; Barcellos, Abusado, 222–26.

38. Silva, "Depoimento: Itamar Silva," 319–20.

39. Anthropologist Marcos Alvito's pioneering research in Acari uncovered these connections, as well as numerous other manifestations of the ubiquitous presence of the drug traffic and associated violence in the complex. Marcos Alvito, As cores de Acari: Uma favela carioca (Rio de Janeiro: FGV, 2001), 122–23, 51–52.

40. Marcelo Baumann Burgos, "Favela: Cidade e cidadania em Rio das Pedras," in A utopia da comunidade: Rio das Pedras, uma favela carioca, ed. Marcelo Baumann Burgos (Rio de Janeiro: PUC, 2002), 60–70. Baumann Burgos stops short of identifying the ruling cohort of Rio das Pedras as a militia, a term that became more common in Rio de Janeiro following his book's publication. For more explicit treatment, see Alba Zaluar and Isabel Siqueira Conceição, "Favelas sob o controle das milícias: Que paz?" São Paulo em Perspectiva 21 (2007): 89–101.

41. "Moreira quer o fim do tráfico," Jornal do Brasil, July 1, 1987, Cidade, 9; Luis Carlos Cascon, "Associações: Um trunfo contra os traficantes nas favelas do Rio," O Globo, September 13, 1987, 18.

42. Cascon, "Associações: Um trunfo contra os traficantes nas favelas do Rio," 18.

43. Adair Rocha, Cecilia Minayo, Vitor Valla, and Eliana Athayde, *Favelas e as organizações comunitárias* (Rio de Janeiro: Centro da Defesa dos Direitos Humanos Bento Rubião, 1994), 55–59.

44. Cascon, "Associações: Um trunfo contra os traficantes nas favelas do Rio," 18.

45. APF, "Inauguração de creche vira festa para Jó," in *Recortes de Jornais, pasta 2* (1988).

46. "Lula não empolgou a Rocinha e a Dona Marta," *O Dia*, July 31, 1988, 4.

47. Vânia Bambirra, "Favelas e movimentos de favelados no estado do Rio de Janeiro," *Política e Administração* 1, no. 2 (July–September 1985): 245.

48. "Na lei do morro o crime não tem vez," *O Povo na Rua*, May 9, 1990.

49. "Começa o seminário sobre a violência nos morros," *O Dia*, August 14, 1989, 7.

50. Eduardo Coutinho, "Duas semanas no morro," Documentary film, (Brazil: ISER, 1987).

51. Barcellos, *Abusado*. Barcellos's *Abusado* is a richly detailed biography of Marcinho VP, given the pseudonym Julinho VP in the book. Note: there are two Marcinho VPs in trafficking lore. Santa Marta's was Márcio Amaro de Oliveira. The other, less media friendly and by all accounts more brutal, is Márcio dos Santos Nepomuceno of the Complexo do Alemão.

52. Alba Zaluar, *A máquina e a revolta* (São Paulo: Editora Brasiliense, 1985). Many of Zaluar's *O Globo* and *Jornal do Brasil* columns are collected in Alba Zaluar, *Condomínio do Diabo* (Rio de Janeiro: UERJ, 1996). For Zaluar's own reflections on these years, see César Caldeira, Emílio Dellasoppa, Marcos Bretas and Michel Misse, "Entrevista: Alba Zaluar," *Revista Rio de Janeiro* 12 (January–April 2004): 131–161.

53. Another pathbreaking work of the 1980s, on the fragility of favela associations, is Carlos Nelson Ferreira dos Santos, *Urbanização da Favela Marcílio Días* (Rio de Janeiro: IBAM, 1986). On the inadequacy of facile explanations of inequality as the cause of urban violence, see Edmundo Campos Coelho, "A criminalidade urbana violenta," *Série Estudos (IUPERJ)* 1, no. 60 (1987): 18. Campos Coelho had earlier questioned assumed links between poverty and criminality in "A criminalização da marginalidade e a marginalização da criminalidade," *Revista Brasileira de Administração Pública* 12, no. 2 (1978): 139–161. On the ways in which inequality and discrimination shaped trafficker lives, see Luis Antônio Machado da Silva, "Violência e sociabilidade: Tendências na atual conjuntura urbana no Brasil," in *Globalização, fragmentação e reforma urbana*, ed. Regina Moreu (Rio de Janeiro: Civilização Brasileira, 1994), 147–68.

54. "Antiga profecia de 'Zé do Queijo' é quase uma realidade," *Jornal do Brasil*, August 19, 1987, Cidade, 12a.

55. Burgos, "A falência da prefeitura do Rio de Janeiro," chap. 4.

56. Lígia Mefano, author interview, September 2006.

57. Burgos, "A falência da prefeitura do Rio de Janeiro," chap. 4, 20–25. For Braga's own perspective, see Braga, *Governo-comunidade*, 65.

58. Bolado's full name was Sérgio Ferreira da Silva. Naldo's was Ednaldo da Silva. "No Rio, o pó cala os governantes," *Veja*, June 1, 1988, 20–27.

CHAPTER FIVE. THE UNRAVELING

1. Gustavo de Almeida, "Polícia contra Polícia," *Rolling Stone*, Brazil, December 19, 2007; Ana Beatriz Leal, Íbis Silva Pereira, and Oswaldo Munteal Filho, *Sonho de um polícia cidadã* (Rio de Janeiro: UERJ, 2011).

2. Eliana Sousa Silva, "O contexto das práticas policiais nas favelas da Maré: A busca de novos caminhos a partir de seus protagonistas," Ph.D. diss., (PUC, 2009), 110; Alba Zaluar, "Urban Violence and Drug Warfare in Brazil," in *Armed Actors: Organised Violence and State Failure in Latin America*, ed. Kees Koonings and Dirk Kruijt (London: Zed Books, 2004), 141–42; Luiz Eduardo Soares, João Trajano Sento-Sé, José Augusto Souza Rodrigues, and Leandro Piquet Carneiro, "Criminalidade urbana e violência: Rio de Janeiro no contexto internacional," in *Violência e política no Rio de Janeiro*, ed. Luiz Eduardo Soares (Rio de Janeiro: ISER, 1996), 173–79.

3. Fábio Alves Araújo, "Do luto à luta: A experiência das mães de Acari," M.A. thesis, (UFRJ, 2007), 34–57.

4. Luiz Eduardo Soares, "Rio de Janeiro 1993: A tríplice ferida simbólica," in *Violência e política no Rio de Janeiro*, ed. Luiz Eduardo Soares (Rio de Janeiro: Relume Dumará, 1996).

5. Ângela Pinho, Claudia Carmello, Denise Galvani, Fernanda Sucupira, Leonardo Sakamoto, Lídia Neves, Lúcia Nascimento, Marcio Kameoka, Natália Suzuki, Nelson Lin, Rafael Sampaio, Renata Summa, and Rodrigo Pereira, "Feridas Abertas," *Problemas Brasileiros*, no. 359 (2003): 1–10.

6. Enrique Desmond Arias, *Drugs and Democracy in Rio de Janeiro: Trafficking, Social Networks, and Public Security* (Chapel Hill: University of North Carolina Press, 2006), 134–40.

7. Patrick Neate and Damian Platt, *Culture Is Our Weapon: Making Music and Changing Lives in Rio de Janeiro* (Rio de Janeiro: Penguin, 2010).

8. George Yúdice, *The Expediency of Culture: Uses of Culture in the Global Era* (Durham, NC: Duke University Press, 2003), 135.

9. Arias, *Drugs and Democracy in Rio de Janeiro*.

10. For a positive assessment of the NGO wave, specifically treating Afro-Reggae, see Jeffrey Rubin, "Meanings and Mobilizations: A Cultural Politics

Approach to Social Movements and States," *Latin American Research Review* 39, no. 3 (fall 2004): 106–42.

11. Centro de Pesquisa e Documentação da Fundação Getúlio Vargas (CPDOC-FGV), "Síntese dos trabalhos iniciados nas favelas pelo Viva Rio," in HS 1981.05.00 ib/t, pasta IV (1994).

12. On Reage Rio, see Yúdice, *The Expediency of Culture*, 143–47; and Marcos Alvito, *As cores de Acari: Uma favela carioca* (Rio de Janeiro: FGV, 2001), 151–52.

13. Arias, *Drugs and Democracy in Rio de Janeiro*.

14. Ana Cora Lima and Carlos Collier, "Unidas Pelo Medo," Viva Rio, http:// novo.vivafavela.com.br/publique/cgi/cgilua.exe/sys/start.htm?sid=87&from_info _index=726&infoid=37278, accessed May 23, 2013.

15. Analysis of the evolution of the drug traffic and its broader social consequence has generated a vast and rich literature. See, in particular, Zaluar, "Urban Violence and Drug Warfare in Brazil," 150; Alba Zaluar, *Condomínio do Diabo* (Rio de Janeiro: UERJ, 1996); Luis Antônio Machado da Silva, "Violência e sociabilidade: Tendências na atual conjuntura urbana no Brasil," in *Globalização, Fragmentação e Reforma Urbana*, ed. Regina Moreu (Rio de Janeiro: Civilização Brasileira, 1994), 147–68; Luiz Antonio Machado da Silva, "Um problema na interpretação da criminalidade urbana violenta," *Sociedade e Estado* 10, no. 2 (1995): 493–511; Luiz Antônio Machado da Silva, "Sociabilidade violenta: Por uma interpretação da criminalidade contemporânea no Brasil urbano," in *Metrópoles: Entre a coesão e a fragmentação, a cooperação e o conflito*, ed. Luiz César Queiroz Ribeiro (São Paulo: Perseu Abramo, 2004), 35–36; Michel Misse, "Cinco teses equivocadas sobre a criminalidade," Série Estudos (IUPERJ), in *Violência e participação política no Rio de Janeiro*, no. 91 (August 1995): 1–19; and Michel Misse, "As ligações perigosas: Mercado informal, ilegal, narcotráfico e violência no Rio," *Contemporaneidade e Educação* 2, no. 1 (May 1997): 1–26.

16. Soares, "Rio de Janeiro 1993," 271–72. See also Luiz Eduardo Soares, ed. *Violência e política no Rio de Janeiro* (Rio de Janeiro: Relume Dumará, 1996); and Robert Kant de Lima, *A polícia da cidade do Rio de Janeiro: Seus dilemas e paradoxos* (Rio de Janeiro: Forense, 1995).

17. Misse, "Cinco teses equivocadas sobre a criminalidade," 33; César Caldeira, "Operação Rio e cidadania: As tensões entre o combate à criminalidade e a ordem jurídica," in *Política e Cultura: Visões do passado e perspectivas contemporâneas*, ed. Elisa Pereira Reis, Maria Hermínia Tavares de Almeida, and Peter Fry (Rio de Janeiro: Hucitect, 1996), 50–74.

18. James Cavallaro and Anne Manuel, *Police Brutality in Urban Brazil* (New York: Human Rights Watch, 1997), 15. For analysis of the geography of urban fear this generated, see, for example, Márcia da Silva Pereira Leite, "Para além da metáfora da guerra: Percepções sobre cidadania, violência e paz no Grajaú, um bairro

carioca," Ph.D. diss., (UFRJ, 2001); Luiz Eduardo Soares, ed. *Violência e política no Rio de Janeiro* (Rio de Janeiro: Relume Dumará, 1996); and Robert Kant de Lima, *A polícia da cidade do Rio de Janeiro: Seus dilemas e paradoxos* (Rio de Janeiro: Forense, 1995). On the fetishization of spectacular violence, see Ben Penglase, "Lost Bullets: Fetishes of Urban Violence in Rio de Janeiro," *Anthropological Quarterly* 84, no. 2 (spring 2011): 411–38.

19. Although Garotinho appeared as the lead author, it was openly acknowledged that he had merely commissioned the study. Anthony Garotinho, Luiz Eduardo Soares, Barbara Musumeci Soares, João Trajano Sento-Sé, Leonarda Musumeci, and Sílvia Ramos, *Violência e criminalidade no Estado do Rio de Janeiro: Diagnóstico e propostas para uma política democrática de segurança pública* (Rio de Janeiro: Editora Hama, 1998).

20. Enrique Desmond Arias, Mark Ungar, "Community Policing and Latin America's Citizen Security Crisis," *Comparative Politics* 41, no. 4 (July 2009): 409–29.

21. Luiz Eduardo Soares, *Meu casaco de general: Quinhentos dias no front da segurança pública em Rio de Janeiro* (São Paulo: Companhia das Letras, 2000). For a generous analysis of Soares's actions, see Jurandir Freire, "Aposta contra os ressentimentos," *Folha de São Paulo*, July 16, 2000, *Revista Mais*, 17.

22. Antônio Carlos Carballo Blanco, "Grupamento de polícia em áreas especiais: Uma experiência piloto," Monografia, (UERJ, 2002). Arias and Ungar, "Community Policing and Latin America's Citizen Security Crisis."

23. Itamar Silva, "Depoimento: Itamar Silva," in *A Favela fala: Depoimentos ao CPDOC*, ed. Dulce Chaves Pandolfi and Mário Grynszpan (Rio de Janeiro: FGV, 2003), 343–45.

24. Marcus Cardoso, "Como morre um projeto de policiamento comunitário: O caso do Cantagalo e do Pavão-Pavãozinho," Ph.D. diss., (Universidade de Brasília, 2010); Arias and Ungar, "Community Policing and Latin America's Citizen Security Crisis."

25. Selma Schmidt, "Poder Paralelo: Relatório da Assembléia indica que 400 dirigentes de entidades se associaram a bandidos," *O Globo*, 20 Jun 2002, 20. Schmidt's article reported on an investigation commissioned by Carlos Minc as chair of the Rio State Assembly's Human Rights Committee. The article reports over one hundred association presidents killed and over four hundred forced to leave their communities. The full committee report was never published, and the state assembly has no copy. These numbers seem unrealistically high. For further analysis of traffickers expelling association presidents from their favelas, see Misse, "Cinco teses equivocadas sobre a criminalidade."

26. Mário Sérgio Brum, "Entrevista: Eliana Sousa Silva," Interview, (Rio de Janeiro: Laboratório de História Oral e Imagem, Universidade Federal Fluminense, 2005); Mário Sérgio Brum, "O povo acredita na gente: Rupturas e continuidades

no movimento comunitário das favelas cariocas nas décadas de 1980 E 1990." M.A. thesis, (Universidade Federal Fluminense, 2006), 181.

27. "Marcello ignorou avisos," *Jornal do Brasil*, February 5, 1999, 20.

28. Alba Zaluar and Isabel Siqueira Conceição, "Favelas sob o controle das milícias: Que paz?" *São Paulo em Perspectiva* 21 (2007): 92–98.

29. Adauto Lúcio Cardoso, "O Programa Favela-Bairro: Uma avaliação," in *Seminário Programa Habitare: Avaliação de projetos IPT em habitação e meio ambiente. Assentamentos urbanos precários*, ed. Rose Marie Zenha and Carlos Geraldo Luz de Freitas (Rio de Janeiro: FINEP, 2002).

30. Jorge Fiori, Elizabeth Riley, and Ronaldo Ramírez, "Physical Upgrading and Social Integration in Rio de Janeiro: The Case of Favela Bairro," *DISP*, no. 147 (2001): 54–59; Mariana Cavalcanti, "Of Shacks, Houses and Fortresses: An Ethnography of Favela Consolidation in Rio de Janeiro" (University of Chicago, 2009); McCann, *Throes of Democracy: Brazil since 1989* (London: Zed Press, 2009).

31. Sérgio Ferraz Magalhães, *Programa Favela-Bairro* (Rio de Janeiro: Secretaria Municipal de Habitação-Prefeitura da Cidade do Rio de Janeiro, 1993); Sérgio Ferraz Magalhães, "A Cidade na Incerteza," *O Globo*, July 19, 2007, 7.

32. Arias, *Drugs and Democracy in Rio de Janeiro*, 192.

33. Teresa Caldeira, *City of Walls: Crime, Segregation and Citizenship in São Paulo* (Berkeley: University of California Press, 2000).

34. See, for example, Caldeira, *City of Walls*; and Sérgio Adorno, "A violência na sociedade brasileira: Um painel inconcluso em uma democracia não consolidada," *Sociedade e Estado* 10, no. 2 (1995): 299–342.

35. The regime's intent in expanding public universities was both to prepare a technocratic sector and to contain radicalism. On the campus Left and its challenges, see Victoria Langland, *Speaking of Flowers: Student Movements and the Molding of 1968 in Military Brazil* (Durham, NC: Duke University Press, 2013).

36. Janice Perlman, *Favela: Four Decades of Living on the Edge in Rio de Janeiro* (New York: Oxford University Press, 2010), 220–46.

EPILOGUE

1. Zuenir Ventura, *Cidade partida* (São Paulo: Companhia das Letras, 1994).

2. Ventura's book also generated several rebuttals from social scientists emphasizing the connections between favela and city, most directly in Adair Rocha, *Cidade Cerzida: a costura da cidadania no Morro Santa Marta* (Rio de Janeiro: Museu da República, 2005). For an innovative longitudinal study analyzing these connections and their influence on individual fortunes in three favelas, see Janice Perlman, *Favela: Four Decades of Living on the Edge in Rio de Janeiro* (New York: Oxford University Press, 2010).

3. Hermano Vianna, unpaginated prefatory material, in Guilherme Bryan, *Quem tem um sonho não dança: Cultura jovem brasileira nos anos 80* (São Paulo: Record, 2004).

4. Olívia Rodrigues Cavalcante, author interview, April 2011.

5. Rodrigo Serrano-Berthet, Flávia Carbonari, Mariana Cavalcanti and Alys Wilman, "Bringing the State Back into the Favelas of Rio de Janeiro: Understanding changes in community life after the UPP pacification process," Sustainable Development Sector Management Unit Report, World Bank, Washington, DC, October, 2012, 14–15.

6. Serrano Berthet, et al, "Bringing the State Back Into the Favelas of Rio de Janeiro," 15.

7. Marcelo Baumann Burgos, Luiz Fernando Almeida Pereira, Mariana Cavalcanti, Mário Brum and Mauro Amoroso, "O *Efeito* UPP na percepção dos moradores das favelas," *Desigualdade e Diversidade: Revista de Ciências Sociais da* PUC-Rio, 11, August-December 2012, 69.

8. Like any good slang, *treta* has various meanings. Used as an adjective in this context, it refers to skill in deploying clever strategies.

Bibliography

PRINCIPAL ARCHIVES CONSULTED

AGC: Arquivo Geral da Cidade do Rio de Janeiro
APERJ: Arquivo Público do Estado do Rio de Janeiro
APF: Arquivo do Pastoral das Favelas
BN: Biblioteca Nacional, Rio de Janeiro
CPDOC-FGV: Centro de Pesquisa e Documentação da Fundação Getúlio Vargas
IBAM: Instituto Brasileiro de Administração Municipal
IUPERJ: Instituto Universitário de Pesquisas do Rio de Janeiro

AUTHOR INTERVIEWS CITED

Athayde, Eliana
de Brito, Gibeon
Mefano, Lígia
Muniz, Paulo Roberto
Rodrigues Cavalcante, Olívia
Segala, Lígia

NEWSPAPER ARTICLES CITED

Andrade, Carlos Drummond de. "A boca do túnel." *Jornal do Brasil*, October 11, section 2:5.
"Antiga profecia de 'Zé Do Queijo' é quase uma realidade." *Jornal do Brasil*, August 19, 1987, Cidade, 12a.
"Apadrinhamento em CIEPS leva Brizola à irritação." *Jornal do Brasil*, April 10, 1986, 7.
"Brizola inicia obras em morro e pede cooperação." *O Globo*, October 5, 1983, 8.
Brizola, Leonel. "Instaurou-se a crise." *Jornal do Brasil*, August 30, 1987, 7.

"Cai por terra a promessa de Brizola de construir 500 CIEPS até o fim do mandato." *O Globo*, January 25, 1987, 1.

"Caó promete 1 milhão de lotes em 5 anos." *Última Hora*, October 20, 1983, section 2:1.

Cascon, Luiz Carlos. "Associações: Um trunfo contra os traficantes nas favelas do Rio." *O Globo*, September 13, 1987, 18.

"Começa o seminário sobre a violência nos morros." *O Dia*, August 14, 1989, 7.

Duque, Helena, Regina Barreiros, and Vera Perfeito. "Violência não tem fim nas classes mais necessitadas." *Jornal do Brasil*, August 3, 1986, 22.

"Estado compra Borel e dá lotes a favelados." *Jornal do Brasil*, May 27, 1984, 13.

"Favelados do Vidigal entram na justiça contra remoção." *A Notícia*, December 26, 1977, 3.

Freire, Jurandir. "Aposta contra os ressentimentos." *Folha de São Paulo*, July, 16, 2000, *Revista Mais*, 17.

"Fundação remove mais três famílias do Vidigal mas só duas vão para Antares." *Jornal do Brasil*, January 12, 1978, 16.

"Governador vai a Ipanema e toma posse do Panorama." *Jornal do Brasil*, February 3, 1984, 5.

"Impasse no Andaraí: CIEP ou área de lazer." *O Globo*, February 4, 1986, 3.

"Juiz condena Brizola por CIEPS na beira da estrada." *O Globo*, July 18, 1986, 13.

"Líderes da Rocinha reafirmam queixa contra violência." *Jornal do Brasil*, August 19, 1987, Cidade, 12b.

"Lula não empolgou a Rocinha e a Dona Marta." *O Dia*, July 31, 1988, 4.

Magalhães, Sérgio Ferraz. "A cidade na incerteza." *O Globo*, Jul 19, 2007, 7.

"Mais um caso de invasão de terrenos na Rocinha." *O Globo*, January 19, 1984, Barra, 1.

"Marcello ignorou avisos." *Jornal do Brasil*, February 5, 1999, 20.

"Moreira quer o fim do tráfico." *Jornal do Brasil*, July 1, 1987, Cidade, 9.

"Morro Dos Cabritos tem lavanderia comunitária." *O Dia*, November 10, 1982, 10.

"Na lei do morro o crime não tem vez." *O Povo na Rua*, May 9, 1990.

"O dia a dia da Rocinha: Uma cidade de contrastes." *O Globo*, January 27, 1985, Grande Rio, 1.

"O novo dia a dia de Maria Helena." *O Globo*, November 1, 1984, Barra, 1.

"O prefeito e o Vidigal." *Luta Democrática*, December 29, 1977, 4.

"Pedetista não vê socialismo." *Jornal do Brasil*, January 15, 1986, 8.

"Polícia acha armas e drogas na casa de Tom Zé." *O Globo*, July 7, 1985, 14.

"A polícia militar e as comunidades." *Favelão*, 3, no. 18 (January 1985): 9.

"Polícia prende traficantes de entorpecentes." *Jornal do Brasil*, April 20, 1987, Cidade, 3.

"Polícia soltou o dirigente comunitário de Mangueira." *O Dia*, June 8, 1988, 10.

"Prefeito: Loteamento na Rocinha é ilegal." *Jornal do Brasil*, May 26, 1984, 12.

"Projeto cidadão no Borel." *O Dia*, August 2, 1982, 10.

"Propaganda política do PDT." *Jornal do Brasil*, November 14, 1982, 5.

"[Quarenta] 40 assassinatos e crianças no crime organizado Dos Tóxicos." *Jornal dos Sports*, March 8, 1985, 7.

"Rocinha cai no Samba para comemorar a posse de Maria Helena." *O Globo*, October, 11, 1984, Barra, 1.

"Rocinha ganha 28 bicas de água." *O Globo*, August 2, 1982, 7.

"Rocinha: Polícia procurava mulher e encontrou Jorge Charuto." *O Dia*, Mar 26, 1984, 10.

Schmidt, Selma. "André." *O Globo*, June 2, 2006, section 2:1.

———. "José." *O Globo*, June 1, 2006, section 2:1.

———. "Poder paralelo: Relatório da Assembléia indica que 400 dirigentes de entidades se associaram a bandidos." *O Globo*, June 20, 2002, 20.

Tabak, Israel. "Pobreza e repulsa à ação policial fazem a marginalidade do Juramento." *Jornal do Brasil*, January 5, 1986, 12.

"Traficante de droga preso no Sul é um dos maiores do Rio." *Jornal do Brasil*, Jul 19, 1987, 30.

"Uma vida de crimes e fugas." *Extra*, April 5, 2009, http://extra.globo.com/casos -de-policia/escadinhauma-vida-crimes-fugas-399692.html, accessed 28 May 2013.

BOOKS, DECREES, JOURNAL AND MAGAZINE ARTICLES, REPORTS, THESES, AND DISSERTATIONS

Abramo, Pedro, ed. *A cidade da informalidade*. Rio de Janeiro: Sette Letras, 2003.

Adorno, Sérgio. "A violência na sociedade brasileira: Um painel inconcluso em uma democracia não consolidada." *Sociedade e Estado* 10, no. 2 (July–December 1995): 299–342.

Alberto, Paulina. *Terms of Inclusion: Black Intellectuals in Twentieth-Century Brazil*. Chapel Hill: University of North Carolina Press, 2011.

Almeida, Gustavo de. "Polícia contra Polícia." *Rolling Stone, Brazil*, December 19, 2007.

Alvito, Marcos. *As cores de Acari: Uma favela carioca*. Rio de Janeiro: FGV, 2001.

Amorim, Carlos. *Comando Vermelho: A história secreta do crime organizado*. São Paulo: Editora Record, 1993.

Amorim, Carlos, and Eduardo Campos Coelho. "Da Falange Vermelha a Escadinha: O poder nas prisões." *Presença* 11 (January 1988): 106–14.

Amorim, Paulo Henrique and Maria Helena Passos. *Plim Plim: A peleja de Brizola contra a fraude eleitoral*. São Paulo: Conrad Livros, 2005.

Amoroso, Mauro. "Caminhos do lembrar: A construção e os usos políticos da memória no Morro do Borel." PhD diss., Fundação Getúlio Vargas–Centro de Pesquisa e Documentação de História Contemporânea do Brasil, 2012.

Araújo, Fábio Alves. "Do luto à luta: A experiência das mães de Acari," M.A. thesis, Universidade Federal do Rio de Janeiro, 2007.

Araújo, Maria Silvia Muylaert de. "Actors' Strategies in a Case Study Favela: Rio Das Pedras in Rio de Janeiro." Report no. 1549, Rotterdam, Netherlands: Institute for Housing Studies, 1990.

———. "Possibilidades e limites de uma política pública habitacional: O programa 'Cada Família Um Lote.'" M.A., thesis, Universidade Federal do Rio de Janeiro, 1988.

———. "Regularização fundiária de favelas: Imóveis alugados. O caso do programa 'Cada Família Um Lote' no Rio de Janeiro." *Revista de Administração Municipal* 3, no. 195 (1990): 26–35.

Arias, Enrique Desmond. *Drugs and Democracy in Rio de Janeiro: Trafficking, Social Networks, and Public Security*. Chapel Hill: University of North Carolina Press, 2006.

Arias, Enrique Desmond, and Daniel M. Goldstein, eds. *Violent Democracies in Latin America*. Durham, NC: Duke University Press, 2010.

Arias, Enrique Desmond, and Mark Ungar. "Community Policing and Latin America's Citizen Security Crisis." *Comparative Politics* 41, no. 4 (July 2009): 409–29.

Bambirra, Vânia. "Favelas e movimentos de favelados no estado do Rio de Janeiro." *Política e Administração* 1, no. 2 (July–September 1985): 241–53.

Barcellos, Caco. *Abusado: O dono do Morro Dona Marta*. São Paulo: Record, 2004.

Bastos, Bruno Aragão. "O povo unido jamais será vencido: História do Morro da Formiga." Monografia, Universidade Federal Fluminense, 2008.

Belchior, Bruna, and Marieta Pinheiro de Carvalho. "Entrevista: Mina Seinfeld De Carakushansky." In *Sonho de uma polícia cidadã: Coronel Carlos Magno Nazareth Cerqueira*, edited by Ana Beatriz Leal, Íbis Silva Pereira, and Oswaldo Munteal Filho, 89–102. Rio de Janeiro: UERJ, 2011.

Bias, Mauro de. "O Bispo Vermelho?" *Revista de História*, July 10, 2012.

Bittencourt, AnaCris. "Entrevista: Irineu Guimarães." *Democracia Viva* 35 (June 2007): 64–72.

———. "Entrevista: Itamar Silva." *Democracia Viva* 42 (May 2009): 36–51.

Blanco, Antônio Carlos Carballo. "Grupamento de polícia em áreas especiais: Uma experiência piloto," Monografia, Universidade Estadual do Rio de Janeiro, 2002.

Blank, Gilda. "Experiência de urbanização de favela." In *Habitação em Questão*, edited by Lícia do Prado Valladares, 93–120, Rio de Janeiro: Zahar, 1980.

Bomeny, Helena. "Salvar Pela Escola: Programa especial de educação." In *A força do povo: Brizola e O Rio de Janeiro*, edited by Marieta de Moraes Ferreira, 95–127. Rio de Janeiro: FGV-CPDOC, 2008.

Braga, Roberto Saturnino. *Governo-comunidade: Socialismo no Rio*. Rio de Janeiro: Paz e Terra, 1989.

Brasileiro, Ana Maria, and Nanci Valadares. "A Rocinha, o Laboriaux e outras estórias." *Revista de Administração Municipal* 30, no. 167 (April–June 1983): 72–81.

Brizola, Leonel et al. "Carta de Lisboa." Manifesto, PDT, http://www.pdtsp.org.br/index.php?option=com_content&task=view&id=474&Itemid=66, accessed 23 May 2013.

Brum, Mário Sérgio. "Cidade Alta: História, memória e estigma de favela mum conjunto habitacional de Rio de Janeiro," Ph.D. diss., Universidade Federal Fluminense, 2011.

———. "Entrevista: Eliana Sousa Silva." Interview, Rio de Janeiro: Laboratório de História Oral e Imagem, Universidade Federal Fluminense, 2005.

———. "O povo acredita na gente: Rupturas e continuidades no movimento comunitário das favelas cariocas nas décadas de 1980 E 1990." M.A. thesis, Universidade Federal Fluminense, 2006.

Bryan, Guilherme. *Quem tem um sonho não dança: Cultura jovem brasileira nos anos 80.* São Paulo: Record, 2004.

Buarque, Chico. "Estação derradeira," song, Marola Edições Musicais, Rio de Janeiro, 1987.

Burgos, Marcelo Bauman. "Dos parques proletários ao favelabairro: As políticas públicas nas favelas do Rio de Janeiro." In *Um século de favela*, edited by Alba Zaluar and Marcos Alvito, 25–60. Rio de Janeiro: Fundação Getúlio Vargas, 2003.

———. "A falência da prefeitura do Rio de Janeiro." M.A. thesis, Universidade Federal do Rio de Janeiro, 1992.

———. "Favela: cidade e cidadania em Rio das Pedras." In *A utopia da comunidade: Rio das Pedras, uma favela carioca*, edited by Marcelo Baumann Burgos, 21–90. Rio de Janeiro: PUC, 2002.

Burgos, Marcelo Bauman, ed. *A utopia da comunidade.* Rio de Janeiro: PUC-Rio, 2002.

Burgos, Marcelo Baumann, Luiz Fernando Almeida Pereira, Mariana Cavalcanti, Mário Brum and Mauro Amoroso, "O *Efeito UPP* na percepção dos moradores das favelas," Desigualdade e Diversidade: Revista de Ciências Sociais da PUC-Rio, 11, August-December 2012, 49–98.

Caldeira, César. "Operação Rio e Cidadania: As tensões entre o combate à criminalidade e a ordem jurídica." In *Política e cultura: Visões do passado e perspectivas contemporâneas*, edited by Elisa Pereira Reis, Maria Hermínia Tavares de Almeida, and Peter Fry, 50–74. Rio de Janeiro: Hucitect, 1996.

Caldeira, César, Emílio Dellasoppa, Marcos Bretas, and Michel Misse. "Entrevista: Alba Zaluar." *Revista Rio de Janeiro* 12 (January–April 2004): 131–161.

Caldeira, Teresa. *City of Walls: Crime, Segregation and Citizenship in São Paulo.* Berkeley: University of California Press, 2000.

Cardoso, Adauto Lúcio, "O Programa Favela-Bairro: Uma avaliação," in *Seminário Programa Habitare: Avaliação de projetos IPT em habitação e meio ambiente. Assentamentos urbanos precários*, ed. Rose Marie Zenha and Carlos Geraldo Luz de Freitas (Rio de Janeiro: FINEP, 2002).

Cardoso, Marcus. "Como morre um projeto de policiamento comunitário: O caso do Cantagalo e do Pavão-Pavãozinho." Ph.D. diss., Universidade de Brasília, 2010.

Casaes, Edu. "De olho na política." Depoimento, Viva Rio, http://www.favelatem memoria.com.br/publique/cgi/cgilua.exe/sys/start.htm?infoid=122&tpl=printer view&sid=2, accessed May 28, 2013.

Cavalcanti, Mariana. "Of Shacks, Houses and Fortresses: An Ethnography of Favela Consolidation in Rio de Janeiro," Ph.D. diss., University of Chicago, 2009.

Cavallaro, James, and Anne Manuel. *Police Brutality in Urban Brazil*. New York: Human Rights Watch, 1997.

Cerqueira, Carlos Magno Nazareth. "Discurso de despedida da primeira gestão." In *Sonho de uma Polícia cidadã: Coronel Carlos Magno Nazareth Cerqueira*, edited by Ana Beatriz Leal, Íbis Silva Pereira, and Oswaldo Munteal Filho, 156–62. Rio de Janeiro: UERJ, 2011 [1986].

———. *O futuro de uma ilusão: O sonho de uma nova política*. Rio de Janeiro: Editora Freitas Bastos, 2001.

"Chapéu Mangueira." *Favelão* 3, no. 18 (January 1985): 4.

Chaves Pandolfi, Dulce, and Mário Grynszpan, eds. *A favela fala*. Rio de Janeiro: Fundação Getúlio Vargas, 2003.

Coelho, Edmundo Campos. "A criminalização da marginalidade e a marginalização da criminalidade." *Revista Brasileira de Administração Pública* 12, no. 2 (1978): 139–161.

———. "A criminalidade urbana violenta." *Série Estudos (IUPERJ)* 1, no. 60 (1987): 1–59.

Compans, Rose. "A regularização fundiária de favelas no estado do Rio de Janeiro." *Revista Rio de Janeiro* 9 (January/April 2003): 41–53.

Conselho de Justiça, Segurança Pública e Direitos Humanos. Decreto [Decree] número 6.635. April 13, 1983.

Coutinho, Eduardo. "Duas semanas no morro." Documentary film. Brazil: ISER, 1987.

Coutinho, Márcia. "Regularização de loteamentos." In *Quatro estudos*, edited by Flávio Ferreira, Paulo Fernando Cavallieri, Marcia Coutinho, Fani Baratz, and Yolanda Villela, 39–55. Rio de Janeiro: Prefeitura da Cidade do Rio de Janeiro, 1986.

Cunha, Olívia Maria Gomes da, and Flávio dos Santos. *Quase cidadão: Histórias e antropologias da pós emancipação no Brasil.* Rio de Janeiro: Fundação Getúlio Vargas, 2007.

Diniz, Eli. *Voto e máquina política: Patronagem e clientelismo.* Rio de Janeiro: Paz e Terra, 1982.

————. *Voto e máquina política: Patronagem e clientelismo no Rio de Janeiro.* Rio de Janeiro: Paz e Terra, 1982.

Donovan, Michael G. "At the Doors of Legality: Planners, Favelados and the Titling of Urban Brazil," Ph.D. diss., University of California, Berkeley, 2007.

Duhau, Emílio. "The Informal City: An Enduring Slum or a Progressive Habitat." In *Cities from Scratch: Poverty and Informality in Urban Latin America,* edited by Bryan McCann and Javier Auyero Brodwyn Fischer. Durham, NC: Duke University Press, forthcoming.

Dulles, John W. F. *Resisting Brazil's Military Regime: An Account of the Battles of Sobral Pinto.* Austin: University of Texas Press, 2007.

Ferreira, Flávio, Paulo Fernando Cavallieri, Marcia Coutinho, Fani Baratz, and Yolanda Villela. *Quatro estudos.* Rio de Janeiro: Prefeitura da Cidade do Rio de Janeiro, 1986.

Ferreira, Marieta de Moraes, ed. *A força do povo: Brizola e o Rio de Janeiro.* Rio de Janeiro: ALERJ, 2008.

Fiori, Jorge, Elizabeth Riley, and Ronaldo Ramírez. "Physical Upgrading and Social Integration in Rio de Janeiro: The Case of Favela Bairro." DISP, no. 147 (2001): 48–60.

Fischer, Brodwyn. "A Century in the Present Tense: Crisis, Politics and the Intellectual History of Brazil's Informal Cities." In *Cities from Scratch: Poverty and Informality in Urban Latin America,* edited by Brodwyn Fischer, Bryan McCann, and Javier Auyero, Durham, NC: Duke University Press, forthcoming.

————. *A Poverty of Rights: Citizenship and Inequality in Twentieth-Century Rio de Janeiro.* Palo Alto: Stanford University Press, 2008.

Franco, Francisco de Mello. "Depoimento." In *Capítulos da memória do urbanismo carioca,* edited by Américo Freire and Lúcia Lippi Oliveira, 190–201. Rio de Janeiro: Folha Seca, 2002.

Freeman, James Patrick. "Face to Face but Worlds Apart: The Geography of Class in the Public Space of Rio de Janeiro." Ph.D. diss., University of California, Berkeley, 2002.

Freire, Américo. "Novo sindicalismo e movimentos sociais." In *A força do povo: Brizola e o Rio de Janeiro,* edited by Marieta de Moraes Ferreira, 128–50. Rio de Janeiro: FGV, 2008.

Freire, Américo, and Lúcia Lippi Oliveira, eds. *Capítulos da memória do urbanismo carioca.* Rio de Janeiro: Fundação Getúlio Vargas, 2002.

Garotinho, Anthony, Luiz Eduardo Soares, Barbara Musumeci Soares, João Trajano Sento-Sé, Leonarda Musumeci, and Sílvia Ramos. *Violência e criminalidade no estado do Rio de Janeiro: Diagnóstico e propostas para uma política democrática de segurança pública*. Rio de Janeiro: Editora Hama, 1998.

Gay, Robert. "The Broker and the Thief: A Parable (Reflections on Popular Politics in Brazil)." *Luso-Brazilian Review* 36, no. 1 (1999): 49–70.

———. "The Even More Difficult Transition from Clientelism to Citizenship: Lessons from Brazil." In *Out of the Shadows: Political Action and the Informal Economy in Latin America*, edited by Patricia Fernandez-Kelly and John Shefner, 195–218. State College: Penn State University Press, 2006.

———. *Popular Organization and Democracy in Rio de Janeiro: A Tale of Two Favelas*. Philadelphia: Temple University Press, 1994.

———. "Toward Uncivil Society: Causes and Consequences of Violence in Rio de Janeiro." In *Violent Democracies in Latin America*, edited by Enrique Desmond Arias and Daniel M. Goldstein, 201–225. Durham, NC: Duke University Press, 2010.

Goldstein, Donna. *Laughter out of Place: Race, Class, Violence and Sexuality in a Rio Shantytown*. Berkeley: University of California Press, 2003.

Gomes, Mércio Pereira. *Darcy Ribeiro*. São Paulo: Ícone Editora, 2000.

Gonçalves, Rafael Soares. "A política, o direito e as favelas do Rio de Janeiro: Um breve olhar histórico." *Urbana: Revista Eletrônica do Centro Interdisciplinar de Estudos da Cidade* 1, no. 1 (2006): 1–23.

———. "Le Droit, la politique et l'évolution des faveas à Rio de Janeiro: La precarité juridique du discours officiel." In *Ville visible, ville invisible: La jeune recherche urbaine En Europe*, edited by J. Boisonnade, 37–63. Paris: Harmattan, 2008.

———. "O debate jurídico em torno da urbanização de favelas no Rio de Janeiro." *Revista Internacional de Direito e Cidadania* 2 (October 2008): 139–48.

Gondim, Linda Maria de Pontes. "Planners in the Face of Power: The Case of the Metropolitan Region of Rio de Janeiro, Brazil." Ph.D. diss., Cornell University, Ithaca, NY, 1986.

Green, James N. *We Cannot Remain Silent: Opposition to the Brazilian Military Dictatorship in the United States*. Durham, NC: Duke University Press, 2010.

Guillermoprieto, Alma. *Samba*. New York: Random House, 1990.

Hollanda, Cristina Buarque de. *Polícia e direitos humanos: Política de segurança pública no primeiro governo Brizola*. Rio de Janeiro: Revan, 2005.

Holston, James. *Insurgent Citizenship: Disjunctions of Democracy and Modernity in Brazil*. Princeton, NJ: Princeton University Press, 2008.

Instituto Brasileiro de Geografia e Estatística (IBGE), "Instruções para revisão do trabalho da base organizacional geográfica," Rio de Janeiro, 2000.

Keck, Margaret. *The Worker's Party and Democratization in Brazil*. New Haven: Yale University Press, 1992.

Kehren, Mark. "Tunnel Vision: Urban Renewal in Rio de Janeiro, 1960–1975." Ph.D. diss., University of Maryland, 2006.

Lacerda, Alexandre Magno González de. "Hegemonia e resistência: Imprensa, violência e cultura popular." M.A. thesis, Universidade Federal Fluminense, 2009.

Lago, Luciana Corrêa do. "O movimento dos loteamentos do Rio de Janeiro." M.A. thesis, Universidade Federal do Rio de Janeiro, 1990.

Langland, Victoria. *Speaking of Flowers: Student Movements and the Molding of 1968 in Military Brazil.* Durham, NC: Duke University Press, 2013.

Larangeira, Emir. "A Facção." In *Polêmicas*, 1–13, Rio de Janeiro, emirlarangeira. com.br, 1995, accessed May 28, 2013.

Leal, Ana Beatriz, Íbis Silva Pereira, and Oswaldo Munteal Filho. *Sonho de um polícia cidadã.* Rio de Janeiro: UERJ, 2011.

Leeds, Elizabeth. "Cocaine and Parallel Polities in the Brazilian Urban Periphery: Constraints on Local-Level Democratization." *Latin American Research Review* 31, no. 3 (1996): 47–83.

Lefebvre, Henri. *Le Droit à la ville.* Paris: Editions du Seuil, 1968.

Leite, Márcia da Silva Pereira. "Para além da metáfora da guerra: Percepções sobre cidadania, violência e paz no Grajaú, um bairro carioca." Ph.D. diss., UFRJ, 2001.

Lima, Ana Cora, and Carlos Collier. "Unidas pelo medo." Viva Rio, http://novo .vivafavela.com.br/publique/cgi/cgilua.exe/sys/start.htm?sid=87&from_info _index=726&infoid=37278, accessed May 23, 2013.

Lima, Robert Kant de. *A polícia da cidade do Rio de Janeiro: Seus dilemas e paradoxos.* Rio de Janeiro: Forense, 1995.

Lins, Paulo. *Cidade de Deus.* São Paulo: Companhia das Letras, 2002.

Lippi, Lucia, and Marly Motta. "José Arthur Rios: Depoimento." In *Capítulos da memória do urbanismo carioca*, edited by Américo Freire and Lúcia Lippi Oliveira, 60–77. Rio de Janeiro: Folha Seca, 2002.

Magalhães, Sérgio Ferraz. *Programa favela-bairro.* Rio de Janeiro: Secretaria Municipal de Habitação-Prefeitura da Cidade do Rio de Janeiro, 1993.

Mainwaring, Scott. "Grass Roots Popular Movements and the Struggle for Democracy: Nova Iguaçu, 1974–1985." In *Working Papers*, 1–48, South Bend, IN.: Kellog Institute, Notre Dame University, 1985.

Matos, Cláudia Neiva de. "Bezerra da Silva: Singular e plural." *Ipotesi* 15, no. 2 (July/ December 2011): 99–114.

McCann, Bryan. "The Political History of Rio de Janeiro's Favelas: Recent Works." *Latin American Research Review* 41, no. 3 (October 2006): 149–162.

———. *Throes of Democracy: Brazil Since 1989.* London: Zed Press, 2009.

———. "Troubled Oasis: The Intertwining Histories of the Morro Dos Cabritos and Bairro Peixoto." In *Cities from Scratch: Poverty and Informality in Urban Latin America*, edited by Brodwyn Fischer, Bryan McCann, and Javier Auyero. Durham, NC: Duke University Press, forthcoming.

Melo, Marcus André BC de. "Políticas públicas e habitação popular: Continuidade e ruptura, 1979–1988." *Revista de Administração Municipal* 36, no. 191 (April/June 1989): 44–59.

Mendes, Vera Lúcia Pedra Clímaco. "Tanta gente sem terra e tanta terra sem gente: Movimento do Mutirão de Nova Aurora, 1979–1995." M.A. thesis, Universidade Federal do Rio de Janeiro, 2006.

Mignot, Ana Chrystina Venancio. "CIEP—Centro Integrado de Educação Pública: Alternativa para a qualidade do ensino ou nova investida do populismo na educação." *Em Aberto* 8, no. 44 (December 1989): 45–63.

Misse, Michel. "As ligações perigosas: Mercado informal, ilegal, narcotráfico e violência no Rio." *Contemporaneidade e Educação* 2, no. 1 (May 1997): 1–26.

———. "Cinco teses equivocadas sobre a criminalidade." In *Violência e participação política no Rio de Janeiro, Série Estudos* (IUPERJ) no. 91 (August 1995): 1–19.

———. "Malandros, marginais e vagabundos: Acumulação social da violência no Rio de Janeiro."Ph.D. diss. IUPERJ, 1999.

Monteiro, Marcelo. "DNA das urnas." *Favela Tem Memória*, July 7, 2004, http://www.favelatemmemoria.com.br/publique/cgi/cgilua.exe/sys/start.htm?infoid=101&sid=4&from_info_index=1, accessed May 23, 2013.

———. "Paraíso cobiçado." *Favela Tem Memória*, July 5, 2004, http://www.favela temmemoria.com.br/publique/cgi/cgilua.exe/sys/start.htm?sid=4&infoid=77&from_info_index=6, accessed May 23, 2013.

———. "Um papa no morro." *Favela Tem Memória*, September 9, 2003, http://www.favelatemmemoria.com.br/publique/cgi/cgilua.exe/sys/start.htm?sid=4&infoid=41&from_info_index=6, accessed May 23, 2013.

Moraes, Rodolfo. "Intervenções governamentais sobre movimentos de invasões de terrenos urbanos: Estudo de casos no município do Rio de Janeiro em 1983." M.A. thesis, Escola Brasileira de Administração Pública, Fundação Getúlio Vargas, 1988.

Motta, Marly Silva da, Américo Freire, and Carlos Eduardo Sarmento. *A política carioca em quatro tempos*. Rio de Janeiro: FGV, 2004.

MR-8. *Resoluções políticas do Segundo Congresso do Mr-8*. São Paulo: Quilombo, 1980.

Neate, Patrick, and Damian Platt. *Culture Is Our Weapon: Making Music and Changing Lives in Rio de Janeiro*. Rio de Janeiro: Penguin, 2010.

Neuwirth, Robert. *Shadow Cities: A Billion Squatters, a New Urban World*. New York: Routledge, 2005.

Niemeyer, Oscar. "CIEPS na concepção do seu arquiteto." *Diário Oficial*, Caderno Especial de Educação (1985): 3.

"No Rio, o pó cala os governantes." *Veja*, June 1, 1988, 20–27.

Oliveira, Hélio de. "Depoimento: Hélio De Oliveira." In *A favela fala: Depoimentos ao CPDOC*, edited by Dulce Chaves Pandolfi and Mário Grynszpan, 253–74. Rio de Janeiro: FGV, 2003.

Oliveira, José Martins de. "Depoimento: José Martins De Oliveira." In *A Favela fala:*

Depoimentos ao CPDOC, edited by Dulce Chaves Pandolfi and Mário Grynszpan, 31–56. Rio de Janeiro: FGV, 2003.

Oliveira, Sonia. "Associação de moradores: Formatos diferenciados de participação política e representação de interesses." M.A. thesis, IUPERJ, 1988.

Penglase, Ben. "The Bastard Child of the Dictatorship: The Comando Vermelho and the Birth of 'Narco-Culture' in Rio de Janeiro." *Luso-Brazilian Review* 45:1 (February 2008): 118–45.

———. "Lost Bullets: Fetishes of Urban Violence in Rio de Janeiro." *Anthropological Quarterly* 84, no. 2 (spring 2011): 411–38.

Pereira, Walter. "Depoimento: Walter Pereira." In *A favela fala: Depoimentos ao* CPDOC, edited by Dulce Chaves Pandolfi and Mário Grynszpan, 275–97. Rio de Janeiro: FGV, 2003.

Perlman, Janice. *Favela: Four Decades of Living on the Edge in Rio de Janeiro.* New York: Oxford University Press, 2010.

———. *The Myth of Marginality: Urban Poverty and Politics in Rio de Janeiro.* Berkeley: University of California Press, 1976.

Pinho, Ângela, Claudia Carmello, Denise Galvani, Fernanda Sucupira, Leonardo Sakamoto, Lídia Neves, Lúcia Nascimento, Marcio Kameoka, Natália Suzuki, Nelson Lin, Rafael Sampaio, Renata Summa, and Rodrigo Pereira. "Feridas Abertas." *Problemas Brasileiros*, no. 359 (2003): 1–10.

Pires, José Luís. *Minhas Verdades: Histórias e pensamento de um negro favelado.* Rio de Janeiro: Refluxus, 2004.

———. *Minhas verdades: Histórias e pensamento de um negro favelado.* Vol. 2. Rio de Janeiro: Refluxus, 2007.

Pirozi, Francisca Medeiros. "Depoimento: Francisca Medeiros Pirozi." In *A favela fala: Depoimentos ao* CPDOC, edited by Dulce Chaves Pandolfi and Mário Grynszpan, 57–74, Rio de Janeiro: FGV, 2003.

Porfirio, Pedro. *O poder da rua.* Rio de Janeiro: Vozes, 1981.

"Projetos para revitalização e reurbanização da Rua Nelson Mandela." Working paper, Rio de Janeiro: Instituto ComÁfrica, 2004.

Queiroz, Leda Lúcia. "Movimentos sociais urbanos: O Movimento Amigos de Bairro de Nova Iguaçu." M.A. thesis, Universidade Federal do Rio de Janeiro, 1981.

Queiroz Ribeiro, Luiz César de and Luciana Lago. "The Favela/(Formal) Neighborhood Contrast in the Social Space of Rio de Janeiro." DISP, no. 147 (April 2001): 39–47.

Regina Novaes, Christina Vital, Cristiane Ramalho, Manuel Ribeiro, and Rita de Cássia. "O Galo e o pavão." *Comunicações do* ISER 58, no. 22 (2003): 5–49.

"Resoluções do IV Congresso da FAFERJ." *Favelão* 3, no. 18 (January 1985): 5.

Ribeiro, Belisa. *Bomba no Riocentro.* Rio de Janeiro: Codecri, 1982.

Ribeiro, Darcy. *Espaço Democrático* 1, no. 16 (June 1–7, 1984): 1–12.

———. *Mestiço é que é bom*. Rio de Janeiro: Editora Revan, 1996.

———. *Nossa escola é uma calamidade*. Rio de Janeiro: Salamandra Editora, 1984.

———. *O livro dos* CIEPS. Rio de Janeiro: Bloch Editora, 1986.

———. *O povo brasileiro: A formação e o sentido do Brazil*. São Paulo: Companhia das Letras, 1995.

Ribeiro, Manoel. "O morro: Territórios, espaços e pertencimentos." In *O galo e o pavão*, edited by Regina Novaes and Marilena Cunha. 45–49. Rio de Janeiro: ISER, 2003.

Rocha, Adair. *Cidade Cerzida: A costura da cidadania no Morro Santa Marta*. Rio de Janeiro: Museu da República, 2005.

Rocha, Adair, Cecilia Minayo, Vitor Valla, and Eliana Atahyde. *Favelas e as organizações comunitárias*. Rio de Janeiro: Centro da Defesa dos Direitos Humanos Bento Rubião, 1994.

Rodrigues, José Augusto de Souza. "Imagens da ordem e da violência na cidade do Rio de Janeiro." M.A. thesis, IUPERJ, 1993.

Rodriguez, Gilberto. "Depoimento." In *A Construção De Um Estado: A Fusão Em Debate*, edited by Marly Motta and Carlos Eduardo Sarmento, 220–30. Rio de Janeiro: FGV, 2001.

Rubin, Jeffrey. "Meanings and Mobilizations: A Cultural Politics Approach to Social Movements and States." *Latin American Research Review* 39, no. 3 (Fall 2004): 106–42.

Sader, Emir. "A polícia é um caso de polícia." *Teoria e Debate* (December 1, 1987): 1–4.

Sales, dom Eugênio. "Urbanização das favelas." *Jornal do Brasil*, June 13, 1981, 11.

Santos, Carlos Nelson Ferreira dos. *Movimentos urbanos no Rio de Janeiro*. Rio de Janeiro: Zahar, 1981.

———. *Processo de crescimento e ocupação da periferia*. Rio de Janeiro: IBAM, 1982.

———. *Urbanização da Favela Marcílio Dias*. Rio de Janeiro: IBAM, 1986.

———. "Velhas novidades nos modos de urbanização brasileira." In *Habitação em questão*, edited by Lícia Valladares, 17–43. Rio de Janeiro: Zahar, 1979.

Santos, Eladir Fátima Nascimento dos. "Tecendo redes: Narrativas sobre a FAFERJ." In *VII Encontro Regional Sudeste de História Oral*, 1–17. Rio de Janeiro: FIOCRUZ, 2007.

Sarmento, Carlos Eduardo. "Entre o carisma e a rotina: As eleições de 1982 e o primeiro governo." In *A força do povo: Brizola e o Rio de Janeiro*, edited by Marieta de Moraes Ferreira, 43–67. Rio de Janeiro: FGV, 1982.

———, ed. *Chagas Freitas: Perfil político*. Rio de Janeiro: FGV, 1999.

Saunders, Doug. *Arrival Cities: How the Largest Migration in History Is Reshaping Our World*. New York: Pantheon, 2011.

Sento-Sé, João Trajano. *Brizolismo: Estetização da política e carisma*. Rio de Janeiro: Fundação Getúlio Vargas, 1999.

Sento-Sé, João Trajano, Ignácio Cano, and Andréia Marinho. "Efeitos humanitários dos conflitos entre facções do tráfico de drogas numa comunidade do Rio
de Janeiro." In *Laboratório de análise da violência*, 1–26. Rio de Janeiro: UERJ, 2006.

Serbin, Ken. *Secret Dialogues: Church-State Relations, Torture and Social Justice in Authoritarian Brazil*. Pittsburgh: University of Pittsburgh Press, 2000.

———. *Needs of the Heart: A Social and Cultural History of Brazil's Clergy and Seminaries*.
Notre Dame, Ind.: University of Notre Dame Press, 2006.

Serrano-Berthet, Rodrigo, Flávia Carbonari, Mariana Cavalcanti and Alys Wilman, "Bringing the State Back into the Favelas of Rio de Janeiro: Understanding changes in community life after the UPP pacification process," Sustainable
Development Sector Management Unit Report, World Bank, Washington, DC,
October, 2012.

Sheriff, Robin. *Dreaming Equality*. New Brunswick, NJ: Rutgers University Press,
2001.

Silva, Eliana Sousa. "O contexto das práticas policiais nas favelas da Maré: A busca
de novos caminhos a partir de seus protagonistas," Ph.D. diss., PUC, 2009.

Silva, Nelson do Valle, and Gláucio Ary Dillon Soares. "O charme discreto do
socialismo moreno." *Dados: Revista de Ciências Sociais* 28, no. 2 (1985): 253–73.

———. "Depoimento: Itamar Silva." In *A favela fala: Depoimentos ao CPDOC*, edited
by Dulce Chaves Pandolfi and Mário Grynszpan, 299–360. Rio de Janeiro: FGV,
2003.

———. "Depoimento: Itamar Silva." In *Morar na Metrópole: Ensaios sobre habitação
popular no Rio de Janeiro*, edited by IPLAN, 54–60. Rio de Janeiro: IPLAN, 1988.

Silva, J. Paulo da. "Tóxico leva PM a cercar de novo Pavão e Pavãozinho." *Jornal do
Brasil*, July 7, 1985, 21.

Silva, Jorge da. *Controle da criminalidade e segurança pública*. Rio de Janeiro: Forense,
1990.

Silva, Luiz Antônio Machado da. "Sociabilidade violenta: Por uma interpretação
da criminalidade contemporânea no Brasil urbano." In *Metrópoles: Entre a coesão e a fragmentação, acCooperação e o conflito*, edited by Luiz César Queiroz Ribeiro,
291–351. São Paulo: Perseu Abramo, 2004.

———. "Um problema na interpretação da criminalidade urbana violenta." *Sociedade e Estado* 10, no. 2 (1995): 493–511.

———. "Violência e sociabilidade: Tendências na atual conjuntura urbana no Brasil." In *Globalização, fragmentação e reforma urbana*, edited by Regina Moreu, 147–68.
Rio de Janeiro: Civilização Brasileira, 1994.

Silva, Maria Laís Pereira da. *Avaliação do Programa de Eletrificação de Interesse Social*.
4 vols. Rio de Janeiro: IBAM, 1985.

———. *Favelas cariocas, 1930–1964*. Rio de Janeiro: Contraponto, 2005.

Silva, Maria Laís Pereira da and Isabel Cristina Eiras de Oliveira. "Eletrificação de
favelas." *Revista de Administração Municipal* 33, no. 179 (April–June 1986): 6–17.

Smolka, Martim O, and Laura Mullahy, eds. *Perspectivas urbanas: Temas críticos en políticas de suelo en América Latina*. Cambridge, MA: Lincoln Institute of Land Policy, 2007.

Soares, Luiz Eduardo. *Meu casaco de general: Quinhentos dias no front da segurança pública em Rio de Janeiro*. São Paulo: Companhia das Letras, 2000.

———. "Rio de Janeiro 1993: A tríplice ferida simbólica." In *Violência e política no Rio de Janeiro*, edited by Luiz Eduardo Soares, 243–275. Rio de Janeiro: Relume Dumará, 1996.

———, ed. *Violência e política no Rio de Janeiro*. Rio de Janeiro: Relume Dumará, 1996.

Soares, Luiz Eduardo, João Trajano Sento-Sé, José Augusto Souza Rodrigues, and Leandro Piquet Carneiro. "Criminalidade urbana e violência: Rio de Janeiro no contexto internacional." In *Violência e política no Rio de Janeiro*, edited by Luiz Eduardo Soares, 165–195. Rio de Janeiro: ISER, 1996.

Soares, Walther Jacintho. "Nova política para as Favelas." *Jornal do Brasil*, January 8, 1984.

Soto, Hernando de. *The Mystery of Capital: Why Capitalism Triumphs in the West and Fails Everywhere Else*. New York: Basic Books, 2000.

Souza, Amaury de, Olavo Brasil de Lima Junior, and Marcus Figueiredo. "Brizola e as eleições de 1982 no Rio de Janeiro." *Estudos* (August 1985): 1–44.

Treiger, Berta, and Eliane Faerstein. "Efeitos de um projeto de urbanização de favela nas atividades locais de geração de renda: O caso Pavão-Pavãozinho." *Revista de Administração Municipal* 35, no. 187 (April–June 1988): 38–50.

Valladares, Lícia. *A invenção da favela: Do mito de origem a Favela.com*. Rio de Janeiro: Editora FGV, 2005.

———. *Passa-se uma casa análise do Programa de Remoção de Favelas do Rio de Janeiro*. Rio de Janeiro: Zahar, 1978.

———. "Social Science Representations of Favelas in Rio de Janeiro: A Historical Perspective." *Lanic Etext Collection*, LLILAS Visiting Resource Professor Papers, 2008, lanic.utexas.edu/project/etext/llilas/vrp/valladares.pdf, accessed on May 23, 2013.

Ventura, Zuenir. *Cidade partida*. São Paulo: Companhia das Letras, 1994.

"Violência." *Favelão* 2, no. 15 (May 1984): 8.

Weinstein, Barbara. *For Social Peace in Brazil: Industrialists and the Remaking of the Working Class in São Paulo, 1920–1964*. Chapel Hill: University of North Carolina Press, 1997.

Yúdice, George. *The Expediency of Culture: Uses of Culture in the Global Era*. Durham, NC: Duke University Press, 2003.

Zaluar, Alba. *A máquina e a revolta*. São Paulo: Editora Brasiliense, 1985.

———. *Condomínio do Diabo*. Rio de Janeiro: UERJ, 1996.

———. "Urban Violence and Drug Warfare in Brazil." In *Armed Actors: Organised*

Violence and State Failure in Latin America, edited by Kees Koonings and Dirk Kruijt. London: Zed Books, 2004, 139–154.

Zaluar, Alba, and Isabel Siqueira Conceição. "Favelas sob o controle das milícias: Que paz?" *São Paulo em Perspectiva* 21 (2007): 89–101.

Zampa, Vivan, and Bruna Belchior. "Entrevista: Coronel Sérgio Antunes Barbosa." In *Sonho de uma polícia cidadã: Coronel Carlos Magno Nazareth Cerqueira*, edited by Ana Beatriz Leal, Íbis Silva Pereira, and Oswaldo Munteal Filho. Rio de Janeiro: UERJ, 2011, 58–69.

Zampa, Vivian, and Mariana Mello. "Entrevista: Coronel Ubiratan de Oliveira Ângelo." In *sonho de uma polícia cidadã: Coronel Carlos Magno Nazareth Cerqueira*, edited by Ana Beatriz Leal, Íbis Silva Pereira, and Oswaldo Munteal Filho, 103–16. Rio de Janeiro: UERJ, 2011.

Encina, José Carlos dos Reis (Escadinha), 125, 126–27, 135, 141, 146, 168

FAFERJ. *See* Federação das Associações das Favelas do Estado de Rio de Janeiro

Falange Vermelho, 125–26

FAMERJ. *See* Federação de Associações de Moradores do Estado do Rio de Janeiro

favela associations, 5; CIEPs and, 99; communitarian unity, 9, 117, 195; drug-trafficking networks and, 9–11, 15–16, 38, 40, 137, 141–50, 168, 173–74; elections, 37, 88, 128–29; electrification and, 88–89; factions in, 109; goals, 63; institutionalization of, 108; Justice Council and, 104; militia-controlled, 174; Pastoral and, 49, 51, 54, 57; PDT and, 78–81; vs. police, 105; property rights and, 40–41, 57, 82–85, 131; PT and, 69–70; women in, 36, 109

Favela-Bairro program, 28, 175–76, 179, 194

"Favela Fashion Week" (Sapucahy song), 181

favela movement: on adverse possession, 56–57; black mobilization and, 34; Brizola election and, 47, 76, 78, 172–73; in Brizola government, 47, 76–81, 112–19, 172–73; compromise in, 54; in favelas, overview, 35–38; federation model, 62; Freitas response to, 66–67; irregular subdivisions and, 59–61; liberation theology and, 45; locations, 46; middle-class movement alliance, 64–65; military regime and, 65–67; mobilization vs. dictatorship, 5; in Morro dos Cabritos, 47–49; overview, 35–38, 46; steps of, 45–47

Favelão (newsletter), 105

Favela Rubens Vaz, 156

favelas: activism in, 15–17; architecture/infrastructure, 179–80, 193; communitarian vision, 54–59; compared to irregular subdivisions, 29–33; drug-trafficking networks in, 9–11, 35, 38; educational initiatives, 10–11, 90–100, 178; electricity programs, 87–89; flooding in, 152–53; forced relocation from, 5, 76, 84, 128, 192–94; global/regional/local change in, 11–14; growth of, 23; housing projects, 28, 32; land invasions, 77, 78; locations, 25–26, 27; military occupation of, 170–71; populations in, 203n22; race and rights, 33–35; second-class citizens, 33; sewer and water in, 89; use of term, 2, 21–29, 201n1. *See also* specific favelas; specific topics, e.g. property rights

Federação das Associações das Favelas do Estado de Rio de Janeiro (FAFERJ), 51–52, 80–81, 84

Federação de Associações de Moradores do Estado do Rio de Janeiro (FAMERJ), 62

Fernandes, Rubém César, 166

Ferreira, Antônio José, 117

Ford Foundation, 54, 154

Franco, Itamar, 170

Franco, Nelson Moreira, 146

Franco, Wellington Moreira, 138, 171; campaign, 74–75, 132–34, 160; on CIEPs, 156; on drug trafficking, 145–47, 153–54; as PDS candidate, 71

Freitas, Antônio de Pádua Chagas, 43–45, 53, 60, 66–67, 69, 75, 91, 118

Fundação Leão XIII, 7–8, 53–54

garbage strike, 19–20

Garotinho, Anthony, 172

Gato Angorá. *See* Franco, Wellington Moreira

Gávea neighborhood, 2

Gay, Robert, 213n9

Globo (organization), 74–75, 160

Globo, O (newspaper), 146

Goulart, João, 68, 97

Gramsci, Antonio, 64, 144

Group for Democracy, 66

Grupo de Terra e Habitação (GTH), 61

Grupo Eco, 59

GTH. *See* Grupo de Terra e Habitação

Guanabara, 66

Guararapes favela, 62

Guevara, Che, 94

Guimarães, Irineu, 52–54, 62, 65–66, 69–70, 84

Haddad, Jamil, 79

Hobsbawm, Eric, 126–27

Hotel Panorama, 96–97, 99, 113